Sex, Love,
and
Violence

Books by the same author

Strategic Family Therapy

Behind the One-Way Mirror:
Advances in the Practice of Strategic Therapy

A NORTON PROFESSIONAL BOOK

Sex, Love,
and
Violence

Strategies for Transformation

CLOÉ MADANES

W. W. NORTON & COMPANY • *NEW YORK* • *LONDON*

Library of Congress Cataloging–in–Publication Data

Madanes, Cloé.
    Sex, love, and violence : strategies for transformation / Cloé
Madanes.
    p.   cm.
"A Norton professional book."
Includes bibliographical references.
    1. Violence.   2. Love—Psychological aspects.   3. Sex crimes—
Psychological aspects.   4. Psychotherapy.   I. Title.
[DNLM: 1. Love.   2. Models, Psychological.   3. Psychotherapy—
methods.   4. Sex Offenses.   5. Violence.   W 795 M178s]
RC569.5.V55M33   1990   616.85′82—dc20   89-26674

    ISBN 0-393-70096-8

W. W. Norton & Company, Inc., 500 Fifth Avenue, New York, N.Y. 10110
W. W. Norton & Company, Ltd., 37 Great Russell Street, London WC1B 3NU

2   3   4   5   6   7   8   9   0

To J.B.F.

CONTENTS

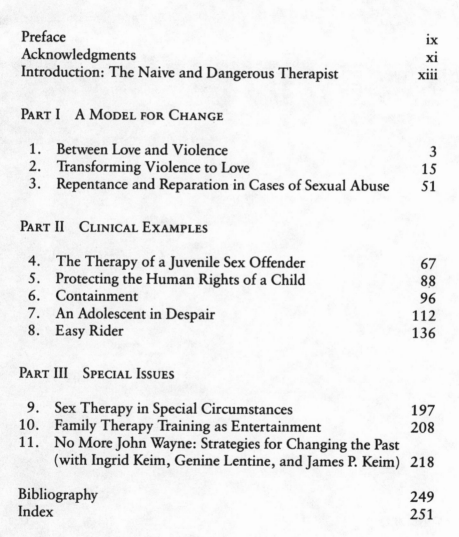

PREFACE

SOME YEARS AGO I was invited by Ronald Laing to give a paper at a meeting in Amsterdam. He said the title of the conference was "Eros and Violence." I said that sounded rather pompous for a professional conference and that, while I could speak about violence and about family therapy, about "eros" I knew very little. A more matter-of-fact title like "An International Conference on Family Therapy" would be better, I suggested. He said that "Eros and Violence" represented the central human dilemma of our time, but that he would consider another title, since perhaps my view represented that of other speakers as well.

After this telephone conversation I thought about how I had admired Laing's work since my college years. I realized that at least I owed him the respect of giving some thought to the subject of eros and violence. I decided to try to figure out what he meant when he said this was man's basic dilemma. Ultimately I wrote a paper about love and violence.

A couple of months before the conference Laing called to confirm the details. He said he was sending the brochure with the new title, "An International Conference on Family Therapy." I said I had written a paper, with great effort, on love and violence, the crucial issue of our time, and that was what I was going to present. Later I learned that the conference had been advertised not only as "Eros and Violence," but also as "Love and Violence," "Eros and Relationships," and "Violence and Family Therapy." As it turned out, the conference took place a few days after the accident at Chernobyl and the radioactive cloud floating over Europe reminded us that the boundaries that separate life and destruction are as tenuous as those between love and violence. The conference was also memorable to me because I had the opportunity to meet the Dalai Lama XIV, Tenzin Gyatso, whose writings have had a great influence on my work.

The paper that I gave in Amsterdam became the main theme of this book, which has also had many titles, from *Love and Violence* to *The Naive and Dangerous Therapist* to *Between Love and Violence*. *Sex, Love, and Violence* was suggested to me by Susan Barrows, my editor at Norton, after she read the book, not knowing that it had been inspired by the Amsterdam conference. I am pleased with the title since the Greek word "eros" can only be translated to English as "sex and love." The book attempts to bring some clarity to the ways in which sex, love and violence are inextricably related, and to give some guidance to the therapist dealing with these issues.

As the book goes to print I hear of Laing's death. I wish I could have talked with him some more about the subject.

ACKNOWLEDGMENTS

THREE CHAPTERS in this work have been published elsewhere in somewhat different form. Chapter 1, "Between Love and Violence," appeared in the British *Journal of Family Therapy*, Vol. 2, 1989, under the title "The Goals of Therapy." Chapter 2, "Transforming Violence to Love," appeared in an earlier version in *Brief Therapy: Myths, Methods and Metaphors*, edited by J. Zeig and S. Gilligan, under the title "Strategies and Metaphors of Brief Therapy." Chapter 10, "Family Therapy Training as Entertainment," appeared in *Handbook of Family Therapy Training and Supervision,* edited by H.A. Liddle, D.C. Breunlin, and R.C. Schwartz under the title "Family Therapy Training—It's Entertainment." A summary version of Chapter 11, "No More John Wayne: Strategies for Changing the Past," co-authored with I. Keim, G. Lentine, and J.P. Keim, appeared in the *Journal of Strategic and Systemic Therapies*, Vol. 6(3), under the title "Strategies for Changing the Past."

The book contains many case examples of therapies. Sometimes I was the primary therapist, but most often I was the supervisor behind a one-way mirror. This means planning the session with the therapist and calling him or her over the phone with instructions, or interrupting a session for a planning meeting. Most of the therapists were professionals who were training in this particular approach to therapy at the Family Therapy Institute of Washington, D.C. (FTI); others were teachers at this Institute. I wish to acknowledge my appreciation of all of them. They are: Lucy Banks, Richard Belson, Marvin Chelst, Yvonne DeCuir, David Eddy, Irene Gaffney, Amy Karlen, Gerald Newberry, Neil Schiff, John Wade, Dava Weinstein, Richard Whiteside, and Stephen Williams.

I am especially grateful to Fran Hitchcock and Susan Barrows, who edited the book, and to Andy Haley, who managed the word processor.

INTRODUCTION:
THE NAIVE AND DANGEROUS
THERAPIST

Cloquet hated reality but realized it was still the only place to get a good steak.

— Woody Allen

I BELONG TO the generation born to therapy during the great years of psychoanalysis. Between the Second World War and the Vietnam War, there was the feeling that therapists were going to discover the essence of human nature. The dark side of mankind would be understood and controlled; atrocities would not be repeated. This book of strategies was written by a mature woman many years later, yet it was generated in the idealism of those times.

The strategies are the result of my attempts to extract the essence of how to change people, and of how to change them in fundamental ways. Therapy is either about the essential or it is about nothing. The therapist strives toward a clarity of consciousness in understanding the stigmatized, the sordid, the perverse, the ugly. This understanding requires complicity in the experience of evil and of pathos. The therapist who struggles to reform the rapist must experience in himself or herself more than an echo of what the rapist experiences. To bring someone out of deep pain one must experience the grief that the other feels. In a family there is always the victim and the victimizer, the good and the evil, the joyful and the pathetic. The therapist is an accomplice to all and loyal to all.

Therapy is not innocent, yet it is a return to childhood. The therapist, with the innocence of a child, honestly identifies with everyone. It is that innocence that makes it possible to bring about change. With this innocence come tenuous boundaries and respect for the power of imagination. Like the innocent little children in Ray Bradbury's story, "The Veldt," the therapist believes that it is possible to create imaginary creatures that will eat up one's own parents.

As we struggle to turn violence into love, to bring order into chaos, to elicit compassion instead of hatred, are we being innocently optimistic? Do we refuse to believe the obvious: that change is difficult if not impossible, and that one thing is certain—pain and death come in the end?

There are two ways to revolt against the real world. One is to commit ourselves prematurely to the deterioration that will ultimately come to us. The other is to rebel. In the "real world," in "maturity," the present moment is sacrificed for the future. The naive therapist prefers the present moment and strives to create one instant, one interchange, that is different, betting against the chance that this moment, this interchange, will not be repeated. The worried little girl saying, "I like me," the lonely wife planning an adventure trip: These new moments contain the death of all previous moments. This is the enchantment of each moment of therapy. The naive therapist who can kill the past is as dangerous as the rebellious children of "The Veldt" who can create the imaginary lions that "really" devour their parents.

Therapy is dangerous because it can reveal the process of rebellion and anarchy but it cannot regulate collective order. When it moves beyond the limited realm of the small social organization, it is no longer therapy, it is political action. As therapists we need to be naive and childish so we can step outside the system and have hope for change. But this stepping outside the system is rebellious and dangerous and goes against the order of society.

Therapy, developed in connection with the decadence of religion, is related to the content of mysticism. The therapist transcends the common boundaries between people and loses herself in imagining other peoples' worlds, their lives. The generalizations about human experience that make it possible to break boundaries are not intellectually complex; they have a childish simplicity. In this naive state of mind, contradictions are not perceived as mutually exclusive. The real and the imaginary, the good and the bad, the communicable and the incommunicable are all the same.

The therapist, presented with a system where each element relentlessly converges into the whole, brings out the rebelliousness of a fragment and makes appear that which did not appear before. The therapeutic work becomes unpredictable—sometimes the therapist is part of the system she creates, and sometimes she is alone with the knowledge that there are no rules, no rites, no obligations. There is nothing but liberty because there are no rules.

Therapy may be nothing more than a search for a moral way of living. But one limitation of therapy is that it is no substitute for the established order of things, even though it pretends to be. When frustration with her limited power commits the therapist to political action, she abandons the work of therapy. Therapy then becomes a minor, childish activity and the therapist an impostor who knows herself to be such.

The therapist shuts her eyes to many things and forgets even herself. But between the clients and the therapist there is clarity and lucidity. The therapist watches herself watching them, and it is her awareness of them that she is watching. She watches for what does not exist. It is what does not exist in a system that determines what does exist. The absence of the warm gesture determines the coldness of the relationship.

It does not matter that therapy unites a client to a therapist who is disappointed, dissatisfied, and humiliated by failures in her personal life. Therapy is no more betrayed by the therapist's unlivable life than it is by the cruel nature of reality. The essence of therapy lies in aiming beyond the possible.

We all live with the desire to survive and to avoid as much as possible the rotten, the dirty, the funereal, the symbolic of death. The therapist is immersed in a world of derangements, of wounds, of the failures that most people try to avoid through their entire activity. Like the comedian, the smiling, optimistic therapist rises above the horror but never forgets it.

I

A Model for Change

1
BETWEEN LOVE AND VIOLENCE

*Many men go fishing all of their lives without knowing
that it is not fish they are after.*

— *Henry David Thoreau*

THERAPISTS NEED shared values to sustain us through changing
times. Currently we are not only divided into schools but also
separated because of the different contexts and populations we
work with. A relatively recent phenomenon is the extraordinary
variety of problems to which therapy is now applied. There is no
one theory of therapy or one set of techniques that can apply to the
whole spectrum of problems brought to therapy. In a complex and
constantly changing society, new problems constantly develop, old
problems are given new priorities, and therapists work in always
changing situations. New theories and techniques must come together with these changes. A set of goals which applies to all
therapy would sustain our integrity and help us through these
times.

Making our values explicit could enhance the humanity of all
persons. Different varieties of therapy, counseling, and social assistance have become so commonplace today that some form of therapeutic intervention has probably touched the lives of every family

in the United States. The same is probably true for most of the economically developed world. Therapists are influencing millions of people not only through their clients and their students but also through the mass media. Magazines, newspapers, radio, television, and movies are influenced in major ways by our field and provide continual psychological recommendations. If we were clear about our values we could be clearer about how we want to exert our influence on these media. Clear goals could also help us do no harm, and not harming is the first consideration of a therapist.

We also need to cultivate a more elevated image of our professional identity. When we write our case studies, we present idealized images not only of ourselves as therapists, but also of the people we work with. Just as we cultivate an elevated image of ourselves as individuals, so as a profession do we create a fiction of our collective identity. The perception we have of our own lives is a kind of fiction that we modify to our needs, to keep our identity intact.

In our own lives as well as in our therapy we cannot understand or even consider a situation without using our imagination to sort and make sense of the chaos of events. But this is only part of the story. As therapists and as human beings we have an amazing ability to transcend the grim and the sordid. Surprizing moments do occur in therapy through acts of dedication, inspiration, and kindness. If we did not idealize ourselves as therapists, and our clients as human beings, we would never be able to extend ourselves as necessary.

These extensions are most needed when we work with children, whom we often have to protect. There are many special problems in working with children. They are usually brought to therapy because someone else wants to change them: the parents, the school, the pediatrician. Their perception of what constitutes their own happiness and well-being often conflicts with the wishes of others. We cannot always encourage children's independence, yet we often have to protect them from those on whom they are dependent. If we are clear and explicit about our goals, our influence on the family and other social institutions will be more positive and effective.

The Human Dilemma

A central question in therapy has been whether there is a basic dilemma that humankind faces and from which all other human dilemmas stem. Philosophy, literature, and religion ask the same question. Various themes have been proposed and have organized our thinking about the human drama. Different schools of thought have proposed that we are doomed to sexual frustration, that we ultimately seek self-destruction, that we can never overcome the trauma of birth, that we are motivated by pure selfishness, that we are overwhelmed by the meaninglessness of life, that we are caught in a web of paradoxical communications, and that all attempts to change bring about more of the same. These are some of the concepts that have been used to explain not only the behavior of people in therapy but also family relations, work difficulties, and social conflicts.

I propose a different idea about what the dilemma of man is. All problems brought to therapy can be thought of as stemming from the dilemma between love and violence. The main issue for human beings is whether to love, protect, and help each other, or to intrude, dominate, and control, doing harm and violence to others. The problem is compounded because love involves intrusion, domination, control, and violence, and because violence can be done in the name of love, protection, and help. The more intense love is, the closer it is to violence in the sense of intrusive possessiveness. Similarly, the more attached and dependent we are on the object of our violence, the more intense the violence.

A mother loves her child. She wants to give him everything; she knows what is best for him. At what point does such love become intrusive and violent? A father spanks his son to teach him not to cross a dangerous street. Isn't this violence love? Violence may also have the function of obtaining love. A child may hit his brother to be punished by his father who otherwise is indifferent to him. The punishment becomes an act of love in that it expresses concern rather than indifference. An adolescent may become violent with his parents when there is a threat of divorce. His violence may bring the parents together against the son, who is expressing his love by saving their marriage, even if they do not want it saved.

How does a therapist steer people toward love and away from violence when there is so often such a fine line between the two?

Reviewing the characteristics of the large number of cases that come to therapy, reveals common elements in the ways family members interact around the dilemmas of love and violence. There appears to be a continuum of four dimensions of family interaction that correspond to different kinds of emotional and spiritual development. Each dimension corresponds to specific types of problems brought to therapy, and for each dimension there are specific strategies of choice to solve the problems.

One dimension involves people struggling for control and power over their own lives and over the lives of others. Family members oppose each other in antagonistic ways, so that the presenting problem can best be understood as an attempt to gain power over significant others. Power is used for personal advantage, people are mainly motivated by the wish to satisfy selfish needs, and relationships are mostly exploitative. Each individual's goal seems to be to dominate for his or her own benefit. The main emotion of family members is fear. The therapist needs to redistribute power among family members and to change how power is used, moving people away from selfish desires and towards the wish to be loved. Typical problems are delinquency, some forms of drug abuse, behavioral problems, and bizarre behavior. The strategies of choice are changing the involvement of parents and other relatives, negotiating privileges and obligations between family members, changing who benefits from the symptom, and rituals and ordeals. These strategies, as well as some of the ones mentioned later, are described in the strategic therapy literature (Madanes, 1981, 1984; Haley, 1973, 1980, 1984, 1987).

The second dimension involves the difficulties resulting from a desire to be loved. Family members are involved in a struggle to be cared for that often leads to self-inflicted violence. A child may seek punishment as a way of obtaining attention. A spouse may develop an incapacitating symptom in the hope of eliciting concern from the other spouse. Rivalry, discrimination, antagonism, and disagreements are often based on a desire to be specially favored. The wish to be loved and appreciated can bring out the best qualities in people, but it can also result in irrationality, selfishness and harm. The main emotion among family members is desire. Needs never seem to be fulfilled and there is always frustration and discomfort. The therapist needs to redistribute love among family members and to change how love is used, changing the wish to be loved to the desire to love and protect others. Typical problems are psychosomatic symptoms, depression, anxiety, phobias, eating disorders, and loneliness. Interactions are characterized by excessive demands and criticism. The strategies of choice are changing the way parents are involved with their children, prescribing the symptom or some aspect of the symptom, prescribing a symbolic act, and prescribing the pretending of the symptom.

The third dimension involves the desire to love and protect others. The wish to love and protect can bring out our highest qualities of compassion, devotion, generosity, and kindness. It may also elicit intrusiveness, possessiveness, domination, and violence. Intrusion and violence are often justified in the name of love. The parent who punishes for the child's "own good," the lover who dominates to protect, the teacher who criticizes to enlighten: These are all examples of love that may lead to violence. A family member powerless to take care of a loved one resorts to indirect means of caring. A child distracts a parent from his problems by developing unreasonable fears or by ruthlessly attacking those around him. The parent, concerned, may temporarily take respite from her own problems to take care of the child. By arranging this respite the child is offering love and protection to the parent, but this love is at the cost of the child's sacrifice and compromises his own desires, accomplishments, and fulfillment. This love is also violent in its manipulation.

The main emotion among family members involved at this level is despair. The wish to love and protect others is the highest human inclination, yet the seeds of violence are contained within that desire. The therapist needs to change how family members protect and love each other and who takes care of whom, introducing the wish to repent for the violence inflicted in the context of a loving relationship. Typical problems presented to therapy are suicide threats and attempts, abuse and neglect, guilt, obsessions, temper tantrums, and thought disorders.

The strategies of choice are to reunite family members, orienting them towards the future and arranging deeds of reparation, to change who is helpful to whom, and to empower children to be appropriately helpful to their parents.

In the fourth dimension the main issue between family members is to repent and to forgive. When individuals have inflicted trauma on each other and have suffered injustices and violence, interactions are characterized by grief, resentment, lies, secrecy, deceit, self-deprecation, isolation, and dissociation. The main emotion is shame because of what one has done, because of what one has refrained from doing, or because one cannot forgive. If family members are to continue to relate to one another, the therapist needs to reapportion the shame. Often the victims are blamed, and that must change. As the therapist clarifies who did what to whom, the wish to avoid responsibility and blame must change to the desire to become compassionate and to develop a sense of unity with others. Typical problems are incest, sexual abuse, attempted murder, and sadistic acts. The strategies of choice are to create an atmosphere of higher emotions, to find protectors for the victims, and to elicit repentance, forgiveness, compassion, and a sense of unity with others.

Not every therapist need agree with this conceptualization of the problems brought to therapy. But we could search for similarity rather than emphasizing difference.

Morality and Therapy

Many therapists are uncomfortable discussing goals of therapy because goals are necessarily tied to moral values. There is an antinomian tendency in psychotherapy that goes back at least to Freud, if not to the early hypnotists. In this view, morality and therapy are independent and even in opposition.

Therapy developed as a worldwide movement during the transition from the elitist pseudomorality of the Victorian era to the terrifying excesses of the fascist regimes supported by institutionalized religion. Perhaps historical contexts determined that therapy would be a humanism carefully divorced from the hypocrisy of religion and morality. But an exaggerated version of this view prevails today. At a higher level, somewhere above it all, is the valiant therapist, a radical demystifying society's stereotypes, confronting suppressed truths, fighting against repression, liberating the unconscious, thinking circularly and never attributing blame, interested in everything that is fun, including sexual fulfillment, creativity, and self-realization. Beneath this mythic being, crouching inside a dull church, the moralist endlessly repeats platitudes: "Love thy neighbor," "Respect your parents."

The antinomy persists because it is gratifying to imagine that as therapists we must be daring, courageous, shocking—rebels against society. It has been argued, not without reason, that therapy is an art and not a science. If so, the old opposition between art and morality applies to therapists as well as to other artists. We have in fact cultivated this self-gratifying view of our profession; the lack of any explicit connection with morality is flagrant in the therapy literature. Instead what is emphasized is the amoral view that values neutrality, the expression of hostility, and the lifting of repression. But is it possible to do good therapy without moral reference points?

The Goals of Therapy

There are some goals common to all therapies:

1. *To control action:* Most people come to therapy because they want to change their own behavior or that of significant others. They want their children to behave better or to learn more; they want to be better parents or to succeed at work; they want to reorganize their lives or they want to change the way they interact with others. They are concerned because they cannot help behaving in ways that are harmful to themselves or to others. To encourage the control of action is an explicit principle of therapy. Therapists want to promote the deliberate control of behavior by the person engaging in the behavior, rather than by others or by uncontrollable impulses.

2. *To control mind:* When people come to therapy disinterested in changing their behavior, they usually come because they want to change the way they think or feel. They are bothered by anxiety, fears, delusion, obsessive thoughts, sadness, etc. Most of the therapist's work consists in changing the context of a person so that

thoughts and feelings will change. It used to be thought that there was some meaning to these unpleasant thoughts and that free association was worth encouraging and exploring. Today it is known that what is important is for a therapist to encourage the discipline of controlled emoting and thinking, to control mind so negative thoughts can be replaced by positive ones and so people do not waste time, miserably obsessed with unpleasant or unproductive ideation.

3. *To control violence and anger:* This is often not an explicit goal of therapy. However, of all the actions and feelings to be controlled, these are the most important. No one comes to therapy to be hurtful and mean. People come to therapy to bring out the best in themselves. Therapists of all schools struggle to bring out what is good in a person, and none intends to promote violence and anger.

In the past therapists used to think that there was an anger within that needed to come out and be expressed and so eliminated. It was thought that unexpressed anger would be harmful to the person containing the anger. Today it is known that the expression of anger *is* the anger, just as the expression of violence is the violence. Therapists need to transform anger into positive actions and to encourage the patience and tolerance necessary to survive in our families and in society.

It might be argued that some problems brought to therapy could be solved through the expression of violence and anger. For example, a man who beats his wife could be encouraged to attack his son instead; a school counselor could encourage a frustrated teacher to express his or her anger towards a child who is not learning. These are examples of common approaches to life's difficulties, but they are not examples of therapeutic interventions. To encourage anger and violence is not therapeutic.

4. *To encourage empathy:* It is impossible to be a therapist without a heightened sense of empathy for the situation of others. It is the ability to put oneself in the other's place and sympathize with the other's misfortunes that makes therapy possible. It is also this ability that enables us to live in a family and in society. All therapists encourage empathy towards others as a part of a well-adjusted and emotionally satisfying life. To feel for others develops intelligence and a sense of justice. Empathy develops creativity, since by

identifying with others it is possible to develop a range of experiences that go beyond what can be experienced in one lifetime.

In the past therapists only promoted empathy within the nuclear family. Later they began to include the extended family. Some began to promote feelings of empathy towards all those who share the same ethnic background. Today therapists tend to minimize the importance of family of origin or ethnicity as compared to what the whole human race has in common. When one's forebearers are the whole of humankind, one carries within oneself unlimited potential. In contrast, when the emphasis is on one particular family tree, the human potential of each person appears limited.

Empathy with a client was less emphasized when psychotherapy was developing as a profession. Therapists struggled to define a professional identity. As part of this effort they developed what came to be known as "the therapeutic posture": a certain sense of superiority, distance, and arrogance toward the client. Today, when the profession is firmly established, this posture is being abandoned in favor of respect. Empathy and respect were sometimes lost when a therapist labeled people in ways that set them apart as inherently different. Now there is a growing realization that given the right circumstances, the therapist might find herself or himself in the same situation as the client.

5. *To encourage hope and humor:* Only death is unsolvable. In therapy there is always the possibility that a problem will be solved. No one is incurable and no situation is hopeless. Therapists today distinguish between their own ignorance or inability to solve a particular problem and the possibility that the problem may be solved irrespective of the activities of the therapist. If the therapist is hopeful, then the clients can be hopeful about their own lives.

A situation can be hopeless or hopeful depending on the point of view. For example, a retarded person will not become president of the United States, but he can lead a productive life and take care of himself; in that sense, he or she is not hopeless. It is the therapist's task to create a framework where goals can be attained and hope is possible.

Humor, together with intelligence and empathy, is what makes the human condition bearable. Often the problem in therapy is how to raise people from the grimness of their situation to a higher level of being. In this regard, humor is invaluable. It enables us to come out of ourselves and laugh at our own predicament. Humor also conquers fear and empowers. The realization that suffering is inevitable and death comes in the end can only be countered with a sense of the absurd.

6. *To promote tolerance and compassion:* Therapists today agree on the importance of promoting tolerance of individual differences and desires. The explicit encouragement of tolerance promotes good relationships between parents and children, husbands and wives, friends, neighbors and coworkers, blocking the intrusiveness that is often at the root of anxiety, fears and emotional disturbance.

Tolerance and compassion constitute a protective environment in which young persons can grow and develop in their own particular ways. Intolerance and intrusiveness lead to expulsion, punishment, and control by others. When families do not contain and protect their members, agents of social control and total institutions take over and often violate human rights.

Sometimes attempts to encourage protectiveness and to prevent intrusions from agents of social control lead to the very intolerance the therapist is trying to avoid. For example, to prevent hospitalization a therapist might encourage parents to physically and emotionally control a child in ways that may be as damaging as similar intrusions on the part of a hospital staff.

7. *To encourage forgiveness and kindness:* The only way we can survive from day to day without emotional breakdown is by forgiving and forgetting. We must forgive our parents, our children, our friends, our teachers. We must also forgive ourselves for our mistakes. When people come to therapy they are often stuck in a situation in which they cannot forgive. Therapists know that it is therapeutic to introduce the idea that forgiveness is possible. Not to forgive is only possible when there is total separation. If family members are to continue to relate to each other they must forgive. Sometimes what needs to be forgiven is minor resentment; sometimes it is extreme cruelty. Nevertheless, it is important to consider forgiveness and to offer the possibility of reparation.

Sometimes a ritual can be performed to mark the end of a period of resentment and the beginning of a period of forgiveness. The bad and unkindly actions of others can be taken as an opportunity to practice forgiveness and to develop tolerance. These ideas can be used to contain problems within families instead of resorting to agents of social control, and to promote the flexibility in point of view that is necessary to discourage violence. Kindness and compassion, empathy and forgiveness are not qualities of an individual but interactions that develop and are sustained in the context of the family.

To encourage kindness in ourselves and in others is consistent with every model of therapy. The practice of altruism is at the basis of all therapy, since therapy itself is a calling that requires an interest in doing good for others. It is possible to disagree with a certain form of altruism, such as unnecessary self-sacrifice, or with the object of altruism, such as a particular population, but there is no question that unselfish good deeds promote self-esteem and improve relationships.

Related to the concept of altruism is the idea of reparation and restitution. Therapists often encourage deeds of reparation toward those whom one has deliberately or unwittingly hurt. To actually perform unselfish acts that involve sacrifice is more therapeutic than talking to a therapist about guilt and depression.

8. *To promote harmony and balance:* With ever more complex lives, exposed by the media to images of all kinds of possible lifestyles, in a culture that presses for hard work and material success, it is all too easy to become narrowly focused. Some people develop their intellect at the cost of their emotional life. Others fulfill their creative potential but live in torment and disorder. Some find that they have sacrificed independence and accomplishments for the sake of the ones they love. There are people who protect themselves from being hurt by withdrawing and withholding their love for others. There are those who give so much that they elicit envy, jealousy and hatred, instead of gratitude.

A goal of therapy is to bring harmony and balance into people's lives. To love and to be loved, to find fulfillment in work, to play and enjoy: All are part of a necessary balance. Instead of being torn by conflicting emotions and disturbing relations, we all want to be in harmony within ourselves and with the rest of the world. An important goal for all clients is to lead a balanced life in harmony and not in conflict. Some people choose a goal in life that requires a path of conflict and rebellion, but even for those it is still possible to live in harmony and to find balance so that conflict is part of one harmonious whole. To prevent excess, avoid deprivation, and find harmony in life is a goal of all therapy.

Conclusion

As therapists we need to make explicit our values and our goals to sustain us through changing times, to consistently exert our influence in positive ways, to maintain a high morale, and to protect our clients, particularly children. In the context of a therapy approach where the unit is the family and where a therapist deliberately plans to exert power so that people influence each other in positive ways, it becomes apparent that all problems brought to therapy can be understood in terms of how family members interact around issues of love and violence. One cannot avoid taking a moral posture about whether love or violence between people should prevail and so bringing morality into the field of therapy. By doing so we can unite around common goals and values.

2
TRANSFORMING VIOLENCE
TO LOVE

Action is the only reality, not only reality but morality as well.

— Abbie Hoffman

IN A STRATEGIC approach to therapy, the therapist takes responsibility for what happens in the therapy room and plans a strategy for each particular case. The main therapeutic tool is the directive, which is to strategic therapy what the interpretation is to psychoanalysis. Diagnostic labels are not used. No one is labeled chronic or hopeless. Humor is frequently used because it helps to raise people to a higher level of being.

An interactional view assumes that to solve a problem, it is necessary to change the social context in which the problem takes place. This context is usually the family.

Besides considering the social context, the therapist needs to understand metaphorical communication. This is central to therapy. If we did not express ourselves metaphorically, people would state their problems clearly and therapists would have no difficulty in understanding them. But things are not so simple. Messages are not always what they appear to be. We are all familiar with the idea that a message can be a metaphor for another message. For example, if I say, "You give me a headache," I may be referring to more than one kind of pain.

A more unusual idea is that the interaction between two people can be a metaphor for another interaction. For example, a husband may come home upset and worried, and his wife may try to reassure and comfort him. If their child develops a recurrent pain, the father may come home and try to reassure and comfort the child in the same way that the wife was previously reassuring and comforting him. The father's involvement with the child is a metaphor for the wife's involvement with the husband. Also, one interaction replaces the other, because when the father is helping the son, the wife is not involved in helping the husband.

There are several interactional functions of metaphors. The first is to communicate: A son's violence, for example, may be expressing the mother's rage. A second function is to displace: A mother's frustration with her son may be a metaphor for her frustration with her husband, and may replace that frustration. A third function is to promote closeness and attach people to one another: A quarrel between father and daughter may be a metaphor for the resentments between husband and wife which are expressed only through the daughter, in this way bringing the spouses together. When communication is metaphorical, problems are difficult to solve because messages do not refer to what they ostensibly refer and people are caught in endless repetitive sequences.

I will describe the four different dimensions of family interaction that were presented briefly in Chapter 1 and the metaphors that are characteristic of each one. Each dimension corresponds to specific types of problems. I will also present strategies to use for each dimension and the therapeutic metaphors that apply to each strategy. Some of these strategies are classic; some are new and published here for the first time.

I. To Dominate and to Control

At the dimension of control people are interested mainly in dominating each other and in struggling for control and power. Typical problems are delinquency, some forms of drug abuse, behavioral problems, and bizarre behavior. Control and dominance are insured through intimidation and exploitation. The therapist needs to redistribute power among family members and to change how power is used, so that, instead of punitiveness, protection and caring can prevail.

Many of the first family therapists understood the problems presented to therapy at this level as a power struggle. Therefore, some of the typical family therapy techniques were developed with the idea that people mainly relate to each other to control each other and to compete for power. Some of the strategies that I will describe for this dimension are the oldest in family therapy.

Communication among family members at this level centers around metaphors of crime, war, and punishment. Distance between relatives is presented as total separation when, in fact, there is intense involvement. Differences are seen as irreconcilable when, in fact, personalities clash because they are similar.

Characteristic of what one finds here is a young adult who is a drug addict, delinquent, out of control. The problem presented to therapy may be a young person who is physically threatening to the parents, who beats up on people, or who breaks into houses. Perhaps the problem is bizarre behavior that is frightening the family because there is a threat of violence.

One family came to therapy because their 17-year-old son was spraying gasoline around the foundation of the house and playing with matches. He also threatened his mother and was obnoxious in many ways. The parents were also loud and obnoxious and had been violent with each other in the past. It would have been possible to hypothesize that the son was worried about the many problems of the parents and was trying to help them by calling attention to himself. This was probably true but not the most relevant way of thinking. What was urgent was to gain power over the young man's behavior so the family would not burn up in a fire.

The therapeutic strategies of choice for this first dimension of family interaction are: correcting the hierarchy, negotiations and contracts, changing benefits, and rituals and ordeals.

Correcting the Hierarchy

This strategy basically consists of organizing the parents to take charge of the family. When adolescents or young adults are antisocial or out of control (delinquent, drug addicted, or violent), and the parents are reasonably benevolent, they can be put in charge of establishing control over their offspring by agreeing on rules for them and consequences if the rules are not followed. Likewise, grandparents and other relatives can be put in charge of the children. The idea is that the older relatives will provide the necessary kindly guidance to reorient the young person to socially acceptable behavior. In so doing, the older relatives will come together in agreement and resolve conflicts that may have initially caused the young person's outrage. The therapist introduces metaphors of the rules and regulations that ensure truce, peace, and survival, and of fair punishment and compensation (see Haley, 1980; Madanes, 1981).

A goal of the therapy is to restore the parents to a position in the hierarchy where they can be protective and helpful to the child. The therapist needs to bring out the tolerance and kindness of the parents, with the view that ultimately parents want to empower their children. Both parents and children need to be encouraged to forgive each other for the abuses of power which may have occurred when the hierarchy was confused. The ruthless striving for personal advantage must change to desire to be loved and this love must be provided within the family. This includes parental love as well as the love of siblings and other relatives.

Sometimes, in order to restore the parents' protectiveness, it is necessary to take power away from professionals. A protective services worker may be intruding into a family and causing strife and violence, a probation officer may be divesting parents of authority, or school teachers may oppress or discriminate against a child. The therapist needs to defend the family's rights—for example, by transferring power from a protective services worker to a grandmother or from a probation officer to a father—and to organize parents to protect a child and defend his or her integrity against the court system or the school system. (A case example that illustrates the struggle to protect the human rights of one child is presented in Chapter 5.)

Negotiations and Contracts

When people are trying to dominate and control, the therapist needs to help them negotiate and reach agreements. Negotiations about money, children, relatives, leisure time, and sex are part of every marital and family therapy. The therapist helps family members express their preferences and compromise with each other. These negotiations are often written as contracts between family members. All the work of the therapy may consist of negotiating a contract and encouraging the family to respect the terms.

Negotiations are particularly important when violence is related to disagreements about money. One solution is to make a contract about money that discourages violence. For example, in a case where a husband was abusing his wife, he was asked to put a thousand dollars in an escrow account. The husband then signed a contract with the therapist that if he hit his wife again, she would get all the money to give to her mother or to her children from a previous marriage. If he did not hit her, at the end of the year the couple would use the money to go on a vacation together.

There are many possible variations of this strategy, but the principle is simple: to make the consequences of the violence more unpleasant to the victimizer than to the victim. Between husband and wife or parent and child agreements can be made so that confrontation is prevented. Arguments about money may be metaphorical of disagreements about sex; sexual unhappiness may be expressing conflicts with in-laws, and so on. Sometimes it is possible to link the symptoms of two family members in a contract so that both will change. For example, if a son is delinquent and a father is obese, and if the father and son love each other, it is possible to set up a contract by which for every week that the son does not do a delinquent act the father will lose two pounds. This type of contract works when there is love and helpfulness between father and son, so that each will give up his symptom as a sacrifice for the good of the other.

Changing Benefits

Sometimes a family rewards hostile acts with attention and concern. In these cases it is useful to reverse the situation so that hostility by one family member results in gratification rather than suffering for others. For example, when one brother is very good and another brother is very bad, the therapist can arrange that every time the bad one misbehaves, the good one will get a present or a special privilege. Instead of the bad brother being punished, the good brother is rewarded. Not only is the presenting problem solved, but the relationship between the siblings changes.

Rituals and Ordeals

Rituals are useful in marking the transition from one stage of family life to another or to indicate a transition in a relationship. The drama of the ritual should be commensurate with the severity of the problem presented to therapy. For minor problems, a birthday party or a trip to visit relatives may be appropriate. A serious transition may require, for example, a ceremony of renewal of marital vows.

Rituals are particularly indicated when people have to overcome very bad things they have done to each other. The ritual signifies that the past is over and that this is a new beginning. In a therapy where the husband had abused the wife and she had attempted to murder him, the spouses were asked to cut off their hair, put it in a jar, take the jar to the top of the mountain where George Washington had taken his wife, Martha, when he was courting her, and to bury the jar under a certain tree. Together with their hair they would be burying their past and all the horrible things they had done to one another. Yet, knowing where their hair had been buried, they could return to that place under the tree when they needed to remember the past so that they would not repeat it.* Cutting off people's hair might seem extreme, but when the problem is attempted murder, cutting off the hair is not very serious. The more extreme the problem, the more extreme the ritual that the therapist devises. Rituals are metaphors that bring people together in positive ways.

The ordeal is a strategy devised by Milton Erickson to make it more difficult for a person to have a symptom than not to have it. A man with insomnia, for example, may be told that if he does not fall asleep by a certain time he has to get up and scrub the floors. The ordeal should be more unpleasant than the symptom but beneficial to the symptomatic person (Haley, 1984).

*This strategy was devised by Neil Schiff, Ph.D.

Ordeals are particularly appropriate for problems of self-inflicted violence, for obsessions, and for compulsions. It is a strategy that should not be used for certain problems, for example, for depression or drug abuse. Substance abusers and depressed people do not have the motivation to carry out an ordeal and the therapist will have difficulty motivating them. An ordeal can be used with people who can be motivated, who come to therapy voluntarily, and who are very clear that they want to overcome the symptom. A drug abuser usually does not come to therapy voluntarily and it is often not clear that he or she wants to get rid of the symptom.

Ordeals are effective with compulsions and obsessions because these often occur with people who are methodical, motivated, and hardworking. They compulsively do something that is not something they like or want to do. So, at the request of the therapist, they can do something else that is also something they do not like and do not want to do. The secret for using this strategy successfully is to motivate the person to apply the ordeal.

Characteristically, the first ordeals described by Erickson followed certain steps. The therapist first finds out clearly what the symptom is, that is, what the problem behavior consists of. For example, if a woman washes her hands compulsively, the therapist asks her to keep a log for a week or two of how many times she washes her hands each day. This establishes a baseline. Then the therapist establishes how many times the woman thinks it would be normal to wash her hands. Compulsions and obsessions are usually a matter of too much or too little of a certain behavior, and the therapist goes by the client's judgment of what is normal. Then the therapist finds out what the woman thinks she should be doing more of in her life. She might say, for example, that she should clean the house better, she should exercise more, read more professional journals, clean the closets, etc. Finally, the therapist suggests that for every day that the woman indulges in the symptomatic behavior more than what she herself has defined as normal, she has to do one of those things that she mentioned she should do more of, but she has to do this behavior in an inconvenient way. For example, she has to set the alarm for two in the morning, get up and clean the house for one hour. The therapist uses the client's own goals and the information the client has volunteered.

Interactional ordeals are particularly interesting. An ordeal could be for a husband to give his wife—or better yet, his mother-in-law—a present every time the undesirable behavior occurs, or to give money to his wife's children from a previous marriage. The ordeal is something that the person dislikes but that would improve his relationship with significant others. The therapist sets up a win/win situation. If the symptom does not occur, the problem is solved; if the symptom occurs, the penalty improves relationships with the family.

A woman came to therapy because she had a serious problem of procrastinating on writing her thesis. She was working on her Ph.D. for a prestigious European university but found all kinds of excuses to write things other than her thesis. This was not difficult to do because she worked as a journalist. I sympathized with her problem and asked her about her family, her friends, her life in Europe, how she got along with her siblings, and so on. The woman said that she had a stepsister in Europe whom she disliked intensely. I changed the subject back to her dissertation and asked how many pages a day she could reasonably expect to write. She said four. I told her there was a solution to her problem but first she had to promise that she would follow the directive. She was not going to like it but I was not going to argue with her. She knew how important it was to finish her Ph.D. and further her career. The woman accepted and I said, "Every day that you don't write four pages, I want you to write a $100 check to your sister and mail it to her with a note saying, 'With all my love,' or 'Thinking about you!'" The woman said that was the last thing in the world she wanted to do and immediately began to negotiate exceptions. I agreed that if there was an international crisis and she had to fly somewhere to report it, that would not count. She was not expected to write on the airplane or while reporting. But she had to keep a log of her jobs and flights which I would carefully check every time she came to a session. The dissertation was finished in a few months and the sister never got a check.

II. The Desire to be Loved

In the first dimension people are motivated by a desire to dominate one another in order to satisfy selfish needs. At the second dimension, people are motivated by the desire to be loved. Typical problems are psychosomatic symptoms, depression, anxiety, phobias, eating disorders, and loneliness. Family members are involved in a struggle to be cared for that often leads to self-inflicted violence. A child might seek to be punished as a way of obtaining attention, even of a negative kind. A spouse may develop an incapacitating symptom in the hope of eliciting concern from the other spouse.

Rivalry, discrimination, and antagonism are often based on a desire to be specially favored. Interactions are characterized by excessive demands and criticism. The therapist needs to redistribute love among family members changing the wish to be loved to the desire to love and protect.

Communication centers around metaphors of internal strife, pain, and emptiness. Characteristically, when one person is upset, another gets sick. Anger at others becomes internal pain. Family members may intrude on each other's bodily functions, determining, for example, what another should or should not eat; at the other extreme, they may be totally indifferent to basic needs for love and comfort. Boundaries are ill-defined and people feel for each other at a visceral level in symmetrical ways. The complementarity that is necessary for an individual to feel loved is lacking. Metaphors are about being identical, about body parts and functions, and about physical illness. There is a preoccupation with sex and with material possessions. Blackmail and manipulation replace direct confrontation. Conversation is often about unsatisfied needs and desires.

The therapist's strategies of choice include introducing metaphors of make-believe and playfulness to move conflicts away from the concrete, physical level at which they are experienced and toward a more abstract, mental and relational realm. Symbols are introduced as props and actions are performed symbolically. In one case, where a mother was asked to care for a sick child, she was given a nurse's uniform to wear as a symbol of giving love through action instead of through identification. In another, a 12-year-old firesetter and his father set controlled fires, playing with make-believe danger instead of burning up with frustration and anger.

Spouses are made to disagree, complain, and reassure each other in prescribed ways. Symptoms are acted out between family members instead of experienced internally. A bulimic, for example, mushes up food and flushes it down the toilet in the family's presence instead of secretly bingeing and vomiting. A depressed man pretends to be depressed and is comforted by his wife, who cannot be certain whether he is or is not pretending.

The therapist arranges for metaphors of contentment and reassurance to replace the metaphors of emptiness and desire. Reality and fantasy are deliberately confused. The message "this is pain" is replaced by the message "this is play." When people are irrationally grim, the introduction of playfulness can elicit new behaviors and bring about new alternatives. What makes change possible is the therapist's ability to be optimistic and to see what is funny or appealing in a grim situation.

For this dimension, where people are seeking to be loved, the best strategies to use are: changing the way parents are involved with their children, prescribing the symptom or some aspect of the symptom, prescribing a symbolic act, and prescribing the pretending of the symptom.

Changing a Parent's Involvement

A therapist may observe that a child's disturbing behavior has the function of involving an otherwise distant parent, who interacts with the child by punishing him or her. The strategy is to engage the parent with the child in positive ways, such as playing together, so the child need not misbehave to maintain a relationship with the parent (Haley, 1976; Minuchin, 1974).

Instead of being distant, a parent may be overinvolved with a child's symptom but not around other areas of a child's life. A strategy is to keep parent and child intensely involved with each other around other issues. For example, a bulimic daughter was intensely involved with her father, a physician who constantly criticized the young woman's eating habits. She constantly mortified him by eating junk foods, vomiting and using laxatives. The strategy was to insist that every day father and daughter have a conversation about politics—the father was very liberal and the daughter was very conservative. These conversations could become very heated. But there would be no more comments about food. The father would not criticize the daughter's habits and she would not tell him what she was doing to her body. The overinvolvement of father and daughter changed from food to politics, their relation-ship became more interesting, and she overcame her bulimia.

A related strategy is to change the memory of an adult's involve-ment with his or her parents in the past. This strategy is useful with people who are tormented with low self-esteem because of memories of being victimized by their parents. The strategy is to say that there must have been someone kindly in the person's childhood who has perhaps been forgotten but who must have existed and whose influence explains the good qualities that the person presents today. One can suggest that perhaps it was a grandmother, an uncle or an aunt, maybe even a school teacher. Slowly the person will begin to remember someone and to build upon this memory. Our childhood memories are not more than a few isolated episodes to which we attribute meaning and continui-ty. We assume that because we remember one episode, it is repre-sentative of many similar episodes which must have taken place. When a new memory of a kindly person is retrieved, the therapist can say that, if one or two kindly actions are remembered, there must have been many more. The therapist can also suggest that every time a bad memory comes to mind, it should be counteracted with the newfound memories of the kindly grandmother, for ex-ample, so that the person will carry inside the image of the good grandmother to counteract the image of the cruel parent.

This strategy is based on a favorite therapy by Milton Erickson: the February Man (Haley, 1967, 1973). A young woman consulted Erickson because she was afraid of having children. She had been neglected as a child by wealthy parents who had left her to the care of governesses and servants. She was afraid that because of her sad childhood she would be a bad mother, not having had the experi-ence of being nurtured herself by a kindly adult. Erickson put her in a trance, regressed her to a young age and conversed with her, introducing himself as a friend of the family. He chatted with her in kind and sympathetic ways. Every session for several months the same procedure was repeated, but the age regression was made to consecutively older ages. The therapy ended when the young wom-an had sufficient memories of this kindly older man, whom she called the February Man, that she was no longer afraid of being a bad mother.

The strategy of changing memories is similar, but does not require a trance. The person is encouraged to search in the past for a kindly person and to expand on that memory. The technique establishes a solid base for the benevolence and kindness that the therapist is presently encouraging.

Prescribing the Symptom

Prescribing the symptom was the first paradoxical strategy described in the therapy literature (Frankl, 1960). If a person came to therapy to get over a symptom, the therapist asked him to have more of the symptom. For example, if he had stomachaches, he was asked to have more stomachaches, to have them at a certain time, in a certain place and so on. A natural development of this strategy is to have parents prescribe the symptom to a child. If a child is a firesetter, the father will make him set fires under his supervision several times a day, so that setting fires becomes an obligation, like homework.

Another variation of this strategy is to prescribe where, when, and how the symptom will take place. A depressed man can be asked to get up early in the morning to sit in a special chair and be depressed. This strategy is particularly useful with couples who quarrel a great deal. They are instructed that every day at a specified time they are to meet in a specified room. For 7 minutes one spouse, looking the other in the eyes, will complain, criticize, and express all of his or her resentments and disappointments. At the end of the 7 minutes the other spouse is only to answer, "I'm sorry, dear," and nothing more. Then it is the other one's turn to complain, and the first one is to say only, "I'm sorry, dear." Neither is to complain or criticize the other, except for those specific 14 minutes and in the manner prescribed. Under the guise of improving communication, communication is in fact blocked and negative sequences are discouraged (Madanes, 1984).

Another possibility is to provide a script to be carefully repeated so that communication is predictable, precise, and positive. The script can be prescribed to a couple, to siblings, or to parents and children. A therapist can instruct spouses on what to say to each other so communication will be satisfying for both. Most people just want to hear their spouse say, "Thank you dear," and "I'm sorry, dear." When these lines occur with sufficient frequency most couples will report good communication and great improvement in their relationship. A simple "I'm sorry" or "thank you" can make a spouse feel understood and powerful.

Parents can be provided with a script to correct obnoxious adolescent behavior. For example, whenever the teenager says something sarcastic or angry, the parents are to say, "I know that you love me, dear; you don't need to be so passionate." The adolescent is taken by surprise and disconcerted, particularly when the rudeness and sarcasm have become habitual.

A script prevents interactional sequences from escalating into hostility. Most people believe that communication is the expression of thoughts and feelings. The opposite is also true. When we say something, we begin to believe it, and then we feel accordingly. When people say positive things, they tend to feel more positive. The principle is similar to having spouses hold hands in a session. It is very difficult to fight or to feel hateful towards someone whom you are touching. The physical contact changes the feelings and the atmosphere of the session.

Another variation of prescribing the symptom is to prescribe restraint. This is a good strategy when the clients seem more interested in controlling the therapy than in solving their problem (Haley, 1987). This is often the case when clients are therapists themselves or are simply shopping around for a therapist, uncertain about the school of therapy they would prefer, about whether the therapist should be male or female, and about whether they should be in therapy at all. These clients usually want to interview the therapist rather than be interviewed. The approach is for the therapist to say that he or she could solve the problem presented to therapy, but that perhaps it would be best not to do so because the consequences of solving the problem may be worse than the problem itself. For example, if the problem were solved, a woman might become a better mother than her own mother; for many women this is very difficult to tolerate. If the problem were solved, a wife might find that her husband is too successful and the marriage might be threatened, and so on. All the possible consequences of solving the problem should be reasonable and probable. As this type of conversation continues session after session, people solve the problem themselves and demonstrate that they can tolerate the consequences.

A lesbian couple who were both studying to become therapists came to HMI shopping for a therapist. They said that on the same day they were going to interview two more therapists to decide which they preferred. The presenting problem was that one of them had anxiety attacks and terrible fears so that she could hardly leave the house. She was also afraid of being alone and of the dark. The strategy was to talk to them only about what the possible consequences could be for each and both of them if the symptoms were resolved. For example, the therapist suggested that anxieties and fears are traditionally a feminine symptom, particularly so in this case, since one of the young woman's greatest fears was of being raped. If she were to abandon the symptom, she would be abandoning the last vestige of a traditional feminine position. This might mean that she would totally assume a lesbian identity, and what would her mother think? The young woman was very annoyed at the thought that this had anything at all to do with her mother or even with the issue of femininity. The therapist said perhaps it did not. Perhaps it was the father who would become upset. Maybe the two women would break up, since one would no longer be the strong, normal one and the other the weak, crazy one.

The therapist reassured both women that she was not predicting that any of this would happen; she was just worried that it might. She was certain that she could solve their presenting problem but she was concerned about whether she should, since the consequences of solving it might be worse than the problem itself. The women protested that this was not so and that they really wanted to solve the problem. The therapist said that maybe, if the anxiety and fears disappeared, the young woman would become a better therapist than her girlfriend and the competition between them would become intolerable.

The idea in this strategy is that everything that is proposed as a consequence is annoying and irritating but has some truth to it. In this case, the more the therapist expressed reluctance to conduct the therapy, the more the young women insisted that this was the therapy they wanted. After three or four sessions conducted in the same way, focusing only on the possible consequences of solving the problem, the fears and anxieties had disappeared. The therapist apologized for not having been of more help and behaved as if puzzled by the rapid resolution of the problem.

Prescribing a Symbolic Act

When people are involved in compulsive self-destructive behaviors, an effective strategy is to ask them to perform repetitively an act that is symbolic of the self-destructive act but lacks the self-destructive consequences. Self-destructive behaviors are usually a misguided attempt to punish someone who does not provide enough love and attention. So the symbolic act should involve a certain punitiveness towards those whom the person is symbolically punishing. This strategy is particularly useful with bulimics and with people who engage in acts like pulling out their hair or sticking pins in themselves.

In the case of a bulimic, for example, the therapist can organize the family members to buy all the junk food that she prefers for bingeing (fried chicken, cookies, cheap ice cream, french fries, etc.) and set it out on the kitchen counter. In the presence of the family members, the bulimic is to mush up all the food with her hands symbolizing what goes on in the stomach when it digests the food. When it is all mushed, she is to throw it down the toilet. If the toilet clogs, the family member the bulimic most loves or resents (for example, the father) is the only one allowed to unclog the toilet. The act symbolizes not only what the bulimic does to herself but also what she puts her family through (Madanes, 1981).

Another way of using symbols is the strategy of prescribing the metaphor. Here the therapist selects the most important elements of a situation, translates them metaphorically, and presents them as the ingredients of a story, essay, or play for the couple or individual to develop.

For example, a couple quarreled to the point of violence over issues of organization, control, power, and money. They both had doctorates in the social sciences and worked as consultants to social service organizations. After listening to their marital troubles, the therapist said that he would like to address them at their high level of competence rather than treat them as the average couple. Given their high level of expertise in issues of organizational and interpersonal difficulties, he wanted each of them to write an essay about how he or she would advise an imaginary organization to solve difficulties such as conflicts between the directors and threats to leave the organization. Each spouse was given an imaginary problem to resolve; each problem was metaphorical of the couple's own difficulties. The next session, after they read their essays, they explained how the solutions they had found to the problems of the imaginary organization could be applied to their marriage. They could easily think of solutions at a metaphorical level, and once the solutions were obvious they could apply them. For example, the wife began to encourage her husband with positive comments, they chose to meet out of the house in a pleasant atmosphere, and the husband took pains to explain clearly what he wanted from his wife.

Milton Erickson used to tell stories based on the patient's situation that would contain suggestions for solutions to the patient's dilemma. The strategy of prescribing the metaphor is similar; however, the clients create their own metaphors and find their own solutions. The therapist only provides the metaphorical theme that represents the client's current situation.

A very rebellious 12-year-old boy was in therapy with his obnoxious mother, who drove him up the wall. The boy was failing completely in school even though he had an IQ of 150. The therapist said that she wanted to tell him a story and that he was to think about a possible end to the story. This is the story: "There was a computer factory where computers were being manufactured in an assembly line. For some reason one day a couple of workers in the line got distracted and put the pieces of one particular computer together in a different way. And this particular computer turned out to be the first computer that could actually, really think. But nobody knew it, and if somebody did not operate him properly, there was no way that the computer could let anyone know that he could really think by himself. So there he was on the shelf, waiting to be purchased, with all the other computers, and everyone thought that he was a computer just like the others. But he was different. And so he was sitting in the store hoping that somebody who would realize that he could think would come and buy him." The boy had to finish the story.

In the next session the boy and the therapist discussed various possible endings to the story. It was clear that, even though he did not say it explicitly, the boy understood that the metaphor referred to his own situation and he felt understood. Solutions to his problems were discussed from then on in the context of how difficult it is to communicate when one has a special kind of intelligence. The mother was helped to develop more sympathy for his plight.

Prescribing the Pretending of the Symptom

A child may have stomachaches to obtain love and dedication from the parents. A husband may become depressed so that his wife will comfort him. In these cases the function of the symptom is a personal gain for the symptomatic person and the benefit consists of receiving love. The therapist can arrange for the child to pretend to have the stomachache and for the parents to comfort him or her as if it were a real stomachache. The depressed husband can be asked to pretend to be depressed and the wife to take care of him as if his depression were real. When the benefit is obtained for the pretend symptom, then the real symptom is no longer necessary (Madanes, 1981).*

III. To Love and to Protect

In the first dimension people are motivated by the desire to dominate, and at the second dimension they are motivated by the desire to be loved. In the third dimension, people are motivated by the desire to love and protect others. The wish to love and protect can bring out our highest qualities of compassion, generosity, and kindness. It may also elicit intrusiveness, possessiveness, domination, and violence. Such intrusion and violence are often justified in the name of love. Typical problems presented to therapy are suicide threats and attempts, abuse and neglect, guilt, obsessions, temper tantrums, and thought disorders. The therapist needs to change how family members protect and love one another, encouraging repentance for the violence inflicted.

---

*This strategy, as well as several others in this chapter, are presented only briefly here because they were previously published in somewhat different form.

Communication between family members centers around death, hopelessness, exhaustion, loss of control, and guilt. Characteristically, when one person in the family is upset, another wants to die. Metaphors are of imprisonment, entrapment, and loss of freedom. People feel they have lost control of their own thoughts and their own lives, since an individual's actions have life or death repercussions on other family members. There is competition among some family members for the position of most guilty and most self-destructive, while other family members are idealized as kindly and worthy of love and protection. The therapist needs to introduce metaphors of togetherness, love, fun and happiness, reversing who is helpful and who needs to be helped. In therapy family members playfully enact situations where parents are helpless and children are helpful. Love is redirected and accepted. As children comfort and advise their parents, hope replaces despair. The family members who are out of control or suicidal recover self-control as they advise and help the others.

For this dimension the best strategies are reuniting family members, changing who is helpful to whom, empowering children to be appropriately helpful to their parents, and orienting people toward the future and deeds of reparation.

Reuniting Family Members

When a problem brought to therapy is related to the pain of separation and exclusion from a loved person, the task of the therapist is to reconcile and reunite family members and to heal old wounds so that separation is no longer necessary. If parents and children have become estranged from each other, particularly mothers and children, no matter what the age, no matter what the presenting problem, one must assume that the symptom is related to the estrangement. The main effort of the therapy must be to bring people together again.

For example, a woman came to therapy because of anxiety attacks and panic that she thought were related to conflicts with her lover. However, she had three adult sons who had disappeared from her life and did not write or call. She did not know whether they were dead or alive. The therapist organized her to find the sons through contacts with her separated husband, friends, relatives, and police. There was a family reconciliation where everybody came together at the mother's house and resumed communication. The woman recovered from her anxiety attacks.

Sometimes parents want to expel their children literally or emotionally. In these cases containment is part of the strategy of reuniting family members. In fact, often, before one can do anything else in therapy, one has to arrange for the family to contain the children without expulsion. It is important to understand that in the parents' mind expulsion may not be contradictory with wanting to love and protect their children. Parents with very low self-esteem may love their children and precisely because they love them, want to give them away to others, that is, to people who they think will be better parents.

Sometimes one spouse loves the other and wants to stay in the marriage while the other is rejecting, resentful, and refuses to come to therapy. In these cases, the best strategy may be to coach the loving spouse on how to win back the other one, how to understand the other spouse, how to respect his or her freedom, how to give the kind of love that the other one wants, etc. Similarly, sometimes it is necessary to coach a parent on how to deal with a child, and sometimes it is necessary to coach a child on how to put up with, sympathize with, and take care of a parent.

When a young person is so alienated that self-inflicted violence has reached the point of a suicide threat, and the therapist judges that the relatives truly want the young person to live (rather than secretly desiring the person's death), hospitalization can be prevented by organizing a suicide watch in the home. All dangerous instruments, such as knives, scissors, etc., are removed from the house and family members take turns at watching the suicidal young person 24 hours a day. The suicidal person, moved by all this love and concern, eventually abandons the suicide threats. The relatives are encouraged to be loving and kindly and to sacrifice themselves in providing this watch. In some cases the suicide threats are just that and the person has no intention of committing suicide. The suicide watch acts as a deterrent because it limits the person's freedom to an intolerable degree.

In establishing a suicide watch it is not a good idea to put one spouse in charge of the other. Since the suicide threat may be an attempt to escape an unfortunate marriage, the suicide watch may increase the feeling of intrusiveness and subjugation and escalate the violence. When an adult, married or not, threatens suicide, it is best to organize the family of origin rather than the spouse to conduct the suicide watch. This is part of the same idea of containment and of helping people to stay together when they fall into despair because they cannot take care of each other.

Changing Who is Helpful to Whom

Sometimes the function of the symptom is to help someone else and the benefit for the symptomatic person is altruistic. For example, the daughter of a depressed mother may make a suicide attempt; the mother is then forced to come out of her depression to help her daughter. The girl's suicide attempt is helpful to the mother in that it makes her pull herself together and behave like a mother to a daughter who needs her. The strategy here is to ask the mother to pretend to be depressed and the daughter to pretend to help the mother in age-appropriate ways, for example, by saying reassuring things, entertaining her with games, expressing love directly, etc. The hypothesis is that the depressed mother is covertly asking the daughter for help and the daughter is covertly helping the mother by attempting suicide. The pretending makes the mother's covert request overt and provides the daughter with appropriate ways of helping her mother that are not self-destructive (Madanes, 1981).

Another strategy is to change who has the symptom. This is an idea based on an important value of American culture: taking turns. In America people take turns at speaking and do not interrupt each other; they stand in line; they take turns at playing, at chores, in love and in sex. When a family presents with an adolescent or adult child who is very bad and other children who are very good, it is natural to suggest to the siblings that it is not fair. Why should only one be bad and ruin his or her life? Why should this sibling get all the attention and take on the task of providing thrills or a purpose in life to the rest of the family? If the other children took their turns, the bad one could be good sometimes and get on with life. The therapist appeals to the love between siblings and to their sense of fair play. This makes explicit an implicit family rule in a way that moves the good siblings to change so that the bad one need no longer be bad (Madanes, 1984).

Empowering Children to be Appropriately Helpful

This strategy is useful when parents present as incompetent, helpless, physically ill, addicted to drugs or alcohol, abusive or neglectful. The children love and protect the parents, but the parents are not giving love and protection to the children. Nothing is asked of the parent or parents. The children are put in charge of one aspect of the parents' life — their happiness. The therapist asks the children: How could your parents organize their lives so that they would be happier? Should they go out more often? To a movie? To a restaurant? Perhaps they could go away for the weekend or have a candlelight dinner at home. Maybe the children could cook and serve the dinner. As the discussion proceeds, the therapist encourages the children to make concrete suggestions, for example, what movie the parents will see, what restaurant they will go to. Children may be put in charge of taking care of themselves and of one parent, of organizing the parents to get along better with each other so they can be happier, of organizing the household and the family's good times. All this is done in age-appropriate and playful ways so that there is no burden to the children; on the contrary, they are relieved to be able to express their love and to take care of their parents. The children are not really in charge. The whole organization is play, more in fantasy than in reality. The parents are moved as they experience their children's love for them and respond in kind, correcting the hierarchy and taking responsibility for themselves and for their children (Madanes, 1984).

This strategy is based on the idea that a family is a very limited organization. Basically, there are parents and children, sometimes grandparents and other relatives. So if one is thinking in terms of who can initiate change or who can help whom, there are only five or six possibilities: One can have parents helping their children, parents helping each other, children helping each other, grandparents or other relatives helping either the parents or the children, and children helping the parents. When no relatives are available and when parents are incompetent or helpless, the children are the best resource, so the therapist enters the system through them. Basically one is looking for the best way to initiate a positive change in the family.

This way of conceptualizing the problem probably originated from working with drug addicts. It is difficult to expect heroin or cocaine addicts to behave maturely as parents to their children. The same is true in cases of great poverty, overwhelming loss, or physical illness. Often the healthiest members of the family are the children.

It might seem that expecting children to initiate change and be helpful to their parents is an excessive burden. But the fact is that in these families the children are already in that situation. All that the therapist is doing is organizing them to be more effective helpers with less personal sacrifice. In fact, it gives children great satisfaction to have a function that is overtly recognized and appreciated as helpful to the parents. (One way of using the strategy of changing who has the symptom and empowering children is illustrated with a case example in Chapter 7.)

Orienting Toward the Future and Deeds of Reparation

Sometimes people come to therapy with feelings of depression, worthlessness, and guilt. They are obsessed with their failure and the lack of meaning in their lives. Instead of arguing with them, the therapist can agree that they may be worthless and guilty; however, since they themselves are not important, they might give more of themselves to others for whom life *is* important. They might select a group of people, preferably those somehow related to their guilt feelings, and do anonymous good deeds for them. For example, a Vietnam war veteran haunted by visions of atrocities witnessed or committed could be sent to donate money, time, and work to organizations that care for Vietnamese orphans. Or, an army commander, depressed and obsessed with guilt over his errors in judgment, which may have led to the loss of his soldiers, can be told to do reparation by donating money and effort to the support and guidance of the widows and children of his men lost in battle. Preferably the good deed will be anonymous, so that it is unquestionably done not for reward or recognition but purely for reparation and altruism.

Probably the first time I used this strategy was when a young, professional, intellectual couple brought their five-year-old daughter to therapy because the school complained that the child was cruel and sarcastic to other children. At home the parents had also observed that she was mean. The therapist noticed that the parents, who were in the process of divorce, were cruel towards each other. The directive was to tell the parents that they needed to model kindness for the daughter so that she could herself be kind. In order to do this successfully, each day each parent had to do an anonymous good deed in the presence of the child. For example, the parent might go to the park and find an animal that needed help, leave a present at somebody's doorstep, or do an anonymous kind act for someone in the family. As the parents did the good deeds, the child changed and became kindly. When the therapy ended, the parents were reconciling.

Another example is the therapy of a 43-year-old black man referred by his therapist, who told him that he had to be totally honest with me, he had to tell me the whole truth. He was in the process of divorcing his second wife whom he had only recently married. He said he was so upset by his two failed marriages that several times he had almost deliberately driven off the side of the highway. He had two teenage children from his first wife, with whom he endured many years of unhappiness. The second wife was a much younger woman, very religious, with whom he had not had any sexual contact before the marriage. Their sexual relationship and their short life together turned out to be disappointing.

I listened to this brief account and said, "Your therapist said to tell me the truth, so tell me the truth." He said, "The problem is that I have been having an affair for many years and that is another source of torment for me." At my insistence, he explained, with great difficulty, that he had started an affair with a nurse when he was a medical resident, almost 20 years earlier. It was an impossible relationship because she was white and he was married. I said, "What was so impossible, so bad about her being white?" He said, "My mother would not approve of it." I said, "You mean you went through medical school, you are a physician, and your mother tells you what to do?" He said, "Well, I am a very religious person." Little by little he told me about his love for the nurse. I kept pressing him: "There must be something very bad about her because just being white could not be the only bad thing about her." He said there was nothing bad about her and even his children wanted him to marry her. However, he had divorced his wife but not married the nurse. He married a black woman instead and moved to another state, but that marriage had not worked.

I said, "There is still something more. You're not telling me the truth. Let's go to the past. Tell me about your childhood." He said that he was brought up very religiously because his father was a minister in a Caribbean country. The father had been defrocked for having affairs with parishioners and was banished from the island. This brought tremendous humiliation to the family and he was raised in poverty with the shame of what had happened to his father. He had left and put himself through college and medical school in the United States.

I said, "I still don't understand how a man as intelligent as you would have this difficulty in being with the woman he loves if she's really not a bad person." He said, "It's a problem with God." I said, "What's the problem with God?" He said, "God would disapprove of this relationship." I said, "Explain to me about this God that you have that is so cruel and petty. What kind of God . . . I mean, do you actually talk to God, does he answer you? Does he tell you, 'Don't see the nurse?' What does God say?" He said, "No, it's God inside of me."

Slowly I pulled out of him that the terrible sinful thing that he was doing was to love the nurse more than he loved God; that was an unforgivable sin. I said that I was a very spiritual person, yet I could not understand what kind of God he had that was so cruel and unreasonable. Why would God care about his love for a woman when there were so many important problems in the world, so much suffering, hunger, and injustice? I asked him to allow me to be silent for a few minutes. I had to try to develop some empathy for him, to feel that I could understand him and think like him, or I would not be able to help him.

After a few minutes of silence, I said that I thought I could understand him. If I ever loved a man more than I love my children, I would think it was sinful. I think I should love my children more than I love anyone else. So, in a sense, my children are to me as God is to him. I was hoping to introduce the image of a more maternal, less punitive God. I said that he had to come out of his depression, his unhappiness, and his guilt not only because we all have the right to the pursuit of happiness but also because I was certain this was affecting his work. He had an important mission and he could not work well with his patients when he was obsessed with these thoughts. He agreed, and I said that God should be more concerned about his work as a black physician than about his love for a nurse.

I told him I wanted him to proceed with his divorce, ask the nurse to live with him or marry him, and tell his mother that he was now an adult and, even though he would always take care of her, he would do with his life what he wanted. However, if at any time he felt guilty and thought about how he should love God more than he loved this woman, he was to take a day off to do good deeds. He had to go to the black ghetto in the city and talk to the children and the teenagers, giving them hope that it is possible to be poor and black and to become a successful, happy doctor. Particularly he should talk to black teenage girls so they would know that there are some black men who are kindly, intelligent, and compassionate. He could also find poor people who needed medical care and give it to them for free.

He said, "I would have a problem with insurance. I couldn't do that; malpractice will not cover me." I said, "We are talking about God here. Do you think that God cares about malpractice insurance?" Reluctantly he said that he would try to do these things. In fact, he had been planning to go off on a mission. I said he could do that if he wanted to, but these particular good deeds he could only do when he was obsessed with guilt about loving a woman. Otherwise he could not do them. The idea was to counter his obsessive, guilt-ridden thoughts with actions that were charitable and important.

I saw him three more times. At the idea of doing the good deeds, he totally stopped obsessing about sinfulness. When he came to the next session, I asked, "What good deeds have you done?" He said, "I haven't had to. I spoke with my mother and she said it was time that I married the nurse. She knew about her for a long time!" I said, "Well, I'm really disappointed because I was really counting on you doing something for the poor. I think you should do these good deeds anyhow." He said, "I don't have time. I'm so busy with my practice and preparing for my mother's visit and the nurse is coming." As far as I know he never did do any good deeds to pay for his guilt.

This approach is indicated when people are overwhelmed with guilt or with obsessions and depression and when love and sorrow toward the victims of violence lead to self-inflicted violence. It can also be used to elicit love for love's sake and as an example for others.

Just as it is useful to bring out the best from the past to remind people of their original love and good intentions towards each other, so it is helpful to project people into the future, suggesting that in 10 or 20 years this day, this week, this month, may or may not be remembered. It is in everyone's power to create good memories of love, caring, playfulness and humor that can be remembered many years from now. The therapist asks people to plan and create such good memories through their actions and interactions. A special celebration or outing, unusual or exciting events, good times with friends — any of these can bring out good feelings that contribute to the positive outcome of therapy.

This is a good strategy for families, and particularly couples, who come in bickering and fighting about every grim, sordid, menial detail of life. They quarrel about who did or did not do the dishes, argue bitterly about who will clean up after the dog, who will take out the garbage, who will straighten out the garage. The therapist cannot help thinking, "For this I studied so many years? To talk about these things?"

The strategy is carried out in steps. First the therapist asks the spouses about the best moments of their lives that they remember. For example, what were the best moments of their courtship? Their honeymoon? If the therapist insists, even the most bitter people will come up with wonderful stories about things that they did many years before. Then the therapist emphasizes that 10 years from now who did the dishes or took out the garbage is not going to be remembered. Only that which is special, unique, or unusual is remembered. So at the end of the session, the therapist directs the couple to do something in the next week or two that will be remembered positively 10 years from now. For a few sessions, the therapist gives only this directive at the end of each hour. This strategy brings out the best in people and raises them out of their grimness.

The following is an example of how to carry out this strategy. A couple came to therapy with a serious problem. The wife was severely diabetic and was drinking herself to death. She drank a half bottle of vodka a night and was not paying attention to her diet or her medications. The husband was not quite violent, but he was a very tall, big man who had violent temper tantrums. He would take a plate of spaghetti and smash it against the wall. The wife was a tall, bloated woman who came to the sessions wearing shorts with curlers in her hair. They talked endlessly about messes: the attic, the garage, cleaning up after the dog, taking out the garbage.

The therapist was a nice young man. As he struggled with this couple he seemed to be getting more and more depressed. They were the kind of people that make the most dedicated of therapists think: "For this I struggled through a Ph.D.?" As the supervisor, I had the challenge of motivating the therapist to become more interested in the couple.

One day, after several sessions, I said to him, "Today I would like you to go in and ask the wife whether she has seen the movie or read *Gone With the Wind*. She is going to say, 'Why are you asking?' Answer that she and her husband remind you so much of Rhett Butler and Scarlet O'Hara. They also have this passionate relationship, always fighting. Like Rhett the husband is always on the verge of violence; Scarlet is always trying to change him but she never succeeds, she never changes him at all!"

When the therapist asked this, the husband immediately looked at himself in the mirror. The only resemblance he had to Clark Gable was his mustache, but he started to stroke it. The wife said, "*Gone With the Wind* is my favorite novel! I've read the whole book five times. I've seen the movie probably eight or nine times. And Scarlet *did* change him." The therapist said, "No. She didn't. I'll bet you $10 that you won't find a passage in the book that shows that she changed him. I'm surprised that, if you know the novel so well and you are so similar to Scarlet, you continue trying to change your husband instead of just enjoying his unpredictability and the passionate relationship that you have with him." She said she would read the book again. But this had already set the context for a different type of interaction. They were identifying with a cultural stereotype of a romantic, passionate couple. The therapist had momentarily raised them to a higher level of being.

Then the therapist proceeded: "I'd like you to tell me, what are the best memories of your life together? Way back in the past when you first met, what were the best times that you had together?" First they could find nothing. The therapist insisted: "There must have been some good times. Perhaps your honeymoon, the birth of the first child." Slowly they began to remember. The husband told how they went on their honeymoon to a place in Florida where there were dolphins. One day he went by himself to the dolphin lagoon and learned the signals that the trainer gave to the dolphins for the show. The next morning he took his wife on a walk, gave the signals, and the dolphins came out of the water and put on a show just for her. Listening to this, the therapist began to get interested in the man. The wife softened as she remembered the episode.

Then they remembered a couple of other charming incidents in their lives. The therapist told them that in the next two weeks he wanted them to just do one thing, and that was to have one good experience that would be remembered 10 years from now. Who did the dishes, who took out the garbage, who cleaned the attic, was not going to be remembered 10 years from now, but an unusual event, like what had happened with the dolphins, would be remembered always.

That day was the first snow of the winter. When they left the session the husband built a big snowman right at the door of the institute, which is something we always remember. This couple discovered wonderful things to do in Washington. For two months, the only directive was to create good memories. All conversation about the relationship and her diabetes was abandoned, except as it related to the good memories that they were creating. In less than three months the wife's health was greatly improved. She had quit drinking even though the therapist had never talked about the drinking, and she was taking care of her diet. They thanked the therapist and the therapy ended.

Another approach is the Hemingway strategy. This strategy is useful with very intelligent, educated, depressed people. Those are the people who have gone to the best schools. They have high degrees, and money—everything in life—and are bored, depressed and overwhelmed with a sort of existential anguish. They don't get along with their spouse and they don't like their work, or they have panic or anxiety attacks or psychosomatic problems. The therapist says to such people that naturally they are depressed: They are intelligent. One thing is certain in life. There is going to be suffering, pain, and in the end death. The world is full of injustice and horror. Anybody who is intelligent is depressed. This is a natural condition of humankind. What is surprising is that anyone would wonder why they are depressed.

Still, when one has decided to go on living, one may as well look at life in a different way—like Hemingway. Hemingway was a very intelligent, creative man. He had everything and he was very depressed, in fact, suicidal. He wrote about suicide from his early years but did not do it until his old age, when he was very ill. He decided to stay alive, he decided he might as well have an interesting life and embarked on a life of adventure. He fought wars and went on numerous safaris. Wherever there was something interesting and difficult happening, he was there. Why not live like that?

So one begins to plan an adventure with these clients. As they begin to plan adventures, they begin to think about the world differently. For example, one might say, "There are many problems in South Africa. Since you don't care whether you are dead or alive, why don't you go to South Africa to help bring some justice." As the person has to argue whether that is really what s/he wants to do, s/he begins to think and plan to do something meaningful.

IV. To Repent and to Forgive

In the first dimension people are motivated by the desire to dominate, at the second dimension people are motivated by the desire to be loved, at the third dimension the motivation is to love and protect. In the fourth dimension the main issue between family members is to repent and to forgive. Typical problems are incest, sexual abuse, and sadistic acts.

Communication among family members is sparse and centers around secrecy. They are afraid of revelations that will bring on more shame; however secrecy perpetuates problems, maintaining inappropriate coalitions and making incest and abuse possible. Metaphors are of ignorance and lack of conscience, empathy and responsibility. People behave like predators and victims.

The therapist introduces metaphors of spirituality and unity, emphasizing symbols of compassion and higher emotion. Family members are moved step by step from abuse to repentance, reparation and protection of one another. Reality and responsibility are emphasized, as secrecy and hypocrisy are replaced with open communication and sincerity.

For this dimension the best strategies involve creating an atmosphere of higher emotions, finding protectors for the victims in the family, and eliciting repentance, forgiveness, compassion, and a sense of unity with others. Since repentance and forgiveness are the topic of Chapter 3, only the other strategies are discussed here.

Creating a Positive Framework

This includes improving the quality of life and creating an atmosphere of higher emotions. The therapist makes an effort to improve communication, assertiveness, and the ability to give and receive love.

Often a therapist needs to raise people from the grimness of their situation into a better way of being. It is useful to start every session, as well as to remind people during the session, that they have come to therapy out of love and concern for each other and that they are seeking a better way of being and of relating to each other. These comments by the therapist prevent angry interactions and petty hostilities among family members.

Humor and the use of the absurd are an important part of this strategy. When people are irrationally grim, the introduction of playfulness can elicit new behaviors and bring about new alternatives. What makes change possible is the therapist's ability to be optimistic and to see what is funny or appealing in a grim situation.

Finding Protectors

In cases of abuse and neglect, the very existence of the family unit is threatened. The therapist needs to look for strong, responsible people in the extended family or in the community and transfer responsibility to them and away from professional helpers. The transfer needs to happen gradually and in stages so that ultimately, under the care of the protector, family members will be able to forgive each other. For example, if an adolescent has been abused by a father, a responsible uncle or grandmother can be put in charge of supervising the family to make sure that this will not happen again. At first the family will be supervised by both the protective services worker and the uncle, then only by the uncle who will report to the protective services worker, and finally by the uncle alone with the worker remaining available to reopen the case if necessary.

Finding a protector is useful not only in cases of abuse and neglect, but also when parents are overwhelmed because of physical illness, emotional, or financial problems. It is also the strategy of choice with multiproblem families with single parents. The parents are asked to appoint a godfather and/or godmother for each child. This can be done no matter what the religion of the family, since the concept of the godparent or equivalent is prevalent in our culture, although this is a particularly effective approach with Catholic families. The godparents can be found among relatives, friends of the family, or members of the community. They will provide emotional and spiritual guidance to their godchild, advice, a friendly containment of the child, a sympathetic ear, and when possible, help with school, an orientation towards getting a job, and material help as well. The child will be responsible to the godparents for his or her behavior, and the godparents will coordinate their efforts with the parent and with the therapist through visits and by telephone.

In this way, the therapist breaks up the family unit into a series of units composed of each child and godparents, along with the basic unit of the children and the parents. The therapist talks with these different subgroups separately and sometimes together. If there are no relatives to serve as godparents, people from the church or from the community may be enlisted. The burden of responsibility is then divided among many adults in the natural network of the family and the children's lives are enriched.

This strategy follows a basic principle: When the therapy is not going well, expand the unit, bring in more people. With an expanded unit, the therapist is dealing with a different level of problem, working with a different hierarchy, in a different situation. One gains new information and new points of view. The therapist is in fact creating a tribe, and then, instead of working with the nuclear family, working with the tribe. She is organizing an extended network that will protect the children and decentralize the parents.

Typically, the sequence in therapy is as follows. If a therapist is not making progress with an individual child or young adult in therapy, the parents are brought in. If there is still no progress, the therapist brings in the siblings, then the grandparents, the uncles and aunts, the relatives, and ultimately, members of the community. Eventually a level is reached where change takes place, because every time new people are approached there are new points of view and different resources. Each time that new people are brought in, the therapist emphasizes that the parents are enriching their child's life by arranging for these new influences. In this way the parents are encouraged to feel that the involvement of others is their success, not their failure, and the hierarchy of the family is respected.

In families where parents reject their children, rejection may be overt, as in cases of physical abuse, or covert and difficult to discover, as in cases of emotional abuse. Some parents establish coalitions with agents of social control against their children. For example, some parents denounce their children to the police with false charges and then refuse to bring the child home even when the court judges in the child's favor. Some parents institutionalize their children in mental hospitals with false reports of violence and homicidal threats. Other parents reject their children in more subtle ways, with scathing criticism, excessive demands, and unsavory interpretations of the child's behavior and motivations. Often the parents have also been rejected as children and the extended family cannot be engaged.

The therapist needs to confirm the child's reality and to encourage positive behaviors of love and tolerance from parents to children and from children to parents. It is useful for the therapist to find ways for the parents to benefit from containing, rather than expelling, the children. Giving the parent a monetary reward for being kindly may be worthwhile.

A single mother of a 10-year-old boy beat her son brutally. Her boyfriend also beat him. The boy had been placed in foster homes and hospitalized several times. Previous interventions by therapists and the Department of Social Services had failed. The mother said that when she beat her son she had out-of-body experiences; she could see herself doing it from the ceiling where she was floating in the air. She could not control her behavior.

After several sessions, during which all attempts to improve the relationship were unsuccessful, the therapist told the woman that the institute was so concerned that we had decided to pay her $10 a day for each day that she or her boyfriend did not hit the boy. She would be paid once a week, in the therapy session, $70, but if she had hit the boy even once, she would lose all $70 for that week. The therapist believed she was an honest person and would take her word for whether she had hit him or not. The boy's report would also be taken into consideration and obvious marks would be noticed, but basically she would be on an honor system.

The son would be paid $1 a day for every day that his mother did not hit him. He would make $7 a week, but he also would lose the whole amount if his mother hit him even once during the week. Paying the boy for not getting hit would take care of the issue of provocation. In this way the family's income was practically doubled, since the mother was on welfare. The contract was in effect for three months, then had to be discontinued because of the high cost to the institute. The boy was never abused again. The mother accepted that she could control her behavior as well as that of her boyfriend, the relationship with her son improved, and she took steps to find a job and improve her life.

Sometimes antagonism and violence are so pervasive that the best a therapist can do is to arrange for separation. To block all contact between spouses may be the only way to prevent violence. Some couples come to a therapist with the question, "Should we separate or should we stay together?" Most therapists prefer not to give such advice and instead to offer assistance in clarifying issues and thinking about problems. However, when there is violence, the therapist needs to take a position, assess the possibility of change, evaluate the risks involved, and advise the couple on whether to separate or not to separate.

Sometimes a therapist needs to support a spouse in leaving a marriage and in finding protection and support with extended family or friends. A therapist might also encourage a spouse to press charges against the other spouse or to seek a court injunction against any further contact. Sometimes a therapist might want to recommend only a temporary or limited separation to prevent violence while resolving conflicts. In certain cases a therapist may want to bring in a grandparent or another relative to live temporarily with the couple. Often the presence of a third person, a witness, prevents violence. Therapists need to know how to evaluate the risk of violence in a relationship and how to make recommendations to prevent physical abuse.

Clarity about when to recommend a separation is even more important in cases of violence against children. To expel a parent or to remove a child from the home may be the only protection for an abused child. It is usually better to expel a parent than to remove a child. Sometimes it is necessary to make it illegal for the parent to see the child at all. If a child must be removed from the home, it is usually preferable to find a placement with relatives rather than with strangers. Keeping a child within the natural network with a caring grandmother or aunt is always better than placing the child with strangers.

Compassion and Unity

Eliciting compassion and a sense of unity is useful when working with individuals who have been the victims of trauma and injustice and are obsessed with trying to remember and to understand why this happened to them. After spending the necessary time helping the person recover and understand childhood memories, it is important to reach closure and end the subject. The therapist says that, even though it was very painful, what really happened to that particular person is not so important. For example, whether or not this particular woman was sexually molested as a child is not as important as the fact that so many millions of women have been abused through the centuries. Each one carries within her the memory of all those women who suffered, and her pain is each woman's pain. If a man was abandoned by his mother, what matters is that so many children suffer terrible injustice and torment without reason or explanation. It is important for each person to make some contribution towards ending that pain. The adult has more in common with the therapist or with a friend than with the abused child he once was. This appeal to separate from the past while at the same time developing a sense of unity with the rest of humanity helps people to disengage from past traumas and get on with their lives. This approach brings out the best in people in ways that make one happy to be a therapist.

A 55-year-old physician consulted about family difficulties, anxiety, psychosomatic problems, and depression. After several sessions, he told me that the root of his problems was in his miserable childhood. He was raised in a lovely home in the country with servants and all kinds of comfort. One day, when he was eight years old, his father unexpectedly summoned him and his brother to the study and announced that their mother was leaving and that the two boys were to be placed in a Jesuit boarding school that same day. The mother did not say goodbye and there was no further explanation. Life in the boarding school was harsh and he suffered frequent physical punishments from the Jesuits. He remembered that every day for years he cried as he wrote to his mother, begging her to tell him what he had done to drive her away. He was certain that he was responsible. She never answered his letters. When he came out of the boarding school, at age 18, he found her, but she refused to give him an explanation, as did his other relatives. He never had found out the truth and now his parents were dead.

I discussed with him various possibilities of discovering the truth but he had tried everything, to no avail. At this point I said to him that millions of little boys had suffered terrible abuse and neglect over thousands of years. There is no justification and no explanation for that pain. What matters is to prevent suffering from continuing. I said that he knew that, and this was why he had become a physician, devoting his life to easing human pain. I said that, even though he must look back at that little boy crying in a monastery with sorrow, he was no longer that little boy. He had more in common with me or with any of his friends than with that sad little boy. That child was dead but the people in the present were very much alive and important to him now. He accepted this view, and was able to make some important changes in his life. He comes back to see me once or twice a year and I remind him of how to think about his past.

Conclusion

I have presented my favorite strategies for changing metaphors of strife and conflict to metaphors of love. All problems brought to therapy can be said to stem from the dilemma between love and violence. This dilemma appears in different dimensions as the fear of a struggle for power, as the desire to be loved, as the despair of not being able to love and protect, and as the shame of not repenting and not loving compassionately. The therapist looks for the love that is missing, changing violence into love and anger into compassion. When people are involved in a struggle for power, the therapist moves them to want to be loved. When the wish to be loved has led to self-inflicted violence, the therapist uses the strategies that lead to the desire to love and protect others. When love has deteriorated into violence, the therapist encourages family members to accept blame and to repent. That is, the therapist chooses a particular strategy by figuring out whether people are motivated by a struggle for power, by a desire to be loved, by the wish to protect, or by guilt and blame.

3
REPENTANCE AND REPARATION IN CASES OF SEXUAL ABUSE

I want to know what love is. I know you can show me.

—Lou Gramm

THE PROBLEM OF incest and sexual abuse has reached crisis proportions in our society. No therapist can avoid treating the offenders or victims. Faced with the need to supervise the therapy of juvenile sex offenders who are not institutionalized, I have developed a standard approach to ensure that further harm will not occur and that therapy sessions will be therapeutic. The method consists of sixteen steps that can be used with a variety of cases of sexual offense, not just with juveniles. Here I describe the steps and how to use them when the abuse has been committed by an older brother who has sexually molested a younger sibling. I then explain how to apply the method to different situations: for example, when the offender is the father; when the offense happened in the past; when the offender is not allowed to have contact with the victim; and in a variety of other situations. The strategy is therapeutic for both the victim and the victimizer.*

---

*I mostly refer to the victim as "she" and to the victimizer as "he" because this is the most frequent distribution of gender, although there are many male victims and female offenders.

Sixteen Steps to Reparation in Cases of Sexual Abuse

In the situation of an older brother who molests a younger sister or brother, the first step is to obtain an account of the sexual offense. The therapist gathers the whole family together and begins by asking the parents to describe exactly what happened. Who did what to whom, how, when, where, how often: everything that they know. Then the therapist goes around the circle asking one by one what each knows, starting with the siblings, and then moving to the offender and the victim. The therapist can encourage the victim to talk but there should be no pressure on her. The pressure should all be on the offender and on the rest of the family. The therapist must feel comfortable using explicit language because it is very important to be clear about exactly what happened.

This is usually the first time that the whole family has talked about the abuse. Even when there has been police interrogation, the family members may not have talked, since those interviews are usually individual. This is also therapeutic in the sense that it prevents denial by the offender. There is tremendous group pressure when everybody explains all they know and all they knew. It is very difficult for the offender to deny what he did.

The guiding principle for the therapist is that there can be no secrets in these families. Incest is possible because it is secret, so in these families all secrets must be violated. In a normal family, people have secrets from each other without severe consequences. In families where sexual abuse occurs, people characteristically try to keep secrets from each other and from the therapist. When there has been incest one cannot allow any more secrets, because a secret can deteriorate into another incestuous relationship. Part of not having secrets is to use very explicit language and to be comfortable in addressing all subjects.

Paper and crayons as well as dolls and toys are provided for younger children to use to represent what happened. Sometimes parents will ask that young children be excluded. If the offense is such that younger children could be victimized, it is best to insist that they be included. Otherwise, one can go along with the parents' wishes and keep them out of this session, but not necessarily out of other sessions.

Step two involves the therapist asking each family member why what the offender did to the victim was wrong, starting with the offender. The offender usually has trouble explaining why it was wrong. He will say it is against religion, it was wrong because he was caught, it is against the law, and so on. Then the therapist asks the parents to explain other reasons why it was wrong. The parents will say it was wrong because it was painful, violent, an intrusion on the person.

In step three the therapist agrees with them that it was wrong for all those reasons and then says that it was wrong for one more, very important reason. It was wrong because it caused the victim spiritual pain. Depending on the religious and cultural background of the family, the therapist uses the expression "spiritual pain" or "pain in the heart." Sexuality and spirituality are related. So a sexual violation is a violation of the person's spirit, and that is why it is particularly wrong. It is more hurtful than a physical attack, like hitting someone over the head. Families never disagree with this view.

The fourth step consists of the therapist saying that a sexual attack also causes a spiritual pain in the victimizer. It is horrible to do something like that to somebody else, particularly to a sibling one loves. The therapist expresses feeling for the pain of the offender.

Step five usually happens spontaneously. Someone in the family tells the therapist that the victimizer and perhaps other family members were also sexually molested by relatives, by strangers, or by friends of the family. Usually there has been incest in several generations. There is rarely just one victim and one victimizer.

The therapist sympathizes with this, and step six is to say that the acts of the offender caused spiritual pain not only in the victim and victimizer, but also in the mother and in other family members. In attacking the victim the offender was attacking his mother, his father, and everybody else in the family, because he was doing this to a child they love.

Step seven is to ask the offender to get on his knees in front of the victim and express sorrow and repentance for what he did. He must do this on his knees and in such a way that it is apparent to everyone in the room that he is sincere and truly penitent. The offender often objects, and sometimes the parents support his objections. The offender wants to say that he is sorry but he does not want to get on his knees because it is humiliating. The therapist needs to say that that is exactly why he should get on his knees. If the offender refuses, the therapist says that therapy cannot proceed until he gets on his knees and that, in fact, the therapist must report to the court that he is not truly penitent and so perhaps therapy is not indicated. The therapist uses the whole leverage of the court, and the alternative to therapy is usually institutionalization. (All our cases have been court involved.)

It may be necessary to have the offender express sorrow and repentance on his knees again and again, until therapist and family are satisfied that he is sincere. Sometimes several sessions are necessary. When the offender gets on his knees and expresses sorrow for what he has done, the victim can forgive him if she wants to, but she does not have to forgive. There should be no pressure on the victim.

In step eight the therapist asks the other family members to get on their knees in front of the victim and express repentance and sorrow for not having protected her. If the offender is resistant to getting on his knees, one might do step eight first, and then go back to step seven. It is important to have a humiliating apology as soon as possible, preferably by the end of the first or second session. This is therapeutic for the offender and very therapeutic for the victim. It establishes publicly, in front of the whole family, that the victim was a victim, that she does not have to apologize, that nobody is interested in what she contributed to the situation, and that she does not even have to forgive. One of the problems of victims is that they tend to define their whole personality as that of a victim. Now the victim can leave the session with a feeling of not being accused and not having to be punished. This is the beginning of not having to think of herself always and only as a victim.

Step nine involves discussing with the parents what the consequences will be if something like this ever happens again. The therapist encourages the parents to settle for the harshest consequence: expulsion from the family, which usually means institutionalization.

In step ten, the therapist sees the victim alone and encourages her to talk about the abuse, to express her feelings, fears, and pain.

The therapist expresses sympathy but emphasizes that when very bad things happen to people, they develop a special quality of compassion that raises them to a higher level of being. They can empathize more deeply with the pain of others. The therapist can also say that, even though this seems terrible now, what happened is just one very small part of her life. It is useful to give a time frame, saying that the offense probably took up just a few minutes in a day that had 24 hours, in a year that had 365 days, out of all the days of her life. While this was happening other important things were happening. She had friends that she liked. Perhaps she liked to dance or liked music or art. The therapist orients the victim towards beautiful things in life and begins to put the offense in that context. It is an unfortunate thing that will eventually be forgotten.

In step eleven, the therapist begins to find a protector for the victim. It is a mistake to think of the mother. Usually the mother in these families is very weak and cannot protect the victim. As an ultimate result of the therapy the mother should be stronger and able to protect the victim, but at this stage in the therapy she is not. It is best to look for another relative, somebody in the extended family. A respectable, responsible uncle or two grandmothers may be very good protectors. The process of setting up the protector is lengthy and continues through the therapy.

Step twelve is reparation. The therapist asks the parents to think about what the offender could do as an act of reparation, even if reparation is somewhat symbolic because there is really nothing he can do to compensate for sexual violence. This should be an act involving a long-term sacrifice, beneficial to the victim. Usually the reparation is that the offender will work and will deposit a set amount of money every month in an account for the education of the victim over a long period of time.

In step thirteen the therapist discusses activities for the offender in order to orient him toward a normal life. The therapist talks about school, sports, relationships with friends, and what is sexually normal. Problems often develop because many of these families are religious fundamentalists who will not allow any sexual outlet outside of marriage, and within marriage only for the purpose of procreation. It is best to spend some time with father and son alone, encouraging the father to talk frankly with the son about sex, sexual impulses, normal sexual outlets, and what to do when an inappropriate sexual impulse arises. These conversations are therapeutic not only for the son but also for the father, who often has sexual problems himself.

However, the only legal sexual outlet for a juvenile is masturbation, and for a fundamentalist masturbation is worse than sexual intercourse and is not permitted. It is sometimes worthwhile to try to influence the elders of the church to give special exception, but this usually fails. The therapist may end up recommending long showers and washing carefully in certain places, hoping that the adolescent will catch the implications. One event that can actually end therapy is when the offender falls in love with an appropriate person of an appropriate age. This applies only to juveniles and is only one sign among many others (age-appropriate behavior, empathy towards others, improved family relationships, etc.). For adult offenders falling in love has nothing to do with being an offender and should not be considered a sign of change in the sexual perversion.

As part of step thirteen group therapy is therapeutic and useful. Many of these boys have difficulties with peer relationships. The group sessions focus on normal peer relationships, on how to present themselves in public, on how to behave towards each other and with other people, and on their strengths.

Step fourteen is restoration of love.* One cannot end these therapies without restoring the mother's love for the offender as much as possible. There are two types of mothers in these cases—the ones who turn against the offender and those who turn against the victim. In both cases one has to restore the mother's love, and this is sometimes very difficult. The therapist can help the mother recall how she loved her child when s/he was a baby and how available she was to help him/her grow and develop, emphasizing how she can still continue to do so. Positive identification can be encouraged by pointing out similarities between mother and child. Special time can be set aside for pleasurable interactions between mother and child when there will be no unpleasant conversation. The child can be encouraged to demonstrate love to the mother, hoping that she will respond in kind.

*This step was suggested to me by Magali Sojit.

Step fifteen involves restoring the position of the victimizer in the family as protector of the younger siblings—not as *the* main protector, but in a protective relationship the way an older sibling should behave towards a younger. One might have the offender advise the younger children on how not to get into trouble, how to avoid strangers in the street, how not to talk to bad people, or how to refuse drugs.

In step sixteen the therapist helps the offender to forgive himself. This is sometimes very difficult. Here one might use the strategy of doing good deeds. The therapist can say that whenever the offender gets obsessed with thoughts about what he did, he should do a good deed for others. In the case of adult offenders there are organizations for abused women, where they can donate their work or their money. Similar good deeds can be set up for juveniles.

Sexual perversion and sexual abuse may happen only sporadically. The consequences, however, are devastating for the victim. Because of this danger, it is best not to end therapy, but to continue scheduling sessions for a long time, even if only every four or six weeks, to keep an eye on the family and detect any signs of trouble that could lead to another offense.

All through the therapy there are three elements that must be remembered. One is secrecy. The therapist must violate all secrets, even though the family may attempt to restore secret coalitions. The second is to dispel the idea of provocation. In all these cases the offender implies or even affirms that he was provoked by the victim, that the victim had a part in this. The therapist must categorically refuse even to consider the possibility. There might have been provocation, but the victim is the victim and the offender is the offender. The third element is that the therapist must understand that, in the mind of the offender, this was a romance. The offender almost has a thought disorder. Somehow he truly believes that this was a romantic relationship. Even when it was violent, even if there was great age disparity, in his mind this was a romance between himself and the victim. One cannot really be sensitive to the offender or understand his thinking if one does not understand this.

Very often it is necessary to repeat the step having the offender on his knees many times, because this is the only way that the family and the therapist can be reassured that this is not going to happen again. In the case of a 12-year-old who had raped his eight-

year-old-brother and his five-year-old twin sisters several times, the
therapist had him expressing repentance on his knees at home
every day. The mother was not convinced that he was not going to
do it again, so he apologized every day for more than a year—in
spite of the fact that, at his own request, he was kept locked up in
his room most of the time. At the end of the first year he attempted
to attack one of his sisters again. The therapist had the family tie
bells to his ankles and his wrists so that they would always hear
where he was. The bells represented taking away the privacy that
he had taken from others. He cried bitterly, but after that he never
attacked his siblings again.

What is curious is that all the time this boy was going to school,
where he never bothered anyone and was liked by his classmates
and teachers. He had been very severely abused himself, under
rather unusual circumstances, as is often the case with sex offenders. The four children were adopted. They had been raised in an
orphanage in Central America. The older boy had been violently
sexually abused by his father, who was dead, as well as by people
in the orphanage. While in the orphanage, the boy was extraordi-
narily protective of his three little siblings. He used to go to the
social worker's office and put the files of the four of them together
on top of the pile, hoping that the social worker would act on their
case and get them adopted together. He eventually succeeded and
they were adopted by a nice American couple. It was only then that
he began to molest his siblings.

When the Offender is the Father
and Other Circumstances

In cases where the offender is the father, the same steps are
followed, including having the father get on his knees and express
sorrow and repentance to the victim. The members of the family
also get on their knees in front of the victim to express sorrow and
repentance for not having protected her. When the offender is an
older sibling, it is usually the offender who resists getting down on
his knees. When the offender is the father, he often gets down on
his knees without argument and cries and repents. It is the mother
who refuses. The mother will say that she did not know anything,

there was no way that she could have known, she has no responsibility, she does not appreciate the implication that she was somehow involved, and so on. The therapist can say that at least she could have had open communication with her child, so that the child would have come to her. She should express sorrow and repentance on her knees for not having had that type of communication with the child. One might even include the grandmother, and have her on her knees for not having had the kind of communication with the grandchild where the grandchild could have gone to her for protection. These steps are very important, because the therapist must give the victim the sense of being righted.

When the offender is the father, it is necessary to add a marital stage that consists of discussing and finding solutions to the marital and sexual problems that are always pervasive in these cases. This marital stage requires many sessions using various strategies with the couple and sometimes involves the extended family.

Sometimes a teenage daughter has strong memories of having been excited by incest with the father, so she has a sense of provocation in the situation, of her own sense of responsibility. The therapist must absolutely insist that the adolescent is a victim in the situation. It is characteristic of sexual abuse that it is often not violent but sexually exciting to the victim. That is part of the offense—part of the violation of the person. A father should take care of his daughter, not arouse sexual feelings in her. He should, in fact, protect her from having sexual feelings towards him, and create the right context for their relationship. It is very important to be very clear about this. If the therapist is confused, it is best to remember that the law punishes the offender; it does not punish provocation.

Sometimes the offense happened in the past and the victim comes to a therapist wanting not only to remember but also to clarify the situation with the parents. The parents are brought in and all the steps are followed in the same way. If the father is dead, all the steps that are possible are carried out with the rest of the family. So the remaining family members get on their knees and apologize to the victim for not having protected her. One brings in all the living family members, even if they have to travel long distances to come to a session. If the relatives insist that the victim's memories are "crazy," they still should apologize because they must have done something that was conducive to those memories. However, total denial by everyone is rare.

In working with these problems one has to use one's common sense and modify the steps according to the severity of the offense. The method was developed for violent cases where there has been rape. However, there are situations like that of a 16-year-old involved in some kind of sexual play with his 14-year-old sister, without rape, without violence. Obviously, going through all these steps would create a problem instead of solving one. The therapist can talk about how sexual play between siblings is wrong because it is incest and about what type of relationship is normal. One can have the siblings apologize to their parents, or have the brother apologize to the parents and the sister. He is the older one, and the boy should take the responsibility, since usually there is some coercion. But one does not go through all the humiliation.

When a young person has sexually molested someone outside the family, there is usually a court order forbidding any contact between the offender and the victim. So it is not possible to have the offender apologize on his knees to the victim. If the therapy is with the offender and his family, the same steps can be followed except that the offender apologizes on his knees to his parents for having done this to another person and for having brought humiliation and shame to the family. Reparation can be done by donating time and/or money to an organization that symbolizes the victim, such as an institution for the protection of children or of battered women. If the therapy is with the victim and her family, the therapist carries out as many steps as possible, including having the family express sorrow and repentance on their knees for not having protected her. There should be no pressure on the victim and no insinuations of provocation on her part should be accepted.

There are other special circumstances. For example, perhaps one is working with an offender whom the court has ordered to have no contact with the children he has molested. The only people in the therapy are the man and his wife. One must modify the steps and have the man apologize to his wife for having done this to the children and to her.

Or, consider the situation when a man has molested his biological daughter and therapy begins while he is in jail. The stepmother and stepsister totally reject the victim and deny any involvement in the incestuous relationship. It would be useless to ask the stepmother and stepsister to apologize on their knees for not having protected the girl. They could be asked to say they were sorry they did not protect her but without getting on their knees. The father could be brought from prison to apologize on his knees, or the family and therapist could visit him there. The grandmothers could also be brought in to express their sorrow on their knees and perhaps arrange for the girl to live with one of them. The steps are modified according to each particular circumstance.

In some situations, families deny everything. For example, the father says he did not do it and the mother says the child invented it. In these cases the court case is usually pending. It is very important to go very slowly and wait. Once the case has gone through the court, the therapy can begin, because then, whatever the outcome, the offender can speak freely. Many therapists make the mistake of becoming indignant; then they lose the relationship with the family and cannot do proper reparation to the victim.

While exercising patience, the therapist sees the victim and different family members individually, trying to piece togther what happened and what they can talk about. The therapist can say, "If you could talk about this, what would you say?" or ask, "How come she had this fantasy, if it was a fantasy?" It is useful to bring in the parents or siblings of the abusive father because often they emphasize to the offender that there is a morality above that of the court, and that he has a responsibility to the family and to the victim. Even when the offender is an adult his mother is very important. The relatives usually talk about other victimizers and other victims in the extended family, making it easier to divulge all secrets. When all else fails, one can have the offender apologizing on his knees to the victim and to the rest of the family for having done something to bring about the suspicion that there had been a sexual offense.

Often there are several abusers and several victims in the family, and one has to decide whom to deal with first. Usually it is best to take one situation at a time, first going through all the steps in relation to the presenting problem. So even though it has been disclosed that there are other victims and victimizers, one finishes these steps, and then perhaps starts them over with another family member. It may not be necessary to go through all the steps again for other family members, although this is the exception. Sometimes it is best just to listen sympathetically and then come back in later sessions to find out more about the other offenses, expressing sympathy and hope that the future will be different and these violations will end in the family once and for all.

Sometimes one can go through the steps simultaneously for several people. For example, in a case with a mother, a grandmother, and three children who had been molested by different family members at different times, but all in the recent past, the therapist went through the steps simultaneously. It may not have been therapeutic to give more importance to the victimization of one than of another.

In all these cases different family members are seen individually at different times. The victim is very much oriented to normal relationships. There are discussions about possible sexual impulses and how to handle them, and about what is appropriate, what is interesting, and what is good. It is best for the therapist to believe that we all have unlimited sexual potential, in that there are all kinds of sexual activities that could be pleasurable. But most of us decide early on that there are certain sexual behaviors that we are not going to engage in. Then we just do not practice them.

The therapist discusses with victim and victimizer how to make an intelligent decision about what sexual behaviors one will never practice. For example, perhaps the victim has sexual fantasies about this or that, for this or that person. However, what would be best is to marry a nice person with whom one can have an ongoing relationship, as well as children. With male offenders it is very important to talk about male sexuality. Most men have sexual fantasies about very young women, in fact women who are almost children, but most men integrate those fantasies in their sexual life with adult women and simply never act upon them with children. If they are controlled in this way, the fantasies are normal. It is the acting out of these fantasies in real life that is abnormal. Of course, in some cases one has to discourage any sort of fantasy.

When one has to separate children from their parents, in most cases, if the father is the offender, it is best to separate him from the family. However, often the mother will not allow that, so it is the child who is rejected. In those cases it is best to place the child with relatives instead of in a foster home with strangers. There almost always are grandmothers, aunts, cousins, or other relatives even if the therapist has to mobilize to find them. Then there is continuity and the child is not with strangers. Usually relatives who take a child with a sense of compassion and charity are better than foster families who are paid. Sometimes it is possible to arrange for the relatives to be paid as foster parents.

It is important to emphasize the detail with which one has to discuss what to do if the inappropriate sex impulse arises again. The therapist needs to take the person through the alternatives, particularly when the offender is an adult. The wife will typically say that he should come to her and talk to her. This is not the right thing to do because the wife is very much part of the problem. The offender will say that he will meditate or he will pray. The therapist needs to say that he must get out of the house immediately, go to church and pray, or go to his mother's house and pray, or go to a restaurant, or go jogging. One has to take the offender through these steps many times and repeat the appropriate things to do. This applies to all sexual perversions. It is very important for the therapist to be easily accessible to the offender by telephone so, if the wrong impulse arises, repeat offenses can be prevented.

This method can be used with cases of physical abuse as well. The parents get on their knees and apologize to the children. Then the therapist proceeds to provide alternatives to the rage and despair that lead to the physical abuse. In these cases it is very important to acknowledge the spiritual pain to the victimizer for having harmed the children.

For example, a prominent scientist was physically abusive to one of his daughters in a way that was almost sexual. The girl attempted suicide. I knew I had to report the father to Protective Services. Instead of reporting him myself, I convinced the father to turn himself in, which is more therapeutic because it places the responsibility on him.* He wrote a letter to the Department of Social Services explaining what he had done. He was not prosecuted, but the therapy proceeded on the basis that he had assumed full responsibility for his acts and was repentant.

*This intervention was suggested by David Eddy.

Conclusion

In cases of incest and sexual abuse there are several important principles to remember:

1. The therapist must emphasize that the sexual offense was a violation of the spirit of the victim.
2. The offender must express repentance sincerely and on his knees.
3. Reparation must take place.
4. All secrets must be violated.

II

Clinical Examples

4

THE THERAPY OF
A JUVENILE SEX OFFENDER

Just sit out there and have them go through the moves.
When you see something you don't like, change it.

— *Joshua Logan (advice to young directors)*

THIS CHAPTER ILLUSTRATES, with excerpts of therapy sessions, the steps presented in the previous chapter. I was the supervisor behind the one-way mirror calling the therapist over the phone with instructions. At the time, the therapist, Lucy Banks, was in training at the FTI. The transcript consists only of what I considered to be the most important highlights of the therapy.

A 16-year-old boy had been sexually molesting his nine-year-old sister over a period of a year. He would go to her room at night and do everything short of rape. He would expose himself, rub himself against her and get on top of her in very frightening and intimidating ways. She had not told anyone about this for a year. Finally she told one of the three middle brothers, who told the parents. They took the child to a psychologist who reported the sexual abuse to the Department of Social Services. At the time the therapy began the boy had been placed in a detention center. He could not come home until the girl said that she was no longer afraid of him, and until the therapist gave permission.

Since this was one of the first cases to which the method described in Chapter 3 was applied, the order in which the steps should be followed was not clear. Today we carry out the steps in a different order. Perhaps it was the resistance in this case that made it clear that the order had to be changed. When one goes through the steps as outlined in Chapter 3, there is little resistance.

The only step that is not in this transcript is the first step, the account of the sex offense, which happened in the first session. It is not included because of the length of the transcript — there were five children and two parents, and each had a turn.

At the beginning of the excerpt that follows, Harold, the offender, is telling about a man who is in jail and cannot get out until after the year 2000. I was on the phone with the therapist at that moment and suggested that the therapist take the opportunity to say to him that his conversation was very relevant because if he were to abuse his sister again he would end up in jail like that man. Present in the room are the parents and all five children. There are three couches: The father, the mother, and Sarah sit on one, the therapist, Daniel and Harold on the other, and Peter and John sit on the third.

Banks: Are you talking about jail?

Harold: Uh-huh.

Banks: Well, I think that's kind of appropriate in a way. You know we've talked a lot here about what has happened in the family. We've talked about what Harold has done. And we've talked about wanting to get Harold back home. But what we haven't really talked about yet is the effect of all this on Sarah. We really haven't got into that except in a very superficial way. This really was a horrible thing to do. A sexual assault like this is a horrible offense to commit on anyone, especially on your sister and especially on a little girl who's nine years old. It's very serious. And as we mentioned earlier, you know sexual assault on someone this young is rape! I mean it's considered rape! With this sort of offense you could go to jail for the rest of your life for rape. And I really want to underscore the seriousness of this.

You know, Harold, you're supposed to be the protector of your little sister, not her rapist. It's very horrible what has happened here. There are a few things that need to happen now. One thing is I need a commitment from each and every person in this family. Peter?

Peter: Yes?

Banks: Are you willing to do the very best you can to help Harold and to help Sarah to make sure that nothing like this happens again? (Peter nods affirmatively and the therapist stands up and shakes hands with him.) John? Are you willing to do the very best that you can to help Harold and to help Sarah to make sure that nothing like this ever happens again?

John: Uh-huh. (The therapist stands up and shakes hands with John. He smiles)

Although this has not been described as one of the steps, it is appropriate in cases where there are several children. It takes so much time to talk to each child that sometimes there are sessions when one barely speaks with each one. If one gets this commitment at the beginning, everyone is involved and all the children know that they are important, even though they may not be addressed in a particular session.

Banks: Daniel, are you willing to do the very best that you can to help Harold and to help Sarah to make sure that nothing like this happens again?

Daniel: I would. (He smiles and the therapist shakes hands with him.)

Banks: Harold?

Harold: Yes. (He grins.)

Banks: A laugh like that could mean the last time you would see your brother!

Harold: I didn't laugh!

Banks: It's very serious. This is not a laughing matter. It's very serious.

Harold: All right. Sure.

Banks: If there is any question in your mind that you really need to think about it — I know that this can make people nervous but it's not a laughing matter. What's happened is horrible and very serious. Mrs. Adams, are you willing to do everything you can to make sure nothing like this ever happens again?

Mother: Yes.

Banks: Mr. Adams, are you willing to do the best that you can to help Harold and to help Sarah and to make sure that nothing like this ever happens again?

Father: Yes.

Banks: Mr. Adams, I have a task for you this week. I would like you this week to think about what could be absolutely the most severe punishment that you can have in store for your son Harold if anything like this—if you were even to have a suspicion of anything like this—were to occur again. And I mean a punishment that would be so severe that this young man won't even want to contemplate something like that again. And I'd like you to give thought to that this week and we can talk about it more in the future. If you ever were to suspect it in the future. The next task, Harold, needs to come from you.

Harold: Yeah.

Banks: And what I want you to do is to come over here to your sister. You need to address your sister. It's very important that at this time you get on your knees, you tell your sister that you know that what you did was horrible, that you are sorry, that you accept full responsibility, and that you'll never do it again.

(Silence)

Banks: Go ahead Harold. It's really something that needs to happen before this family can move forward. Before you can move forward. Go to your sister. It's the manly thing to do.

It is important to say, "It's the manly thing to do," because in a year or two he would be tried as a man and also because this is the crime of a man. It would be a mistake in a situation like this to address him as a boy or to use the word "boy" or "kid" or anything similar.

Banks: It's really the manly and respectable thing to do. Harold, I want you to go do it. (Harold does not move.) Mr. Adams, I'm going to have to call on you to help me with your son. I'd like you to instruct your son to do this. I think you know that it's the only thing for a man who has made such a terrible, terrible error to do.

It is very tense in the room. Daniel moves away from his brother on the couch; he's afraid of the father approaching.

Father: Come on, son. Do what she says. Come on! She can't make progress if you don't.
Banks: He may need some help from you. You may need to go over and bring him to his knees.

The mother is crying and the little girl is comforting the mother. She gives her tissues and pats her on the shoulder. The father stands up and gestures to Harold to stand next to him.

Father: Come on. Do what she says to do.
Banks: Kneel down to your sister's level.
Harold: I don't get on my knees!
Father: Harry, stop it! Now stop it and do what she said! Go on! Get down!

John takes the father's place next to the mother and comforts her together with his sister by putting his arm around her and offering her tissues. There is a long silence while the father patiently stands next to his defiant son.

Banks: You know, Harold, that you've wronged your sister and that you owe her something.
Harold: Yep.
Banks: And this is one small . . .
Harold: (Turning to his sister) Sorry, Sarah.

With two words like that Harold quickly tries to establish a secret coalition with his sister: He turns to her and says, "Sorry, Sarah" as if they were alone. That is what the therapist cannot allow.

Banks: I'm sorry, that won't do it.
Father: That's not . . . come on, Harry, get down and give it.
(Silence)
Father: Say something from the heart, not just "sorry." Would it help if I just said it with you? Come on, it's just the family.

Harold: Yeah, I know.

Father: All right, then, well get down there. Down on your knees! It's not a joke. You know you could be in a lot worse predicament. So get down. You're not demeaning yourself. You are apologizing to Sarah.

Harold: I know. I did.

Father: No, that's not an apology. It's not from the heart. It's not a heartfelt apology! It's not a heartfelt apology at all! It's not saying that you are sorry for what you have done. If you want to return home, then you better start right here.

Harold: Why would I think of doing it again?

Father: I don't know.

Mother: What made you do it the first time?

Harold: I served my time.

Father: No.

Harold: I'm doing my punishment in Westfield Home.

Father: No.

Mother: No. You're not being punished.

Father: That's just being there. That's not punishment.

Harold: It's away from the family though.

Mother: Yes it's away from the family, but you are not being punished for what you did.

Harold: But it's away.

Banks: We need to end this session in about two minutes and this is something, Harold, that you really need to do. And if it doesn't happen in the next two minutes I don't know if I can be helpful. It seems that the only thing that I could report to the court would be that you weren't really remorseful for your crime. That you were sorry because you've been removed from your family, but that you had no remorse for what you did to your sister.

Harold: I said I was sorry to her.

Banks: It has not been convincing to anyone in this room! You have a very serious debt to your sister that you really need to fully recognize. The court needs to know that you truly feel remorse and that's the kind of information that they are asking from me. So that's kind of the bind that you put me in and I can't continue to see you all if it's just going to be a charade.

I need to know that there is really some remorse, to know that it wouldn't happen again. So I would only see you one more time to finish things up if something like this can't take place here. (long pause)

Harold, you know I really think that you are facing a critical point in your life and this right now can be a turning point for you as to whether you're going to live the rest of your life as a man or as a criminal rapist! And that's a very big difference! I think you have it in you to be a man but I don't know. As far as punishment, the court is going to be thinking about that. Your father is going to be thinking about that in terms of punishment from the family, if this were ever to happen again.

There's another thought, another plan. Something else needs to happen, which is that, when Harold is able to, I think it would be a very good idea for him to get a job and for the money from that job to go in a fund for Sarah's use in her future as a sort of reparation, damages so to speak.

Father: That's a good idea.

Banks: But as far as I am concerned there is very little I can do to be of assistance unless there is remorse and unless I see some demonstration of remorse, and we've got two minutes before this session ends. So it's up to you Harold. A man or a criminal.

Mother: What's wrong with getting on your knees?

Harold: I won't do that.

Father: Why not?

Harold: Because.

Mother: Because why?

Father: Tell me why. What's wrong?

Harold: Because I won't get on my knees.

Father: What's wrong? What's wrong with that? That's your sister!

Harold: Well, if I do it's none of your business."

"If I do it's none of your business." He wants to do it alone with Sarah, which would be reestablishing the incestuous secret.

Banks: Mrs. Adams, is there anything else that you can say from the viewpoint of a woman and a mother to help your husband

· 73 ·

in his attempts to convince Harold that he needs to do this? To get his life on a new start?

Father: He's just being stubborn. He knows.

Mother: I don't think what you are asking of him is too much.

Father: No, it's not too much.

Mother: You don't . . . from my viewpoint (she speaks in a very soft, sad voice) I told you I went through the same thing and nobody ever said, "I'm sorry."

She had been molested by her stepfather as a child. The fact that the mother tearfully regrets that nobody said, "I'm sorry," to her, Harold's resistnace to getting on his knees, and the parents' insistence that he do it are all factors that indicate that this is the correct approach to therapy. Each in his or her own way is saying that an apology "on his knees" is significant and necessary.

Mother: You feel you're hurting. You feel you've been punished.

Harold: All right. Sarah. (turning to her)

Father: No that's not the way she wants it. That's not the way she wants it, Harry.

Harold: I'm sorry for —

Mother: Harry —

Harold: — sexually molesting you.

Father: Harry, that's not the way she wants it.

Harold: And I will give you money if you, you know —

Mother: No, Harry.

Harold: — need it.

Mother: Honey, hear me out!

Father: Harry!

Harold is talking right over the parents. It is so important to him to establish a private coalition with his sister that he is apologizing and offering to pay her. He makes the offer intimate and private by ignoring what the others in the room are saying.

Harold: As much as you want.

Mother: You're hurting. But, but, but honey, look at me, look at the damage that it does to somebody! See, I didn't have nobody to turn to, but it does, it leaves scars, Harry.

The mother's choice of words suggests she is unclear about whose pain she is referring to—hers or Sarah's. She is indicating that she experiences the attack on the child as a metaphorical attack on herself.

Father: Everybody is hurt.
Mother: Everybody's affected by this.
Father: The whole family. Not just you, not just your pride.
Mother: I know you're hurting and I feel for you.
Father: It's not just your pride.
Mother: But Sarah is hurting.
Father: Yeah! Her most of all! You're six years older than she is!
Mother: I mean look! Look at the damage it's going to do to her. I'm 36 years old and a couple of months ago I had to let your Dad know who my attacker was, but the point is, it leaves its scars.

It could be that Harold's attack on his sister made it possible for the mother to reveal the secret that she had held inside for so long.

Father: If you don't do it now then that's a scar that you are going to carry plus it's a scar that she has got to carry.
Mother: All we want to do is try to get this family back together and get you the help that you need along with everybody else in this room. That's all. We love you. You know that! I've told you over and over again. The help is here Harry. You've got people that want to help you. Not being nosy, not cut you down, but that want to help you. You know, when I was growing up I didn't have nobody to help me. I had to do it on my own!
Father: Do you want me to get down there with you on your knees, do you want me to get down on my knees too?
Mother: But believe me—
Father: Huh?
Mother: As you're affected by it, so is she. She's the one who has the nightmares still, who comes in the room at night and gets in the bed with me screaming!
Father: Do you want me to get down on my knees too?
Harold: What's the difference? What's the difference? She don't want me home anyways!

Mother: Can you blame her? After what you put her through!?
Harold: Hey! All right! I don't have to come home. I'll stay at
    Westfield.
Mother: Wait a minute. Can you blame her? Can you blame her?
Harold: Tell the court, forget it! Forget it! I don't want to come
    home.
Mother: Harry, can you blame her? Harry, can you blame her?

Harold wanted to be home with the family and he could not come
home until Sarah said she was no longer afraid and until the therapist said that he could come home. "Can you blame her?" asks the
mother. This is the whole drama. Who is to blame? And he was
refusing to accept the blame for what he had done.

Harold: I'll just wait until I get enough money, get my own apart-
    ment.
Mother: Harry! Can you blame her for what has happened?
Harold: No.
Mother: My goodness!
Father: Do you want us to blame her for not trusting you anymore?
Mother: That's like somebody—
Harold: She don't have to trust me!
Mother: Harry!
Harold: (to Sarah) Do you want me home—yes or no?!
Mother: Harry!
Father: You don't put it to her like that.
Mother: That's not the way.
Father: That's not the way to do it.
Mother: No, that's not the answer.
Harold: Do any of you all want me home, yes or no?
Mother: Harry, I think you know that everybody in this room
    wants you home.
Harold: All right. All right.
Mother: But you've got to get the help.
Harold: Well, I've told you, I don't get on my knees. I don't get on
    my knees.
Father: You are just being stubborn. If I get down there with you
    will it help?
Harold: Nope.

Precisely because he objects is why the therapist has to get him on his knees! It is important to have an action that is symbolic enough of total humiliation so that it can be a turning point in the relationship.

Banks: Well, there is nothing here that has indicated to me that you feel remorse for what you have done at all. And I think that's really unfortunate because I think you have a lot of potential if you can get beyond this hurdle.

All this time the little girl has been reassuring and comforting the mother. The attack on Sarah was a symbolic attack on the mother. That is why she and the younger brother are comforting the mother; that is why the mother cries and the little girl does not cry.

Father: You know, Harry, there is nobody that is a tough monkey. There is nobody that is a tough nut. Tough nuts can be cracked!

Banks: I want to call on some other members of the family here to help. I know from having spoken with all of you that everyone in this family wants Harold to be home. And everybody in this family wants Sarah not only to be safe but to feel safe. And I would like each of you three brothers to ask Harold if he would please do this because it is really the only way he's going to get over it. Because you all know and you love them both, but you all know that he owes this to Sarah and it's the manly thing to do. It's the right thing to do. So Daniel, I'd like you to start and I'd like you to ask your brother to do this for those reasons.

Daniel: All right. You know we all love you Harry and we want you home. You are just too crazy to see that. You don't want to get down there because you think it might hurt your pride. You think you're big and bad, but you know you owe it to Sarah. Why don't you just get down there and do it? You know this may be the last time you ever see us. You know we all love you so why don't you just get down there and do it! (He cries, holding his head with one hand.)

Banks: Peter? Ask your brother.

Peter: Why? Why don't you get down on your knees? It's just a simple, easy task. You act like it's so hard to do. Mom and us, we are the ones that have to suffer for what you do. (He stops abruptly, sobbing.)

Banks: John. Can you ask him to do it? Because you want him home and because he owes it to Sarah.

John: (cries softly)

Father: See? Your brothers want you at home. So why is that so hard to do? Why is that so hard?

Harold: Because I don't want to get on my knees.

Mother: Is it going to kill you? Does it mean that your life ends because you get on your knees?

Father: I don't see anybody having a gun or a knife to your head.

Mother: No, I don't see anybody laughing in this room. I don't see anybody making fun of you.

Harold: Don't nobody suppose to laugh at me for it.

Father: Well then do it! Do it! Nobody is going to think less of you because you get down and apologize to her for what you've done.

Mother: You know, you are making it tough! Everybody wants you home. You just have to do this simple thing and that's all!

Father: Maybe he doesn't want to come home at all.

Banks: I am really impressed by the power of this family. I'd like for everyone in this family except for Harold to get on their knees in front of Sarah.

They all kneel in front of Sarah, except Harold. They do it without asking why because it is appropriate at that moment.

Banks: And I'd like for you all to tell Sarah how sorry you are that you were not able to protect her.

Father: (on knees) I'm sorry that I wasn't there for you when you needed me. I was in the house but I was asleep or doing something else.

Mother: I'm sorry I didn't see the signs. I mean, I went through the same thing but I didn't see the signs, and I'm really sorry that this happened to you.

The three brothers apologized sincerely and with feeling. The therapist told Harold that she was giving him one week to consider, and that he must get on his knees in the next session.

They came back the next week and we immediately knew he was going to get on his knees because he seemed to have a less defiant posture, more childish and appropriate. The little girl sat away from her mother, her arms crossed, looking at him. The therapist did not know and did not ask whether the family members had talked together. In fact, they could not have talked very much because Harold was living in a detention center.

Banks: Go ahead and get on your knees, and look at your sister. Take a minute to compose yourself, so that you will be very serious. (Harold obeys.) And what I want you to do Harold is, I want you to apologize to your sister for all of the different things you did. I want you to apologize for exposing yourself, for getting on top of her, for threatening her, frightening her, taking advantage of her.

Harold: Sarah I'm sorry for taking advantage of you. I'm sorry for threatening you. I'm sorry for sexually molesting you. I'm sorry for getting on top of you. I'm sorry for blaming it on you. I'm sorry for not apologizing last time.

What made it certain that he was sincere was that he added, "I'm sorry for blaming it on you and I'm sorry for not apologizing last time." He had not been told to say that. He said it spontaneously and stayed on his knees a few seconds longer than necessary before he sat down across from Sarah.

Banks: Sarah, you know, it's really up to you whether you want to forgive him or not. Do you want to forgive him?

Sarah: (emphatically) Yes.

In my experience the victim always forgives. Sometimes the victim says to the therapist afterwards in private. "I can't really forgive him. I didn't really forgive him!" And then I think the appropriate thing is to answer, "I admire you even more for that, because it means that you are so kind and compassionate that you told him you forgive him even though you really cannot." The therapist praises the victim and takes blame away from her. Usually what the girl answers is, "Well, the truth is, I do forgive him."

Banks: You do. Would you get Harold to look at you, and you can look at Harold and tell him that you've forgiven him.

Sarah: I forgive you.

Banks: Harold?

Harold: Huh? (He is sitting in a awkward, childish, embarrassed posture.)

Banks: I think you owe her something for that. Thanks? It's a lot for her to forgive you for! You could thank her for forgiving you.

Harold: Thank you for forgiving me.

Banks: Okay. I think it's a very big step that Harold has taken. As we talked about last time it's sort of, he was really at a sort of a threshold, deciding what direction his future was going to go in. If he was going to handle this like a man by recognizing what he's done and that it was wrong and that he had to accept responsibility and he had to accept the blame, or whether he was going to live the life of a criminal and a sexual abuser. But I wanted for us to talk a little bit about how to help Harold to understand exactly why what he did was wrong and why he has to accept blame.

Now we reverse these steps. The therapist talks first about why it was wrong and about the spiritual pain. Then the offender gets down on his knees more readily.

Harold: It's rape.

Banks: That's a good point. What is it that makes rape wrong?

Harold: The way you do it.

Banks: What is it about that, about the way you do it that makes it wrong? You know, Mom and Dad, please feel free to help him with explaining.

Father: It's a violent act.

Banks: It's violent, you're right. It's like, that's a really good point, it's like other kinds of physical abuse, like hitting her, only it's much worse. But that's the first reason that it's wrong, because it's violent. Why is it worse than physical violence? Why is it worse than it would have been for him to walk up and hit her over the head? I know it's hard to put these things in words, but—

Father: Because he's taking advantage of her, he's doing something without her consent. And it's not only wrong according to man's law but also according to God's law.

Banks: You are absolutely right. You know, you're putting that beautifully. I'd like you to say that to your son because I really want this to be something that he will remember, these reasons.

Father: Well, one thing you know, we've studied the Bible for a long, long time, since all of you all were born. Your Mom and I have been studying the Bible way, way long before you were born, and even after you were born. You know what God's laws and commandments were. That's the main reason, one main reason because it's wrong. Second, because it goes against man's law and you know as Bible students we have an obligation and a right in the community to set an example for the people. And you were violating her. She's much younger. Even if she were older or even if she were the same age it's her body and she has a right to say no. And because of the violence of it, the whole thing. It's just like if somebody off the street that you didn't even know walked up and just for no reason punched you in your face and started beating up on you.

Banks: That's very well put. Mr. Adams. There is another part of it that maybe you, Mrs. Adams, as a woman, can explain to your son. I think that you touched on it last week.

Mother: Well, you know, like your father said it is wrong, we know that. Sarah is your sister; even if she wasn't, you know, like your father says, she has the right to say no. It's her body and you or nobody else has the right to make somebody do something that they don't want to do, or force them. And I mean, she was a victim, and she's afraid of you, she doesn't trust you, and you do a lot of damage emotionally.

Banks: Exactly. And that damage—I mean, you put that really well—because it's a violation of a very intimate and private part of your sister. So it's not only the violence part of it and the illegal part of it but the violation of her in a very private kind of way. A violation of her spirit. (pause)

There is another thing about this that I know that you all feel, which is what this has done to the family, how it's not

only affected Harold but also Sarah. There's also been a certain violence on this whole family. And I can tell by the looks
on your faces that you feel it. How can you put that so that
your son understands it?

Father: I don't know, I really can't put it in words. It's just that the
last couple of months, it really tore the family apart.

Banks: And in terms of the violence to Sarah, these acts were
violations of the whole family because the whole family, as I
was really struck with last week, the whole family wishes that
they had been able to protect her. That they had been able to
prevent it.

Mother: Yeah.

As the therapist talks about the abuse of Sarah as a violation of the
family, Sarah indicates that she is more relaxed by fixing her hair. It
is childish and appropriate for her to be concerned about her hair
and not as intensely involved in the situation anymore. She is not
sitting next to the mother. She is sitting between Harold and another brother.

Banks: So Harold's abuse of Sarah was a violation of this whole
family because it put you all in this position of not being able
to protect your little girl the way you would have wanted to.
And it brought a certain, perhaps shame, humiliation to the
family.

Mother: Yes.

Banks: Which is very hurtful. Harold, can you understand, can
you say how this behavior, this abuse of Sarah was a violation
to your mother? Why it was wrong to your mother?

Harold: It's her daughter.

He very quickly understands it is a violation of the mother.

Banks: You're right. Can you say why it was a violation to your
father?

Harold: Because it's his daughter too.

Banks: You're right. It's his little girl whom he would have wanted
to protect. What about for your brothers? How is this a violation for your brothers?

Harold: Because it's their sister.
Banks: And what would they have wanted to do for their sister?
Harold: Protect her.

The mother then spontaneously told about how Harold himself was sexually molested when he was 13 years old.

Mother: The kids were left with a friend and one of the neighbors across the street stayed there, spent the night and—
Father: Things got out of hand.
Mother: Things got out of hand.
Father: There was another, there was a boy his age—
Mother: There was a boy his age.
Father: At the time they were 13 and we got bits and pieces of it. He told a little bit.
Mother: Yeah. That nothing happened. He was—
Father: About a year later we found out that it was much more serious than what he had told us. Then we went to, I didn't say anything, you know we are Jehovah's Witnesses and we went to the body of elders in our congregation and explained what had happened and they talked to both of the boys. We thought it was overcome, but I guess—

That was the second session. A couple of months went by. The therapist focused on the normal life of the little girl, defining her and treating her like a normal child and getting away from her as victim. She did the same with the boy. He began to misbehave in normal ways, getting bad grades, cutting classes and getting into fights with other boys in more normal adolescent ways. Many of the fights were because he was falling in love with a girl his age and he was showing off in front of her. That was a positive sign. But there was still a great deal of tension with the mother. It was necessary to make an attempt to restore the mother's love for him. A session was devoted to this.

Harold usually looked at the floor. He rarely looked people in the eyes and seldom looked at the therapist's face. However, once she began to talk about the mother's love, he did not take his eyes off her face.

Banks: And it's a question for you, Mrs. Adams, at what point will
you be able to forgive your son and to love your son in spite of
what he's done?

Mother: I love him. I think Harry knows that. I told him that. I've
been affectionate towards him, even times when he is mad. I
mean really mad. I've forgiven him for what he tried to do to
Sarah but I have not forgotten. I mean, I think that's asking a
little bit too much. I feel that if I hadn't forgiven him he
wouldn't be back in the home.

The other family members were present although they did not
participate. It was important for them to see the restoration of the
mother's love or at least the intent of that.

Banks: You know, I'm not sure if Harold really knows that you love
him and have forgiven him. That he's earned that back. And I
think that that is so important because I don't think that
Harold is going to be all right until he knows that. Until he's
really convinced of that, until he's convinced that you love
him.

Mother: What other ways besides saying it to him and showing it
to him? I mean, the kid is going to believe what he wants. I
don't care how many times I sit and tell Harry I love him, if a
kid is going to rebel and he's got it made up in his mind,
"well, Mom and Dad don't care about me," . . . Okay, I went
through this. And yeah, when you are a kid you feel that,
well, Mom, Dad favors this one, you know—I really don't
think they love me. You've got to show that child, okay?

Banks: And that's what I am saying Mrs. Adams, I don't think it
shows. I wasn't sure whether you had forgiven him and loved
him again. I think that Harold can see very clearly how much
you love his brothers and maybe even especially his sister and
I think that that really shows. But I don't think the love for
Harold has shown.

Mother: And here again I say, how can you sit there and tell me
that I don't love my own child? My first baby I lost, okay?
And it was a fight to keep him.

Banks: To keep Harold?

Mother: That's right. It was a rough go. All my children are special but the first one! I love Harry.

The therapist could have explained more clearly that the issue was that Harold did not *feel* loved. Instead she emphasized how the mother was not showing her love. This misunderstanding was fortunate because it led the mother, angry at the therapist, to state emphatically how much she did care for Harold. Now it sounded convincing.

Mother: I've told it to him, I've shown it to him. I think, instead of saying that you think he doesn't realize that I have forgiven him or love him, you need to ask him.

Banks: Mrs. Adams, I'm realizing that I think I owe you an apology because I think maybe I've said this in the wrong way. Or you might have misunderstood what I meant to say. I'm not saying that you wouldn't love your children. I think you are a wonderful mother, and of course you love your children. I'm saying I don't think it shows to Harold. Can you show him now?

Mother: Yeah, I have no problems with showing affection towards any of my kids.

Banks: Yes, and I've seen that. Come over and hug your son, and kiss your son, and tell him that you love him and forgive him.

Harold: Why do that when she does it at home?

He is protective of her, fearful that this is too threatening to her.

Mother: (The mother stands up, takes Harold by the hand, and embraces him) I love you and I have forgiven you.

Banks: You know, I believe you when you say what you just said to your son. I also belive you when you say that you tell him this at home.

At that moment Sarah, who like the other children had not been paying attention to this interchange, became really interested. This was important because the victim carries the guilt of having separated the mother from her son.

Banks: I'm really concerned that with this particular problem you've been having with Harold, that he needs a special concerted effort to convince him of this, because I'm not sure that it shows completely to him. Even though I know that you've made these efforts and I know that, of course, you love your son, your firstborn, of course! In order for Harold to be able to love his sister the way a big brother should love and protect a sister and in order for Harold to grow up and to be able to love a woman in a productive way and in a good way, to feel good about women, it is very, very important for him to be able to feel and accept his mother's love. That is an essential thing. I really want you to know that I'm not saying that you have not tried to show him. I'm saying that this is a special problem. And there is something I want you to do this week with your son. Every day I want you to spend 15 minutes expressing your love and doing loving things with your son. Talk with him about his life, about what he's done that day, share with him things that you've done that day, tell him about how much you love and support him. And during that time, no matter what else has happened that day, no matter how he may have misbehaved and how you may have had to deal with it outside of that time, during that time no correcting him, no going over what he has done, none of that. Just set aside a special time that's for you and Harold to help him to feel and accept his mother's love.

The therapy continued for four months. Harold fell in love with a 16-year-old girl and began to behave worse. The parents were very strict and, according to their religion, did not let their children go out with people of the opposite sex or go to dances. Harold was running away at night and coming home late, after visiting his girlfriend. The parents were upset but, in fact, this was a very good sign of age-appropriate behavior.

The therapist worked with the parents on their marriage and on problems that probably related to the mother's history of abuse. One of the problems was shame. Such families seem to have very low affect and to be very quiet, probably because of shame. Many directives were introduced to promote good humor and fun. In a session supervised by David Eddy, the therapist told the parents that they looked so dignified and stately, particularly the father, that he wanted them to carry out an experiment. They were to dress up and go for a walk on Embassy Row, a street in Washington. The therapist made a bet with them that people would stop to ask them their country of origin, or their diplomatic assignment, or directions as if they would know the neighborhood. They did this and had a wonderful time because they were actually stopped. There were many interventions of this type with the parents.

Two years later, Harold was finishing high school, there had been no repeat offense, and he was thinking of studying to become a counselor.

Conclusion

The following are the most salient aspects of what was accomplished in these three sessions with this family:

1. The parents collaborated with the therapist in insisting that Harold accept responsibility for his actions, express sorrow and repentance on his knees, and do reparation.
2. The mother revealed the secret of her victimization and of Harold's victimization.
3. The siblings collaborated with the parents in encouraging Harold to accept responsibility and repent.
4. Parents and therapist blocked the possibility of further secrecy between Harold and Sarah.
5. The parents and siblings expressed sorrow on their knees to Sarah for failing to protect her from the abuse.
6. Harold sincerely expressed sorrow and repentance on his knees to Sarah for having abused her, for blaming her, and for not apologizing sooner.
7. Sarah forgave Harold.
8. Everyone in the family recognized the spiritual pain caused by the sexual abuse and how it had been an attack on each member of the family.
9. The mother expressed to Harold her love and forgiveness.

These steps made it possible for the family to continue together with love, repentance, and reparation.

5

PROTECTING THE HUMAN
RIGHTS OF A CHILD

*We don't need no education, We don't need no thought
control, Dark sarcasm in the classroom, Teacher leave
'em kids alone.*

— *Pink Floyd*

TAKING POWER AWAY from professionals is often necessary when
agents of social control are violating human rights. The idea is to
prevent professionals from distributing power inappropriately, defining problems as hopeless, or intruding upon the family so that
the family unit loses control. Sometimes it is necessary to take
power away from professionals to correct the hierarchy at the first
dimension of interaction, where people are mainly interested in
dominating each other for personal advantage. The following story is an example of such a situation.

The father was from South America and worked as a house
painter. The mother was born in Europe. She occasionally worked
as a teacher's aide. There were four children, two older boys who
had finished high school and were working, a 15-year-old daughter
still in school, and a 12-year-old daughter, Margarita, who was
mentally retarded. Margarita had attended a special class in a
regular school, where she was liked by the children, had some
friends, and was doing well. One day she was tested (her IQ was
71) and she was put into a school for severely retarded and handi-

· 88 ·

capped children. She did not like this school, was afraid of some of the children and soon began to refuse to go to school. She could not understand why she had to go there. She wanted to go back to her old class.

The parents could not make her go to school. After several days of absences, the truancy officer contacted the father and explained to him that parents are obligated by law to send their children to school. The father tried to force the girl to go but she refused and on several occasions escaped the father by jumping out the window and running away from the house. The truancy officer insisted that the father was violating the law and had to get the girl to school. He informed the father that in the state of Maryland, where the family lived, there is a fine of $50 a day to parents who do not send their children to school. The father took a belt to the girl and beat her on two occasions. He had never beaten any of his children before. And so the first intervention into the family from a social service agent, the truancy officer, resulted in the girl's being beaten with a belt. The school's intrusion into the family resulted in child abuse.

The marks from the belting were noticed at school and were reported to Protective Services. A worker came to the house to investigate. Each family member was interviewed separately and a report was filed noting that the father and mother disagreed on how to discipline Margarita. The implication was that adequate parents agree on how to discipline children. This veiled accusation that the parents' disagreements were at the root of Margarita's problems disturbed the parents considerably. Child abuse charges were pressed against the father, who was faced with a possible five-year jail sentence.

Now the 15-year-old daughter realized that she had great power over her father. If he disapproved of her friends or of the hours she kept, she could threaten him with complaining to the Protective Service worker. Realizing that she no longer had to obey her father, she began to misbehave. The intervention from a second social agency, Protective Services, resulted in another child's behaving out of control.

The court assigned an attorney to the father, another to the mother, and another to Margarita. It was not clear why the mother should have an attorney herself, since no charges were pressed against her. Probably it was because it had been officially noted that the parents disagreed. The three attorneys were nice young women. They had difficulty talking to the family members, who were undereducated and suspicious. It was much easier for the attorneys to talk to each other, and by talking to each other they somehow developed the illusion that they were talking to the family members. They negotiated with each other and reached agreement very smoothly, deciding that it was best to place the girl in a residential school so that the father would not beat her and so that she could get an education.

The three attorneys also believed that Margarita did not go to school because she was worried about her mother and that she was staying home to keep the mother company. The idea that school refusal is related to a concern about the mother has been proposed by several family therapists. The attorneys' opinion illustrates how "expert opinion" can be misused. The attorneys decided that since (ex officio) the mother was holding Margarita back, the way to help her was to place her in an institution where she could be separated from this bad mother. The fact that they were punishing the victim by separating her from her family did not enter into their considerations.

They could not find a nearby institution that would take this girl. The only place they could find was a home for inner-city delinquent adolescent girls, a five-hour drive from the parents' home. This very frail, timid little girl was going to be the youngest among delinquent adolescents and probably the only one who was not from the inner city, not delinquent, and quite retarded. The third intervention from a social agency, the court-appointed public defenders, resulted in the threat of inappropriate institutionalization for Margarita.

On hearing about this possibility the mother became very depressed. This was her youngest daughter and she was especially attached to her, as mothers often are to a defective child. Margarita said that she would commit suicide if she was placed in that school.

The family members were referred to therapy at FTI. After two or three sessions they began to unite and to be more hopeful. The mother began to look for a private school for the girl as an alternative to residential placement. She was willing to go to work to pay for Margarita's education. The lawyers, however, continued to insist that the child be taken away from the mother and placed in residential care so that she could have an education. We held a meeting at the institute with the three attorneys and the Protective Service worker. All four refused to change their point of view. They believed that the mother was keeping Margarita home from school to keep her company and protect her from her unhappy marriage.

The therapist arranged for the mother to go to school every morning and assist the teachers as a way of demonstrating that she was not keeping Margarita at home. This had no impact on the four professionals, who also refused to reason about the fact that they were in any case talking about a very limited education, since the girl had an IQ of 71 and could probably learn at home everything that she was going to learn. The mother had taught her to clean and cook and had arranged "pen pals" to help her develop her writing and reading skills. The attorneys also refused to consider that separating mother and daughter was a violation of their human rights. It had been the father who had committed a delinquent act, not the mother or daughter.

Since it was impossible to change the attorneys' views, we decided to recommend to the parents and Margarita that they dismiss their court-appointed lawyers because they were not representing them appropriately. The father, the mother, and Margarita wrote separate letters to the judge, dismissing their attorneys and asking that new ones be appointed by the court. Margarita's letter was particularly moving, as she asked the judge not to separate her from her mother. There was no answer from the judge and the attorneys called a hearing.

On the day of the hearing the therapist, the supervisor, and the family appeared in court and were told that the whole file on the family had been lost, including the letters firing the lawyers. They had to wait while there was a search for the file. After a while they were told the file could not be found, the hearing was postponed, and they should go home. There would be no hearing that day. Ten minutes later, the hearing was held, without the family present, and the judge ruled that Margarita should be placed in residential care.

The rights of the child and of the family had been violated. A serious illegality had been committed in holding a hearing without the family members present and in not acknowledging the fact that the three attorneys had been dismissed. Moreover, nobody was available in court to raise the fact that the child was now suicidal. Because of the possibility of suicide, placing her in residential care was life-threatening.

How could we block institutionalization while the court's decision was appealed? We considered the possibility of hospitalizing Margarita in a children's psychiatric ward to prevent her from attempting suicide and as a way of delaying her placement. But we decided against hospitalization because labeling her as mentally ill would add insult to injury, not to mention the trauma of being in a psychiatric ward.

All of this had cost the family a great deal of money even though we did not charge for the therapy. The institute was struggling to keep the family together and help them recover from the depression that had resulted from all these interventions by agents of social control. The brothers and sister were cooperative and helpful but Margarita had now become truly obnoxious and oppositional. The mother began going to school by herself every day with the hope of demonstrating to the court that she was not keeping the girl at home for company. While all this was happening, numerous requests to the department of education for private tutoring went unanswered.

The one person with power in the situation was the judge, but he was refusing our phone calls. Wishing to convey to him that he was violating the human rights of the child, I phoned each of the three attorneys. I politely explained that, while agreeing with them in their concern for Margarita, I believed that this was a human rights issue and I would pursue it as such to the highest court. As soon as I had said this to two of the three attorneys, the judge called me back.

I told him that I understood that the law says that the state has the obligation to offer a child an education. The word is "offer." It does not say "to force" an education on a child. Also, even though it may not be explicitly stated in the law, a child has the right to live with her mother, and this right is implicit in every law that protects children in this country. If he, the judge, had to choose between offering an education and preserving the bond between mother and child, the bond between mother and child is more important.

He said, "Well, not necessarily. The law could be interpreted to say that the state should force an education on a child." I thought this statement was quite remarkable. He added, "It could be interpreted that the education is more important than the mother-child relationship."

I answered that I did not think so and that I believed this was a human rights issue and would pursue it as such. I reminded him that the mother never abused her daughter and that it is a human right of women to live with their children.

He answered, "And how about your famous institute? How come you are so famous and you still haven't made this child go to school?"

I replied, "Because you keep interfering. All we can talk about in therapy is court, hearings, placements, threats. One can't do therapy like this." He asked me what I wanted. I said, "I want court-ordered family therapy for a year and a home tutor until we get Margarita back in school." He said all right, and he hung up.

These requests were granted in a new hearing. The tutoring took place at the institute instead of at the home, so that Margarita would have to leave the house. She eventually went back to school, there was no further abuse, and the family stayed together.

Conclusions

Interventions such as these are relatively uncommon because most therapists think that this kind of problem is not within the area of therapy and belongs to the realm of Social Services. Such thoughts are a misconception. This is what our work is about—to protect children. Taking power away from professionals is often what a therapist has to do before beginning to think about anything else in relation to therapy.

The case of Margarita is an example of a responsible approach to a situation of abuse and neglect. Consideration was given to the priorities in a child's life. To stay in the family, to be loved by a natural mother, as well as by brothers and sisters, and to have the opportunity to correct the relationship with a father who has been abusive obviously take priority as human rights over the desirability of going to school rather than being tutored at home.

To avoid these kinds of problems it is best for therapists to work in very close collaboration with the Department of Social Services, with the court system, with organizations involved with adult and adolescent offenders, and with whoever else might be involved when a case is court-ordered. It is best to bring in the other professionals involved as soon as possible and to reach agreement beforehand, so that it is clear to the family that the professionals are in accord and collaborating with one another. It is unfortunate for family members to realize that professionals are fighting over them, just as it is undesirable for children to notice that parents are in conflict about them.

When a case is adjudicated, it is best to invite the probation officer to a session and ask him or her to summarize the conclusions, the orders from the court and the conditions of probation. Whenever possible, it is desirable to transfer the authority of the probation officer to the family, so that the parents of the family will enforce the rules of probation and contact the probation officer only to report. Even better, sometimes it is possible to make the parents' rules the conditions of probation. In this way the family hierarchy is restored and the officer supports the parents instead of taking power away from them.

Similar arrangements can be made with other professionals, such as physicians and school counselors. It is usually best to meet with the other professionals before the family session, so a common view can be presented to the family. Often school personnel do not want the child to be present in a meeting about him or her. Decisions about a child are made without the child present to express, defend, or represent himself or herself, even though this goes against the principles of democracy that are taught in schools. It is best to insist and to arrange with the school to have the child present.

When a psychiatrist prescribing medication is involved with a client, it is important to ensure that the whole family is informed about possible side effects and the chances of irreversible neurological damage. If family members are capable, we send them to the library to read by themselves about the consequences of the medications.

Often parents feel oppressed and coerced by agents of social control who require family therapy and parent education and who want to tell them how to be parents to their children. The therapist needs to say to them that the ultimate goal is to have all professionals out of their lives. The goal is not just to have the young person behave appropriately, but to stop the intrusion into the family from various social agencies. The best way to do this is to shift power to the natural network of the family. If the therapist can find older, wiser people within the extended family, such as grandparents, uncles and aunts, it is best to transfer authority to them so that they will supervise the family and make sure that parents and children are well. Relatives are usually more stable, interested, and involved than professional workers.

6
CONTAINMENT

*The less effort, the faster and more powerful you will
be.*

—Bruce Lee

A FAMILY WAS referred by the Department of Social Services because
a young mother was trying to place her 11-year-old son, Ben, in a
foster home. She said that he was disobedient and out of control.
The social workers felt so strongly that he should not be placed
that they had gone to extremes to prevent this. One of the issues
between mother and son was that the mother had filled the boy's
closet with her clothes and even kept her sewing machine in his
room, to his great resentment. The Department of Social Services
had even rented storage space with the hope that the mother would
put some of her things in storage instead of placing the son in
foster care.

The mother was a hairdresser who worked out of her own
home. She had never wanted to have children but her husband
convinced her. As soon as she became pregnant, he disappeared
and was never heard from again. She raised the boy by herself. She
was an only child of elderly parents and had no relatives. The
therapist was David Eddy, teacher and clinical director at FTI. I
was the supervisor behind the one-way mirror, planning the inter-

view with him and calling him over the phone with suggestions. My goal for the first session was to bring out the mother's love for her son and obtain a clear commitment that she would never expel him.

The transcript illustrates one way of reuniting mother and child when the issue is at the third dimension of interaction, how to love and protect. Eddy began by asking the mother what problem she wanted to solve.

Mother: Well, solving my anger, you know, I get angry when he doesn't listen to what I feel he should do or is best for him. He doesn't seem to think I'm out for his best interest a lot of the time and, you know, he's not willing to cooperate. And I just get frustrated and sort of throw in the towel, so to say.

This is good sign in that she defines herself as the initiator of a negative sequence. She does not say the problem is his misbehavior. She says, "It's my anger."

Eddy: What do you mean?
Mother: Like, well, the hell with it, I'm not going to deal with this kid. He can go fend for himself. Where I feel like I have a lot to offer him as a parent, and as a nurturer in general but he, because of his behavior, is not allowing me to be more nurturing.

It is apparent that the hierarchy is reversed. The mother talks about the son as though he is in a position superior to her.

Mother: You know what I'm saying?
Eddy: Sure. And so it's a point where you, kind of, what happens? When you get discouraged you just kind of stop?
Mother: I just don't even want to deal with him. I won't cook for him.
Eddy: Is he concerned about his Mom in any way?
Mother: No. I don't think so.
Eddy: Really?
Ben: Concerned about what?
Eddy: About your Mom. I mean that she is overburdened and maybe works awfully hard. One of the possibilities is—I don't

want to run into this too quickly—but one of the possibilities is that he sees how hard you work and all of the efforts you put forth and that he wants to spare you having to work anymore for him so—

Mother: Yeah, well, he doesn't require me to do things like drive him someplace. Yeah, he doesn't put many demands on me that, you know, I see other children doing which I wouldn't consider them a burden, but as an opportunity to interact.

She talks as if the boy is supposed to put demands on the mother to make her feel like a mother.

Eddy: So this is an opportunity for a new beginning for you.
Mother: Right. I feel very fortunate that we got to see you.

The therapist does not comment on the mother-son interaction; he just switches the subject and says that this is an opportunity for a new beginning. This is the right thing to do. He shows that he understood what the mother was saying by picking one word that she used: opportunity, But he changes the subject away from inappropriate behavior and focuses on the future.

Mother: He didn't want to come to see you and I was, you know, I'm disappointed that he doesn't see any value in—
Eddy: You know, I can recall when I was 11 years old, I think if I'd had to be dragged off on a sunny afternoon to sit in some warm office with a guy who is going to tell me how life could be better, I might have felt the same way.
Mother: You know, when things get as bad as they have been between us, I would think that he would want to, you know, improve the situation. You know, where I'm at the point where I feel we can't coexist together, that he's going to have to go and live with somebody who can handle him, because I feel I can't handle him.
Eddy: May I, while you're at this point, ask him a bit about some of the difficulties as he sees it? It's okay?
Mother: Uh-huh.
Eddy: Ben, what are some of the problems as you've seen them? What are some of the problems for you?

Ben: Her sewing machine.
Eddy: Your mom's sewing machine?
Ben: Uh-huh.
Eddy: What do you mean?
Ben: It's in my room! And she puts that thing in my room and it takes up half my room. When my friends come over they think that I sew.
Eddy: Yeah! So you are embarrassed by it.
Ben: And I don't want it in there. It takes up too much room.
Mother: Well, I told you when we move—
Ben: No, even when we move it's like in three years!
Eddy: So what else Ben?
Ben: She always makes me do chores more than she does. She tells me to do stuff that she doesn't want to do.
Eddy: So what kind of chores don't you like?
Ben: Like the dishes. Like vacuuming, because she's always telling me, like on her rug she always wants me to get into certain places and everything.
Eddy: And what other chores don't you like?
Ben: Cleaning my room. Because I'd be able to clean my room if I had enough room!

Ben gave a long description of the many chores that he did.

Eddy: Now what chores don't you mind?
Ben: Taking out the trash, cleaning my room if she didn't have her sewing machine in my room.
Eddy: So if that sewing machine wasn't there you'd have a really clean room.
Ben: Yeah, if she didn't have those shelves with all those clothes. My whole closet has her clothes in it. Doing my laundry.
Eddy: You don't mind that?
Ben: I have to do my own laundry because she does it like every three months.
Eddy: What else? (to the mother) Was that an exaggeration? (She nods.) It was.
Ben: What? You do it every three months. Yes, you do! Look at all those clothes that you have in the hamper. I don't mind clearing off the table. I don't mind using the mop for the floor.

Eddy: So there are about half the chores that you really mind doing and the other half you don't mind doing at all.

Ben: Uh-huh.

Eddy: What are the things that you do that are really helpful to your mom? What do you think she will say the things are that you do that are real helpful?

Ben: I don't know.

Eddy: What do you think?

Ben: Nothing. She doesn't think that anything I do is worth doing.

This is typical of very intelligent children. He does not feel that his mother is interested in anything that is interesting to him.

Mother: When you do all the dishes and do them right, I acknowledge that.

Ben: You have to examine everything. You have to go and find the dishes in the middle and you go search through everything, and if there is a little tiny dot you say, do it over.

Eddy: So your mom is hardworking, right?

Ben: Yeah, kind of. All she has to do is cut it, cut hair, and then she gets $70.

Mother: That is for a permanent.

Ben: But it stinks. It stinks when she does a permanent. I'd rather stay outside. When Steve's over, she's always like, she just, it's like she likes him.

Eddy: And you get jealous?

Ben: No.

Eddy: No?

Mother: He likes him too.

Ben: Yeah, but you like him more than me.

Mother: You think I like Steve more than you? That's not true. You're my son.

Steve was her boyfriend. This was the hook that we were waiting for because the drama between this mother and son is the drama of love and commitment. Is she committed to him? Is she going to keep him as her son? Does she love him as a son or not? When the boy says she likes Steve better, and the mother says, "No, I like you more than Steve, you're my son," the conversation has shifted to the real issue: Does the mother love her son, is she committed to him? This was what we were waiting for. Now the conversation can go in that direction.

The therapist must understand that the fact that the mother says that she likes her son more than anyone else because he is her son is not contradictory with the fact that she wants to place him in foster care. She has such low self-esteem that she does not think that giving him to another woman to raise is rejecting him. In her mind the other woman will be a better person and a better mother to him. One must understand this to work with such mothers. It would have been a mistake to say, "How can you say you love him when you are giving him away?" because she would not understand that logic.

Eddy: Do you think he's embarrassed hearing that?
Ben: What?
Mother: Maybe, yeah.
Eddy: Why don't you tell him now?
Mother: Ben?
Ben: What?
Mother: I like you more than Steve. I like you more than anybody else. Or rather, I love you more than anybody else. But sometimes I don't like what you do, or what you don't do makes me angry.
Ben: She expects me to remember everything.
Eddy: Now Ben, will you sit over by your mom for a minute?
Ben: What for?
Eddy: Because I don't want the words to get lost as they travel across the end of the coffee table.
Ben: Does that one work to? (indicating the camera)
Eddy: Uh-huh. Maybe that'll give you a better angle. It will catch your profile. You have a strong jaw.
Mother: Does that make you uncomfortable?
Ben: It's like Family Feud!
Eddy: Family Feud! (laughs) Do you think I'm a TV host or something?
Ben: Do you do it in VHS?
Mother: It's not Family Feud here, but it's Family Feud when we go home.

Eddy: But that's what we're going to change. Look at your mother when she says this, Ben, it's real important.

Ben: Look at her?

Eddy: Yeah.

Ben: What for?

Eddy: Because what she has to say is very important.

Mother: Ben, do you know why I'm here?

Ben: No.

Mother: Because I want to get along with you better, because I want to have a good relationship with you. Because I care about you.

Ben: It doesn't seem like it to me.

Mother: Sometimes I feel like you don't allow me to be the mother. You want me just to be your person who does things for you. I know that you don't like me. I feel that you don't like me, right?

Ben: Right.

Mother: And a lot of time I don't like what you do or what you say.

Eddy: Tell him what you would like the relationship to be like between the two of you.

Mother: Well, I would like to get along and I would like to be your friend, and your (pause) —

Ben: It's called a mother.

Mother: Right. I want to be your mother but you don't want — it doesn't seem like you want me to be your mother.

Eddy: Take his hand and tell him you are going to love him no matter what.

Ben: Oh, great, this is like —

Mother: He doesn't like me to do that.

Eddy: He's embarrassed like any 11-year-old, but that's okay.

Ben: And it's even on camera.

Mother: So what? Come here.

Ben: Hi Mom. (waving at the camera)

Mother: Come here.

Ben: Yes, yes.

Mother: Now do you want that too?

Ben: What?

Mother: Do you want to get along with me?

Ben: Yeah, but I don't want your sewing machine in my room.

Mother: Well, if I had another place to put it, I'd put it there.

Ben: Well, then find another place, don't keep it in my room.

Eddy: Why don't you tell him that you are going to love him even if he continues to complain about the sewing machine?

This is the second time that the therapist asks the mother to say that she loves her son. Often, if one expresses a positive emotion, then the chances are that eventually one will actually feel it. If the mother says that she really loves her son and will always love him, then she will be closer to really feeling that love for him.

Mother: There's no way that I would stop loving you because you are my son. But I want to get along better. And I feel upset because you don't like me most of the time. You know I feel that you don't like me and I don't like you, but I don't want to be enemies. I want to be, I want to be—

Eddy: And none of that is true, it is? That you don't like each other.

Mother: Well, yeah, it is true.

Eddy: There've been unpleasant things but you love him.

Mother: Right.

Eddy: And you're always going to love him. Tell him.

Mother: Yeah. I really love you and that's why I want to get along better because I feel I have a lot to offer you. But sometimes I'm so angry and upset I—

Eddy: Say things I don't mean.

Mother: Right, say things I don't mean. Do you know that?

Ben: No, but you just told me.

Eddy: Can you get him to look at you?

Ben: Yeah.

Mother: So—

Eddy: Does he know the things that you mean when you say that when you get angry you say things you don't mean?

Mother: Do you?

Ben: Yeah.

Eddy: Does he know that when you have said that you were going to get rid of him that you said that out of anger and that you really don't mean that?

Mother: Do you know that?

Ben: What?

Mother: That when I said that I want you to find another place to live it's because I want to get along with you so bad that I can't bear not getting along. I can't deal with being in conflict.

Ben: I can't believe that.

Mother: You can't believe what?

Ben: That you want me to go to another place because—

Mother: Because I feel that it might be better for you if you were with people who could manage you, because I feel you're too young to be on your own. (to the therapist) He wants to come in at any hour in the evening and he never tells me where he is going or what time he'll be home.

To place the boy in foster care would be devastating not only for the son but also for the mother. He is her only son and all she has in life.

Eddy: So you've gotten frustrated and sometimes you've said things you didn't mean and he's gotten confused and he's not sure what you mean and what you don't, right?

Mother: Do you think that's true?

Ben: No.

Eddy: You think that's true though, right?

Mother: Yeah I, you know, I—

Eddy: You and I know it's true.

Mother: Right.

Eddy: So why don't you tell him that no matter what, you've chosen to come here to solve problems, and that you are never going to give him up?

Mother: Ben.

Ben: Huh?

Mother: Turn around. I don't want—listen!—I don't want to give you up!

Ben: It sure sounds like it to me! You're always calling up all these places.

Eddy: Tell him you won't, no matter what.

Ben: Oh, I know you will.

Mother: Well, the thing is I never wanted it to be permanent. I felt like they could make you see the light. By being somewhere else they could help you understand that at your age you just can't come and go as you please and do what you want because it's not—

Eddy: But you always ultimately wanted your son with you.

Mother: Yes.

Eddy: Tell him.

Mother: But I want you to be with me all the time, but I don't want to be with somebody who doesn't want to cooperate or who's angry at me all the time.

Eddy: Tell him that, no matter what, you are never really going to place him, because I am going to help you solve that.

Ben: I still know that you're still going to threaten me with that.

Mother: (to the therapist) I have threatened him with it a lot.

Eddy: Tell him that you're never going to do it.

Ben: She was doing it. I remember I was coming home one day and she was on the phone like—

Mother: I would like him to understand why I was doing it.

Eddy: I know. I know. And we can get to that, but what I'd like you to do is to make a commitment to him now. Look him in the eye and tell him, "You're my son, I love you, and I'll never give you up."

Ben: Still, I know she'll be lying if she says that. I know that you are still going to do it, because you always—(to the therapist) I even heard her on the phone. I came home and she was talking on the phone with some lady. She started yelling and screaming about something I didn't mean to do.

Eddy: He's distracting you from that now. And he's trying to help you with the tension of saying it. But it's all right. I think it's important that he hear it from his Mom. Could you get him to look in your eyes? Then tell him that no matter what, you are never going to give him up.

Mother: Ben.

Ben: Huh?

Mother: Come here. Turn around and look at me. Because I really care about you and I really love you. Ben.

Ben: Huh?

Mother: You really mean a lot to me. I know it doesn't seem that way a lot of the time . . .

It was important not to minimize what the boy was saying. This was a good first step, but the therapist needed a much stronger commitment from the mother in order to convince this boy. This commitment had to be obtained in the first session so that the therapy could continue in a framework of love, emotional stability, and security.

Mother: But I really, really love you, and I will never give you up.

Ben: Then why were you talking to that lady?

Mother: Because I wanted some help.

Ben: No, that wasn't help! That was social something.

Mother: That was help.

Ben: No, it wasn't help. You said you wanted to place me in some foster home!

Eddy: Well, we're going to put this behind us right now, right? And I have a way to do that.

Ben: Yeah? How?

Eddy: We are going to make a legally binding, notarized and publicly declared document.

Ben: What's that?

Eddy: It's a contract. A legal contract. And your Mom is going to make this contract. She's going to have a copy of it, you're going to have a copy of it, I'm going to have a copy of it, and it's going to be filed with the clerk of courts. And that contract is going to guarantee that your Mom is never going to give you up.

Ben: Even if she dies?

Eddy: Even if she dies.

Mother: Would that make you feel more secure?

Ben: What?

Mother: To have a contract?

Ben: Yeah.

Eddy: All right. Absolutely. Let me get the paper. We'll do it right now!

Ben: Okay.

(Therapist leaves room.)

Ben: Sure better than that lady.

Mother: What lady?

Ben: That lady.

Mother: Yeah?

Ben: Mary Picker or whatever her name is.

Mother: You didn't like her?

Ben: No! She was always on your side.

(Therapist enters room.)

Ben: How's this going to get to the court?

Eddy: Because I am going to have this notarized and I am going to file it with the clerk of courts as a legal document that your Mom makes today that she certifies. In fact, I think it should even be in your Mom's words.

Mother: (holding paper and pen in her hands) I . . .

Eddy: Do you want me to help you with it, since I know this legal stuff?

Mother: Okay.

Eddy: (dictating slowly as the mother writes) "I give my sworn oath and assume my complete legal and loving commitment to my son Ben. I further swear that I will never place him in foster care, give him away, or leave him, under penalty of law." And you should sign it using your full name, and date it up here.

Mother: 20?

Eddy: 20th. I'll sign it as a witness. And I'm going to get it stamped with our seal here and make copies.

Mother: (to Ben) Do you want to read it?

Eddy: How about if your Mom . . . (to Ben) Do you want to read it out loud?

Ben: Me? I'm not a good reader.

Eddy: I bet you are a good reader, but how about if your Mom reads it to you? (to mother) Why don't you look at him as you read it?

Mother: (Trying to sit so that she can read and watch Ben at the same time) I can't see him. Okay. "I give my sworn oath and assume my complete legal and loving commitment to my son

Ben. (Her voice shakes as she begins to cry.) I further swear that I will never place him in foster care, or give him away, or leave him, under penalty of law."

Eddy: Would you like it to say anything else?

Ben: No. (Ben is also moved as he looks at his mother's tearful face.)

Now that she is crying, it is evident that she is feeling the love that she has expressed.

Eddy: I am going to make copies and have it sealed.

(Therapist leaves room.)

Mother: (dries her tears and blows her nose) So, do you like this therapist?

Ben: Yeah! He's better than the other person. Why? Do you like him?

Mother: Yeah. He's supposed to be one of the best around.

Ben: So, are we going to see him every week?

Mother: Do you want to?

Ben: Yeah.

Mother: Okay.

(Therapist comes back into the room.)

Mother: The relationshiip you have with your parent is very, very important because it will affect every relationship you have with people.

Eddy: That's right, and I'm going to help you have a wonderful one.

Mother: And I want him to see the value in that. He doesn't seem to think it's important.

Eddy: Now I'm going to have this signed by the judge and then I'll give you copies after that takes place. I want you to look at Ben one more time—I'm going to have some things I want Ben to do—but first I want you to tell him again how much you love him and look forward to the months and years ahead and how close your're going to be.

Mother: Ben, I really do love you and want to have a fun and loving relationship with you and I want you to feel that you can trust me and come to me whenever you have a problem, whenever you want somebody to talk to. Or if you don't like something I said to you or want you to do, I want you to tell me about it so we can work it out somehow. And if we can't work it out then we could talk to Dr. Eddy and then maybe he could help us work it out. And the reason I'm here is because I love you and I want to get along with you.

Eddy: That's wonderful. Now I'm going to ask you to trade places with your son for just a minute.

Ben: Trade places?

Eddy: You can sit back over where Ben was sitting. I want you to sit where your Mom was, Ben, so you are closer to me for a minute. There are things that a young fellow does when he's 11 that are not the things that he'll do when he's 17 or 18. They are not the things that he did when he was 5 or 6. But I want you to tell your Mom that you are sorry for the things that you did that provoked her and made her say that she was going to get rid of you.

Ben: I'm not good at speeches.

Eddy: I know you're not. I'll help you. Just turn to your Mom and take her hand and tell her you are sorry for the things that you did —

Ben: Okay. (Taking her hand.)

Eddy: —that led her to say she was going to get rid of you.

Ben: I'm sorry about the things that I did (to the therapist), what?

Mother: Why don't you put it in your own words?

One of the problems was that the mother was very critical of Ben. The rest of the therapy focused very much on that. But she had said one very important thing: "I want us to have a fun and loving relationship." Therapy also focused on the fun the two could have together.

Eddy: I think we'll need to think of this like a pump. Sometimes you have to prime it to get things going. I'd like him to use my words for the time being to help him remember and get things going, if that's all right? Would you mind?

Mother: No. But to me it doesn't seem like it has the impact when it's just going through the words.

Eddy: I know, but I think he wants to make sure that they are the right words. And I want to help him get started. I think you also know that this is a young fellow who, if he didn't mean it, wouldn't say it even if I gave him the words!

Mother: Is that true?

Ben: A little.

Eddy: So you are going to mean everything you say to your Mom, aren't you?

Ben: I guess.

Eddy: Take your Mom's hand. Hold it with your hand, not with your shirt. She has a nice warm hand, doesn't she?

Ben: Yeah, it's a hand. It's a human hand.

Eddy: It's a warm hand of a mother who loves you. I want you to tell your mother that you are sorry that you provoked her.

Ben: Okay. I'm sorry I provoked you.

Mother: Do you know what that word means, provoked?

Ben: Yeah.

Mother: Okay.

Eddy: And that you want to have a happy life with her.

Ben: And I want to have a happy life with you.

Eddy: And it's not easy for me to be this earnest.

Ben: Earnest? What does that mean?

Eddy: Sincere.

Ben: Okay, what was it again?

Eddy: It's not easy for me to be this sincere.

Ben: It's not easy for me to be this sincere.

Eddy: Give your mom a big hug and a kiss.

Ben: Okay.

(They hugged and kissed.)

The session continued with a discussion of Mother's Day, which was coming up at that time. The therapist had the contract notarized and signed by the judge. Two weeks later the boy misbehaved again and the mother called Protective Services and said, "I've had it! I am going to put him in foster care." The social worker answered, "You can't! You have a contract signed by the judge." The mother said, "Oh. Just testing, just testing." They continued in therapy and their relationship improved, as did other aspects of their lives. There were no more threats of expulsion.

A year and a half later the son was behaving well, getting good grades in school and working part-time. He was planning to study business and become rich, which the mother was counting on.

Conclusion

The problem was how to reunite mother and child so there would be no more threats of expulsion. At the beginning of the therapy the hierarchy was reversed and the mother was not in the superior position to the child that is needed for her to be able to love and protect her child in a motherly way. One way of correcting the situation was to appeal to a higher authority. The therapist used a "legal contract" and "the judge" who signed the contract as the agents of a higher authority to whom the mother pledged her love and commitment to her son.

There were several reasons for arranging that the mother's commitment take the form of a "legal" contract. She demonstrated from the beginning of the session that she enjoyed complicated, somewhat pompous language, and the son was very intelligent and could understand the meaning of a contract. Also, the mother had been using "the law" (Department of Social Services) to separate from her son. Now "the law" was being used to bring them together in a "legal and loving commitment."

7

AN ADOLESCENT IN DESPAIR

Suicide is painless.

—*From M*A*S*H*—Screenplay by Kurt Vonnegut

A MOTHER CALLED the FTI and said that the family had been referred by the court to family therapy because her 17-year-old daughter, Martine, while working in a department store, had stolen more than $2,000 from the cash register. The mother also mentioned that the previous year the girl had made a suicide attempt and that the two parents were not in good health. The father was somewhat overweight and suffered from severe high blood pressure. The mother was seriously diabetic. There were two other children who were not present in the first session: an older brother, Alex, 19, who was going to college but spending the weekends at home, and a 13-year-old sister, Beth, who was in high school.

I was the supervisor behind the one-way mirror and had agreed not to communicate with the therapist, Neil Schiff, until the first interview was almost over. This resulted in two different ways of understanding the problem presented to therapy. The therapist thought that the problem belonged to the first dimension and was a struggle for control where the adolescent was looking to dominate the parents for personal advantage. I thought that the prob-

· 112 ·

lem belonged to the third dimension and that the girl was trying to love and protect her parents. The reader will be able to appreciate the importance of conceptualizing the problem correctly and choosing the right strategy, which eventually takes place near the end of the first interview.

Schiff: (to the father) Why does Martine do the things she does?
Father: Why she does the things she does we don't know. When I'm home she's very helpful. She's always very giving. She has a lot of friends. Friends in what sense of the word I don't know. If they're true friends or they're there because they need something from Martine I don't know.

Milton Erickson used to say that people will tell you everything that is important in the first five minutes of the first session. When the father emphasized how helpful and caring Martine was he was expressing an essential aspect of the problem.

Father: This is something where we feel there may be a little problem. She argues with her sister.
Schiff: The problem is she may be exploited by friends? That she's not sure of herself so she does more for people than she really should?
Father: That's exactly the way we feel about it. And she argues quite a bit with her sister, for what reason I don't know. I mean, maybe it's a period of time that they're going through, a stage. She seems to look up to her brother. They seem to be very close. And basically we feel that she's a good child. She's got a lot of love in her but she's got problems.

It is a good prognostic sign that the father is able to say something positive about her at this moment.

Father: Either she's trying to gain our attention by doing the things she does, I don't know, or she feels like she's under so much pressure to satisfy everybody that she has to do these things. Maybe it's some kind of peer pressure, so to speak.
Mother: Well basically, what Jim said, I feel the same way. I do feel

that she's a little jealous of Beth. Beth's very thin, vivacious, outgoing, has a lot of friends . . .

What follows is a list of devastating things that the mother says about Martine, starting with how she is jealous of Beth, her younger sister, because Beth is thin, attractive and has many friends.

Mother: And I think she feels pressured because Alex does very well in school. He's always been a high achiever, where Martine is doing very poor in school. (Martine had a learning disability.) But I also think it's because of her self-esteem. She's overweight and every time you try to approach the subject of course she fights it. I know what it's like. I just, myself, lost 40 some pounds.

Schiff: Wow!

Mother: Within the last couple of years. It's really been bad. I've caught her stealing. I've caught her lying. And a few years back, about two years back, when she was babysitting, two of the neighbors came to me to tell me that she had stolen from their house. And what she does with the money I don't know, because she can't even tell me why she did this at the store. She seemed to like her job. She liked being there with the other kids.

Schiff: How do you see the problem, Martine?

Martine: That I have a problem that's been there for a while.

Schiff: You have a problem that's been there for a while.

Martine: Yes.

Schiff: What's the problem?

Martine: Like my parents said, you know, jealousy over the two and just, you know, pressure.

Schiff: Who do you feel jealous of and for what reason?

Martine: Well, Alex, you know, for school wise, and Beth, she's outgoing, you know, she'll come home and be able to go run around and me, I'll come home and I'll sleep or, you know, do something around the house.

Schiff: And how long has it been this way for you?

Martine: A while.

Schiff: A year, two years, five years?

Martine: Well, since I started high school I just, you know, it's the pressure also from the students, you know.

Schiff: What kind of pressure?

Martine: They have a name for being "Top A." You know what I mean? You get looked down on when you're in basic classes like I am.

Schiff: They look down on you?

Martine: Yeah, no one likes to be looked at that way, you know.

Schiff: Do you have friends?

Martine: Yeah.

Schiff: Good friends?

Martine: Yeah. I mean, I know good friends from bad friends. There are people who tend to come to you when they just need something, but I stay away from them.

Schiff: Let me ask you this. How would you order the problems that you have? What would you say is the most difficult problem, second most difficult problem, the third? What's the most difficult problem you have?

Martine: At school.

Schiff: And what at school?

Martine: Just, you know, just studying and performing well.

Schiff: You don't study?

Martine: I do, but I get frustrated and just give up.

Martine does not make one critical remark about anyone. When asked how she sees the problem she says that the mother is right, she is jealous of her sister and of her brother. She has problems at school because she does not do as well as the other kids. She takes all the responsibility herself. In an adolescent this is a sign of clinical depression. A normal adolescent would say "My parents don't understand me, they're too strict, they're not like the other parents, my sister is awful, my brother treats me badly, the teachers at school don't know how to teach." Since I knew that she had made a suicide attempt, I was concerned about her self-criticism.

Schiff: Yes. Have you always had trouble with schoolwork?

Martine: Yeah.

Schiff: You always have. Have you been evaluated, I mean have you been tested so that—

Martine: Yes.

Schiff: And what were—

Martine: That's why I'm in the basic classes. I am a slow reader.

Schiff: What's the second most difficult problem?

Martine: The jealousy over my brother and sister.

Schiff: Okay. And what's next after that?

Martine: The stealing.

Schiff: Let me ask you about the stealing. Whom do you steal from—everybody?

Martine: No.

Schiff: Just certain people?

Martine: Well, I haven't done it in a while. I mean, Macy's—

Schiff: How much did you steal from Macy's?

Martine: I don't know.

Mother: $2,520.

Schiff: Over $2,000!

Mother: Yes. And we don't know what she's done with the money. We figure that it's $700 a month that she spent on what, God only knows. I just can't conceive of it.

Schiff: That's an enormous amount of money. Did they send you to court? What happened as a result of that? Did you have to pay it back?

Martine: Nothing yet.

Mother: I went over to the Youth Division with my husband and talked to the officer who will be handling the case and he said at this point they don't know what they are going to do. We had to contact Macy's to make arrangements for restitution.

Schiff: Yes. So you say the problems are school, jealousy, and stealing. Anything else besides those three that you would regard as a problem?

Martine: Lying.

Schiff: Whom do you lie to?

Martine: My parents.

Schiff: Anybody else?

Martine: I have to the principal at school.

Schiff: Is there anything that you've told me so far that's a lie?

Martine: No.

Schiff: These are serious problems that you mentioned. Is there anything else?

Martine: Just my weight. I'm working on that now.

This kind of interviewing is too harsh for a depressed, suicidal adolescent. It would have been appropriate if Martine had been a rebellious delinquent. I knew that the therapist was not thinking that this was a depressed girl concerned about her efforts to be appreciated, concerned about her parents and so on, because he kept coming back to, "What do you steal? To whom you do you lie?" "Did you lie to me?" If he had thought differently, he would have been helping her immediately to feel better about herself.

Schiff: How much weight do you wish to lose?
Martine: Fifty pounds.
Schiff: Fifty pounds. And you're involved in some kind of a diet program?
Martine: Yes, Weight Watchers with my Mom and Dad.

The therapist then asked the father what he had done to try to help Martine. The father talked about how he was reluctant to punish Martine because he was worried that it was just going to make her behavior escalate.

Schiff: So. You've given her considerable liberties even though she's been doing things that caused you a great deal of concern.
Father: Well, it's not as if we hit her or we do anything physical, it's just that for some reason or another she doesn't want to communicate.
Mother: I did. You have to admit.
Schiff: You do what?
Mother: Hit her. I could kill her. He had to pull me off her the other day. I mean, I just want to kill her when she does things like this.
Father: I don't remember pulling you off her. When was this?
Martine: You weren't home. It was Saturday. Beth wanted to borrow my record and I wouldn't let her, so Mom comes in and she started beating on me.
Father: No I didn't know about that.
Martine: I called Alex to come help me and he couldn't pick me up.

Mother: It probably stems from me because I lose my temper.

Father: Well, I didn't know my wife was using physical —

Mother: You've told me before to leave her alone.

Father: Yeah, well, I mean you know, I just don't feel at this stage of the game that any type of physical punishment is going to do it.

Schiff: Is there anything else that you have tried to do to help Martine that your husband hasn't mentioned? I mean, for example, you said that you have punished her by hitting her. Has that worked?

Mother: No. It just makes me angrier, and then I feel sorry about doing it. But I have a very bad temper. I've even tried sending her to my mother's, maybe getting her out of the house.

Schiff: Where is your mother?

Mother: My mother lives in Florida. I was thinking of sending her to a foster home. I checked into that, but I was told because of her age they wouldn't accept her.

Schiff: If this gets worse, what's going to happen?

Mother: I'll leave. I'll leave. My mother has already told me —

Schiff: You're going to leave him?

Mother: If he is willing to come, that's fine. But she wants me to come down and visit her now and I'm almost tempted to do it.

Schiff: Well, there's a difference between visiting your mother and leaving your family.

Mother: I would leave.

Schiff: You mean the situation is so bad that the kids could cause a separation in the marriage? Is that what you are getting at?

Mother: I won't put up with it anymore! I've always given up stuff for the kids and last November I decided — I'm a diabetic and I wanted to get off insulin, so I joined Nutri-System at great expense. I did it for me. But I had to give it up because of her. (cries)

Schiff: And you did very well, 40 pounds is a lot of weight.

This outburst reveals the level of immaturity of the mother. Normally mothers accept as a fact of life that one give up many things for one's children, especially when they are little. This mother seems to consider that she should not have had to give up things for her children even when they were young. She goes on to say that she lost 40 pounds by joining a very expensive diet system, and she had to give that up because the parents had to repay the money Martine stole from the department store. This is upsetting to her.

Behind the mirror I was looking at the situation. The mother was very immature, violent and ill. The father was ill also and somewhat helpless. The girl had a learning disability and there were two successful siblings. I was thinking that this girl might behave in this way to ensure that she would not be able to leave home, because perhaps she was the one at home who took care of everybody in the family. I was beginning to suspect that she was probably like the servant in the household, doing everything so that the family would function. I knew both parents worked, with the mother working in spite of her illness, out of economic necessity. Very often it is the child with a learning disability who is selected to stay at home and take care of the family, since it is difficult for her to move on and go to college. Martine was also obese, which ensured that she would not be going out to parties and on dates like other girls her age. She also behaved in delinquent and suicidal ways, insuring failure, which would again make it possible for her to stay home. I was thinking that the problem was not that she was a rebellious, antagonistic adolescent, trying to control the parents; rather, the problem was that she had to take care of everybody in the family—a task at which she was destined to fail, because a 17-year-old girl cannot take care of her family.

At this point the therapist sent Martine to the waiting room and asked the parents if there was anything they wanted to tell him in private.

Father: Martine is probably the warmest of all three and she's the first one to want to do something to help. Of the three, she's the warmest. She'll help. She's giving, you know, on one hand. She's dishonest, she steals, okay, on the other.
Mother: Well, I guess the reason I don't come down too hard on her is because I'm afraid that she will do something to herself.
Schiff: When did she try to commit suicide?

Mother: Last year.

Schiff: And what was the precipitating factor?

Mother: We don't know. Probably school.

Schiff: What did she do?

Mother: She slit her wrists.

Father: No, she didn't.

Mother: Well, the way that they claim in school, she didn't slit her wrists straight across, she went up like this.

Schiff: She did it in school?

Mother: Yes.

Schiff: She took a razor blade at school? Where, in the bathroom?

Father: She didn't actually, there was hardly even a scratch on her.

Mother: Well she, it was, it was deep. It was deep.

Schiff: And it was at school this took place?

Mother: In the bathroom.

Schiff: And they called you and they called the rescue squad?

Mother: No they didn't call the rescue squad. They called me.

The parents do not know how the suicide attempt happened — a sign of serious neglect. Here mother says she did it in school; in fact, Martine slit her wrists at home. The mother also minimized the danger, saying that it was not deep because it was vertical, though in fact a vertical cut is more dangerous than a horizontal one. Martine cut her wrists at home, bandaged herself, and went to school. Someone at school noticed the bandages and called the mother. The parents had not even found out what actually happened.

Schiff: So you're afraid if you lean on her she's going to try to kill herself?

Mother: Because she's always threatening that she's going to kill herself. She hates the house and she doesn't want to live — you know, that type of thing.

Schiff: How long has she been talking about that?

Mother: I don't know, say the last couple of years.

The talk about suicide is characteristic of the despair of wanting to help and not being appreciated, of wanting to protect and not being able to, and of feeling trapped in a difficult situation.

Schiff: Do you ever lose your temper with him? (pointing at the father)

Mother: Yes. Yes. And he's lost his temper with me.

Schiff: Has there been any abuse between the two of you?

Mother: He's only hit me once. I'm mostly the one who hits him first.

Schiff: Recently, or was this some time ago?

Mother: Last year.

Schiff: Has the situation with Martine aggravated tension between the two of you or has it brought you together?

Mother: I think it's brought us together more.

Sometimes when you ask people the function of the symptom they tell you. The therapist took the parents to the waiting room and brought Martine alone into the therapy room.

Schiff: The reason that I wanted to talk to you alone, as you probably guessed, was to find out if there were things about the situation, about you, or about your parents, or your family, that are important but that for one reason or another you weren't comfortable mentioning with everybody sitting here?

Martine: Yeah, it's just that I feel like I'm the cause of everything.

Schiff: How long have you felt that way?

Martine: For a while. Like since, I started in junior high. I just felt out, you know.

Schiff: That was what, five years ago?

Martine: I've felt like this for a long time.

Schiff: You felt "out." What do you mean by "out"?

Martine: Out of place.

Schiff: In the family? In what way?

Martine: You know just—Beth being the youngest getting attention, Alex the oldest, you know, being able to do, you know, what he wants, he always had my parents' attention. I just was off by myself.

Schiff: You tried to kill yourself last year. You tried to commit suicide. Did you do it at school or at home?

Martine: At home.

Schiff: What did you do?

Martine: I cut my wrists. And I don't know who told my parents.

To this day I'd like to know. Someone called my Mom. I don't even know, they won't even tell me how they found out.

Schiff: What made you do that to yourself?

Martine: Just, you know, problems, pressure. I've just had it! I just feel like giving up!

Schiff: Where's the pressure coming from?

Martine: Mainly at school.

Schiff: Like what? People hassling you? Is that what you mean?

Even the therapist seems to want to blame somebody else, but Martine continues to blame herself.

Martine: Yeah, you know, I hate being in basic classes and I'll study and study and get an E and then I give up. So I give up easily on everything, I just gave up, because I don't know what I'm going to do.

Schiff: What do you mean, when you get out of high school?

Martine: Yeah. I have a year left. I don't think I'm going to be ready for college, I'm having, you know, such a hard time now, and I see my friends struggling now who are in college and it also doesn't help when my mother, I know she gets hot tempered, she'll call me a failure and a loser, or something.

Schiff: Are you worried about your parents?

Martine: Yeah.

Schiff: What are you worried about?

Martine: About how I know that I hurt them bad and I've always had a feeling of them fighting, and stuff, and I've always felt it was because of me and the stupid things I do.

Schiff: Do you have any ideas about what would be particularly helpful to you?

Martine: Well, I do want to get out of the house for a little bit.

Schiff: You mean move out of the house?

Martine: Just go away.

Schiff: Where do you want to go?

Martine: (sobbing) I was just going to stay with a friend.

Martine starts to cry when she talks about leaving the home. Of course she knows that she cannot; she does not have anywhere to go. It is interesting that in the double bind theory of the origin of schizophrenia, when a person was given incongruent messages, not being able to leave the situation was considered most inducive of despair and of pathology. It is at this thought that she cannot leave home that she starts crying.

The therapist came out of the room to talk with me. I explained to him how I viewed the girl and added that I did not want to put pressure on the parents because I was concerned about their health and about the mother's violence. But there were two people in the family who were not even in the session and they had to be present next time. We planned several interventions.

Schiff: Here's the situation the way that I see it. There is a problem of self-destruction here.

Mother: On her part?

Schiff: It's on everybody's part, not just Martine's part. Do you agree?

Mother: Yes.

Schiff: And Martine is in a situation that is really too much for her to handle. I don't mean simply the problem of having stolen money. She carries a tremendous burden in the family as well, and it's too much for her.

Mother: What kind of burden? You mean, because she has to work?

Schiff: No. I'll get into that in a moment. And I take the issue of anybody attempting suicide very, very seriously. And there are lots of ways of killing yourself. You can do it dramatically in one step by shooting yourself or by taking some kind of medication, or you can do it by eating too much, or by doing things that raise your blood pressure so that you have some kind of medical complication. There are a lot of ways of killing yourself. And everybody in this room, all three of you, in one way or another, are behaving self-destructively and you know that.

And also, part of the problem is that there are two people who are not here. Your son and your daughter should be here in order to help. Martine carries a tremendous burden. If Martine didn't misbehave, the loss of temper that you have towards her, you might have with your husband instead and that might be more of a problem.

Mother: But I lose my temper with the other three also.

Schiff: But more with her than with anybody else. And more with her than with your husband or anybody else and that's a burden for her.

When there are several presenting problems one always address-es first the one that is most life-threatening. In this case it was more important to address the suicide attempt than the delinquency. Whenever somebody presents a symptom and is also suicidal, one needs to intervene to prevent the suicide first. The first priority is to keep a person alive; second, to keep him/her coming to therapy so something can be done to help him/her; only then should one try to produce change.

Father: So in other words you feel that she is, to be blunt about it, she's being picked on more than the others.

Schiff: That's right. You know, she has an image of herself as somebody who's not very bright, doesn't do very well aca-demically, has to buy friends, is always doing something wrong at home, has always been a source of problems, and so forth. But that's propaganda because one of the things is, as your husband said, she's the only one of the kids who's warm, who's compassionate, she's the only one who helps. The oth-er two aren't even here!

Mother: Yes, but that's no fault of theirs. There's no way I could pick Alex up at the university at 6 o'clock and get here at 6:30. I mean, he had exams. There's nothing he could do. He would have been here.

Schiff: If you or your husband had a serious problem, were sick or something like that, Alex would be there. If something's im-portant enough, people make the sacrifice and they make arrangements to take care of that. Beth's just at cheerleading practice. Here her sister is in a situation where she tried to kill herself, the family is such that you talked about, if things don't get better, you were thinking about leaving—that's a terribly, terribly, terribly grave situation! And the only one who's here is Martine! There are some things that need to be done to correct this problem and that's what you came here for. You knew perfectly well before you came that, while you might not like what was said, you sought the services of a

professional person who could do something to help you because the situation is a serious one.

Mother: All right. And it is. It has to be corrected.

Schiff: That's right. Okay.

Mother: I mean, she still has the rest of her life to live.

Schiff: That's right. And so do you. And so does your husband,
and so does Alex, and so does Beth. So there are several
things that I want you to do right now. One is, I want you to
make it clear that you yourself are making a commitment to
work with me, I can't work, and I don't think it's fair to the
other people, if there's a threat that you're going to leave! You
have to say, "I'm not leaving. I'm staying here. I'm going to see
this thing through." She needs to hear that. You're an example
for her. What I want you to say is this: "I will stay for this
therapy. I will see this thing through until Martine is over
these problems. I'm going to stay with Jim and I am going to
stay with the family. I am not going to be a runaway mother."
Would you please say that?

Mother: I am not going to be a runaway mother.

Schiff: I'm going to stay with—

Mother: I'm going to stay with Jim and I'm going to stay with the
family. I really want to see this thing through. I want to see
Martine get better and the family is to be more of a family
unit.

Schiff: Okay.

Mother: Not just five people living in the same house.

Schiff: That's right. Now the next thing—I'm putting a lot of this
on you but I know you can handle this—I want you to turn to
your husband. I want you to hold your husband's hand, and I
want you to tell him that you love him and that you want to
work as closely as possible with him to get Martine over these
problems. (The mother turns to Martine to take her hand.)
No, not Martine, your husband.

When the mother took Martine's hand instead of her husband's,
the therapist should have used that wonderful, affectionate gesture
towards Martine. Unfortunately, he was so focused on what he had
to do next that he missed the moment. He could have had the
mother take both Martine's and her husbands's hand.

Mother: I love you and we'll work it through.
Father: Good. Good. (embarrassed)
Mother: And we'll help Martine. Okay?
Schiff: Okay. I want you to tell me something complimentary about your daughter.
Mother: That she's very loving
Schiff: That loving is enough and also too much. Beth and Alex are going to have to start doing some loving. Beth is going to have to start doing her share. Alex is going to have to start doing his share. Martine is already doing too much.
Mother: It's true, and I will admit that I rely a lot on Martine because for whatever reasons she does it, if I ask her to help me she will, where Beth would balk and won't do it and I just give up and Alex's too busy to be bothered.

The mother said this is true, as if she had totally forgotten all the negative things that she said about Martine only half an hour before.

Schiff: Okay, I want you to say right now, "I'm going to get more out of Beth and more out of Alex."
Mother: I'm going to get more out of Beth and more out of Alex.
Schiff: Okay.
Mother: I would like to see that happen. Seriously.
Schiff: I'm going to help you make it like that.
Mother: I give up too easily.
Schiff: (to the father) I want you to say the same thing.
Father: I want to get more out of Beth and Alex.
Schiff: Okay. Now there's one more thing. I would like for Martine to be on vacation until we meet again. She already does too much. What I mean by that is this: Don't nag her. Don't ask her because she'll do something and the others won't. And if you alone can't do it, you get your husband involved. And don't let up on them until they start. Martine's on vacation. She'll take care of her business, she's a responsible kid.
Father: I agree.
Mother: That's true.
Schiff: So leave her alone. Say only nice things to her. Don't nag

her about, you know, this or that, her weight or what she's doing or is she studying or is she working. She does her part. Leave her alone, talk about nice things with her, and get the other ones to start doing what they should be doing. I want an absolute commitment from you that the next time we meet Alex and Beth are going to be here.

Mother: They will.

Schiff: I don't care if there is a nuclear war, when you show up here and I'm here, they've got to be here, okay? (to Martine) Now, sometimes it's difficult in the beginning and sometimes you feel like giving up. I don't want you to give up. There may be things I don't know much about yet and there may be things that haven't been said that I need to know about. I don't want you to do anything to hurt yourself. You're a very sweet girl and you have a lot of potential and there are not so many compassionate human beings walking around. It would be a terrible, terrible thing to lose somebody like you. So you can't do that, okay? You have to promise me.

Martine: Uh-huh.

Schiff: Is that a deal?

Martine: Uh-huh.

Schiff: Say I promise I won't hurt myself.

Martine: I promise I won't hurt myself. (The therapist shakes hands with Martine).

Schiff: Okay. Now I would like to see you in two weeks.

Alex and Beth were present in the next session.

Schiff: I'm going to ask your mother and father to explain to you what took place here so I can then get on with things.

Mother: Well, last week we discussed what happened with Martine, and what we're going to do to try and help her.

Schiff: Now, you have to get more specific. That was a wonderful beginning.

Mother: That we are all going to try and work with her and not put too many demands on Martine. That everybody in the family is going to have to pitch in, meaning you, Alex, and you, Beth. You'll have to start doing for yourselves.

It is a very good sign that she remembers so well the most important part of the session.

Mother: And for your father, and for me, and your sister.

Schiff: Okay, Alex. Tell me what you're doing in your life at this point. You go to school?

Alex: Yeah. I'm going to the university majoring in computer science.

Schiff: Are you a good student?

Alex: Yeah, I think so.

Schiff: You graduated from high school? Were you a good student there? Good student means what kind of . . .

Alex: B's and C's. In my senior year I slacked off. That's pretty normal.

Schiff: Yes, but you are basically a solid B student.

Alex: Yeah.

Schiff: Okay. In the last couple of years, including this year at the university, you enjoy your studies, you've enjoyed being at the university this year.

Alex: Yeah.

Schiff: Have you worked while you were in school? No. You're working at your work, you're not involved with any projects? Okay, good. In the last couple of years have you been enjoying your social life as well? Do you have a decent social life?

Alex: Yeah, yeah.

Schiff: Yeah? Got a girl friend? Five or six?

Alex: No, just one.

Schiff: Just one.

(Mother laughs.)

Schiff: Five or six is right? Do you have a harem?

Mother: Alex is one on one.

Schiff: Yeah?

Mother: Do one, get rid of one, start the next.

Schiff: What else are you doing besides studying? Do you play sports or anything like that?

Alex: No, no sports. I'll be working in the government this summer and then year round from now on.

Schiff: Yeah?

Alex: With computers.

Schiff: Are you pleased with the way that your life has been going for the past couple of years?

Alex: Yeah.

Schiff: You are. Okay. I'm going to ask you to stand up and to come over here and to shake Martine's hand and thank her for the way that your life has gone for the past couple of years.

Alex: (stands up and goes to Martine) Thank you, Martine.

Martine: (smiling) You're welcome.

Schiff: Okay. Now, are you wondering why I asked you to do that?

Alex: Well kind of, I don't know.

Schiff: Okay. Do you have any idea why I did?

Alex: Well, we're a family and we're supposed to help each other.

Schiff: Uh-huh. And how has she helped you?

Alex: She does everything for me. She's always there when I need her.

Schiff: That's incredible!

It is interesting to note that this brother was just going to school and was not working while Martine, with a learning problem and difficulties in school, had to work to contribute to the family besides doing all the housework for everybody.

Schiff: I mean it's hard to believe, what more could you ask of a human being?

Alex: Not much.

Schiff: Okay. And not only has she been there for you, but whom else has she been there for?

Alex: Everybody in our family.

Schiff: She has been? Now what's her life been like in the past few years?

Alex: I think it could be better.

Schiff: Her life has been a miserable goddamed mess! Right? To be absolutely candid. So while she makes a sacrifice, you know, she's been there for you, she's been there for your parents, okay, her life has been shit! Right?

Alex: Right.

Schiff: (to Beth) Do you enjoy your life, I mean, did you enjoy this year, was it a pretty good year?

Beth: It was fun.

Schiff: Fun? And what about the year before? Fun as well?

Beth: I did better in school though.

Schiff: You did better the year before. But even though you didn't do as well this year, you still had fun.

Beth: Yes.

Schiff: Okay. I'm going to ask you to stand up and shake hands with Martine and thank her for the fun that you've had for the past couple of years.

Beth: Thank you, Martine.

Martine: You're welcome.

Schiff: Okay, now do you know why I had you thank her?

Beth: No.

Schiff: What did your brother just say?

Beth: Because she's always there for you, and she has been.

Schiff: And she has been. Okay. And what's her life been like for the past few years?

Beth: Just bad.

Schiff: That's an understatement right?

Beth: I don't know.

Schiff: It's really been horrible. Isn't that true?

Beth: Yeah, I guess.

Schiff: She's suffered. Martine was not only there for you, you know, overtly, you know, in a way that you could recognize like she was there for Alex if Alex needed anything, she did something for him, but she also supported your parents. So if your parents were upset about things, or upset at each other, or frustrated with the way that their work was going, or something like that, she would distract them and they could get mad at her rather than getting depressed or angry at themselves or angry at each other. She's the one who took that on herself. What I mean to say is this. Martine made it possible for you and your brother to be on a vacation for the past couple of years. She's the one who stayed home. She would keep your parents from going at each other by distracting them and making them pay attention to her and her defects. So she's paid a very high price for you, Alex, and for you, Beth, and for both of you.

That's something we have to change now. And so tonight

we are going to talk about how to change that. We're going to talk about changing it in two ways. First of all, Alex, if you and your sisters are a team, then Martine is a player who has been used too much. So what I want to do is this. I want you and your sisters to plan how responsibilities can be distributed more fairly, not all on Martine's shoulders, in the family. So I'm going to ask you to pull your chair over here. Can you move that? It's a heavy chair. (Alex moves the chair closer to his sisters.) Pull in close.

Okay, now here's the first part of it. Your parents, somebody has to play the role of ruining the family, okay? So that your parents can be distracted from some of the other things that are bothering them. It's also a way of bringing them together, okay, without getting on each other's backs. So what I want you to do is talk about who's going to be the life ruiner. Who's going to be the life ruiner for the next two weeks? And what they're going to do. I want you three to talk about that. Now I'm not talking about murder and I'm not talking about suicide, and I'm not talking about something that's going to put you in jail, but you have to be an effective life ruiner. You have to cause problems and you have to be failing in your own life so that your parents get really upset at you, and you're the one who takes all the heat for a while. Okay? And you have to decide who's going to do it.

Martine: Beth.

Alex: Well, I think I'll be a volunteer since I've been away at school and not at home.

Several strategies were used in this session. The first was changing who had the symptoms. Usually the oldest and most responsible sibling, like Alex, is the one who volunteers first to replace the problem child in ruining the family's life.

Alex: I think I can wreak some havoc.

Beth: Wreak some havoc?

Alex: I think I can distract.

Schiff: How can you do that? Actually, it shouldn't be me saying this. You should be talking to Alex and helping him plan this. And you especially should be doing it because he's doing it for you, you know, he's letting you off the hook. You're going to have a fun time if he's making a mess of himself!

Martine: How are you going to do it?

Alex: Oh, there's lots of ways, like not make my bed, not clean my room, just throw everything all over the place like I do at my dorm. I could come home late at night drunk. Anyway I'll be glad to wreak some havoc and take the load off my sisters.

Schiff: But now another thing you can do, it seems to me, is you can pick on Beth. And you and Beth can fight so Martine and Beth don't have to fight all the time because that's really a burden to Martine. I mean she's been used for that too much. You can give her and Beth a chance to have a relationship as sisters. You can vomit all over the living room and just leave it there, you know, not clean it up. You know? (They laugh.)

Father: Don't give him any ideas.

Alex: (laughs) Right.

Beth: He could leave his bed unmade for a day.

Schiff: How about stealing? Why don't you steal money from your parents?

Alex: No, I don't think I want to steal money. I don't think I want to steal anything.

Schiff: Well, I mean, you know, why not steal, you know you can steal five dollar bills, a hundred dollars. That would be nothing compared with the sacrifices she made. She stole what, $2,400! You see, here's the problem, Martine made a sacrifice, but has it made anything better?

Martine: No.

Schiff: It really hasn't. Your mother is still ready to run away.

It is important to clarify that this way of helping does not really help. Martine's stealing and suicide threats did not really help anyone.

Schiff: Your dad still needs to lose weight for his health right? And she's got herself into deep trouble. It didn't solve her school problems, and there are things in the family that need to be straightened out still. What Martine did didn't solve that. In fact, if we are absolutely candid about it, it didn't solve any problems. It made them worse. Your temper got even worse, your nerves got worse. The financial situation got worse. More pressure. So maybe there's a better way that you can help your parents and each other. Not just by being a life ruiner. That's just a temporary thing.

When a problem is very serious, it is a good idea to use several strategies. There were three strategies used in this session. One was taking turns at who has the problem. The second was a straightforward, fairer sharing of responsibilities in the family, which the therapist arranged next. The third strategy was reversing the hierarchy and having the children advise the parents on how to be happier.

Schiff: What about more positive things? I want you to talk about that.
Alex: Well, first of all I think Martine should come to me for help with her school work.

This is very appropriate because Alex is in college and he is a good student.

Alex: And we all have to participate more in household activities and clean up and distribute it more evenly than it is right now. Divide the household chores.
Schiff: It's obvious that even though there're problems there's a great deal of love among the members of your family. It doesn't always come out but it is obviously there. And I think that you would just take over and you would do for them. When I see your parents again I expect a glow. I want to see Martine smile too. Martine you're an expert. You've got to help your brother and you got to help Beth. You've got to tell them who's going to do what. Come on, you're an expert.

Here was when we found out how great was the extent of what Martine did at home as she explained what had to be done in the household. The siblings then decided who was going to do what. Up until then Martine had been doing everything.

Schiff: (to Martine) And I don't want you to do it all. You just help them to know what has to be done.

Martine: Okay, Beth you have the week after Alex and Alex's going to split the bathrooms upstairs. I had to do the whole upstairs last Saturday because Beth was out and you were lying down or studying or something. You know, you could have helped for a few minutes. I did the whole upstairs.

Schiff: Okay, now this is a very important discussion on a different subject. What I want you to talk about now is how you can make your parents happier. Would it make them happy if the three of you took them out to dinner on a surprise basis? Or if you brought something, you know, if you made a special dinner at home? If they came home from work one night and the table was set and it was real nice silverware out there and candles lit and a really good dinner was cooking, something like that and you were all walking around in party hats with noise makers, things like that, would they like that?

Alex: I think we should come home and take one night out.

Martine: Take one night out and just all go out as a family.

Alex: Have a dinner.

Martine: Maybe to a movie or something. So we don't have to go to dinner, we can go to a movie or go play putt putt or something.

Schiff: You are much younger than your parents and you're optimistic, okay? They've forgotten how to be happy. They have forgotten how to be happy. So I want you to be in charge of their happiness. If you think they would be happy going to a movie then I want you to send them to a movie.

Martine: And go on vacation.

Schiff: Okay, go on vacation. And the only thing they can argue about is what movie to go to, or whether to go to Florida or to California.

Alex: (to Beth) Things are going to change. We've got to grow up, you know.

The brother made a list of the things that they were going to do to make the parents happy.

Schiff: All right now, you all have to put your hands together like this, you know the way the football players do it. Okay, now you have to put the left hands, now you have to raise your right hands. Okay, now you have to say "I solemnly swear I'm not going to let my brother and sisters down, or my parents down, or my family down."

Martine, Beth, and Alex: "I solemnly swear I'm not going to let my brother and my sisters down, or my parents down, or my family down."

Schiff: Okay. Now you each have to sign that piece of paper. (They signed the lists of things that they were going to do.)

The therapy continued for several months and Martine began to do better in school. There were no more symptoms, no more delinquency, and no more suicide threats. She was able to graduate with her class in high school, which at the beginning of the therapy had seemed improbable. The real surprise was that in the graduation ceremony the principal of the school gave the graduation speech about her. He talked about what a wonderful person she was, what an effort she had made and how she had succeeded. It was very moving to the whole family. Martine's relationship with her mother improved and they became good friends. She lost a little weight, and soon found a boyfriend. They got married soon after she graduated from high school and so Martine *was* able to leave home.

Conclusion

The transcript illustrates how it is necessary to understand a problem correctly in order to plan the right strategies. In the first session the adolescent's wish to love and protect her parents was acknowledged and she was protected from the despair that can lead to suicide. In the second session the siblings' collaboration was obtained and Martine was relieved of her unfortunate position in the family. All this was done in good cheer and without undue pressure on any family member.

8

EASY RIDER

You think too much, Boss.

— Zorba (Anthony Quinn) in Zorba the Greek.

THE FOLLOWING EXCERPTS are from the first session of a therapy with a single mother and her two children. Faced with a multitude of very serious presenting problems, I took a very simple, common sense approach.

This case illustrates how to understand a child's situation quickly and how to intervene rapidly to solve the presenting problem. It also exemplifies how to be respectful and optimistic and to promote hopefulness and humor even when faced with many very serious problems.

Cindy was referred to the Institute by the Crisis Center in the local community. She was upset because her nine-year-old daughter, Amy, was threatening suicide. She had said that she wanted to kill herself and to burn in a fire. The mother was also concerned about the "sibling rivalry" (as she called it) between Amy and her 13-year-old brother, Larry. Cindy also mentioned on her first phone call to the institute that she was divorced, that her ex-husband was an "absentee parent," and that she herself was very depressed.

Certain assumptions could be made from Cindy's first telephone conversation with the secretary. Amy might actually be depressed and suicidal and/or Amy's suicide threats might be a metaphor for the mother's despair and depression. If the latter hypothesis were correct, a rapid intervention would free Amy from being the metaphorical expression of the mother's problems. In any case, since suicide threats must always be taken seriously, a quick intervention was called for. Cindy's use of the term "sibling rivalry" suggested that she knew some psychological jargon. We would try to use normal language in the therapy so that the focus would be on change and not on psychological discussions. The fact that Cindy referred to her ex-husband as an "absentee parent" indicated that she had strong feelings about him.

The only additional information was that Cindy was a white collar worker for a large corporation. She had been trained as a nurse but had stopped nursing to help her husband with his construction business.

Cindy was a tall, thin woman, carelessly dressed in jeans. She could have been attractive but she appeared not to care how she looked, wore no makeup, and seemed tense and depressed. Amy was a beautiful, skinny little blonde who looked like her mother. Larry was dark-haired, handsome, and tall for his age. As they walked into the therapy room, Cindy put on her jacket, instead of taking if off, even though the room was warm. She seemed very anxious.

Madanes: So, what's the matter?

The wording of the question conveyed that I was not interested in using psychological jargon or in taking a professional posture to distance myself from her.

Cindy: I've been looking for help for about three weeks. Our family seems to be a real mess right now and I'm having some real difficulties functioning on a daily basis. Amy's having some real difficulties and you may want to talk—she may want to talk to you alone about those, about her feelings. I told her it was okay, that she should feel comfortable and talk about her feelings about me and be very truthful and honest, because I want to get some help for us. We do not have good mental health right now in our house, and it's affecting me. I've taken some time off from work and I don't know when I'm going to be able to get back to work. I'm having trouble awakening, doing simple things like just getting dressed, just taking them to school.

At this point, instead of asking whether she was depressed, I asked if she was worried. Depression has connotations of psychopathology; worrying is more normal. The question indicated that I was interested in her problems but not in psychologizing. I was thinking that Cindy must believe that she was a bad mother and must have very low self-esteem, because she was giving her daughter permission to talk to me alone about her, implying that there were unsavory things that Amy needed to tell me.

Milton Erickson used to say that a client tells you what is most important in the first few minutes of the first interview. Cindy had done just that, and I knew that the goal of the therapy had to be to raise her self-esteem, so that she could come out of her depression and behave and feel like a good mother.

Cindy: I'm having a lot of panicky feelings and I feel terrified at times and almost afraid to leave the home to go to the store, and today sort of explains, I think, some of those feelings. A lot of times I have premonitions of things in my dreams and in waking. And I've been feeling real terrified and haven't understood what was happening. I had a dream—I was telling the children on the way over here because I was concerned. I had a dream that their father called. He's been mostly an absentee parent and is a convicted pedophile. Then he really called and wanted to take Larry away for the weekend. I should have just hung up. But instead we continued to talk and he started calling names, and going right down through the family, everybody in my family.

Madanes: That happened today that he called you?

Cindy: Yes. So I became frightened and I turned off all the lights and (puts her head in her hands and begins to cry). I don't want to talk about this with them in here.

Madanes: (handing her some tissues) It's okay. We'll talk about it

privately. Let's just talk for a few minutes about the things
that it's all right to talk about in front of them.
Cindy: Okay.

If I had asked the children to leave the room at that point, they
would have sat in the waiting room anxiously wondering what was
happening to their mother, whom they had left in tears. Before
taking them out of the room, I had to establish that the mother was
all right, that she was a good mother, that the children loved her,
and that I was a kindly person. Then they could sit in the waiting
room without anxiety.

Madanes: Are your fears mainly in relation to your ex-husband?
Cindy: I think so, a lot of it. I don't know, I couldn't really get a
grip on my fear and this feeling of terror the last few days.
And then when he called, it was like I understood, because I
ran around the house and shut the lights down and drew the
curtains and I felt like he was coming over. I think I stayed on
the phone because I didn't want him to know that I was afraid
of him. I feel that if I hung up he would know that I am
afraid.
Madanes: Are the children going to school now?
Cindy: Yes.
Madanes: They are going regularly to school and you take them
there in the morning?
Cindy: (nods affirmatively)

I wanted to know how much Cindy was actually acting on the basis
of fear. If she was letting the children go to school, it meant that
she was not so worried about their father hurting them.

Cindy: But what's going on at home is that we're having a lot of
difficulties, a lot of sibling rivalry. Amy, I don't know how
much she's reacting normally, because Larry can be very
sneaky and lies to me a lot. So I don't know how much he's
doing. They fight with each other. Now Amy's version is
always much different from Larry's, so I don't know how
much he's not telling me the truth, or how much she's exag-
gerating. I don't know what's happening between them.

Madanes: Let me ask you a question. When you were working, did
  they stay alone in the house until you came home?
Cindy: Oh, no. They go to before and after school care.
Madanes: So when do they fight?
Cindy: Whenever they are together.
Madanes: It's usually when you are there in the house.
Cindy: Yes. I leave them alone occasionally to go to the store, once
  in the evening to go to a P.T.A. meeting. Larry is left alone
  more than Amy now because he's 13.

I realized that Cindy was probably living like a recluse but I was
reassured that she was careful in taking care of the children.

Madanes: (turning to Larry, who is sitting across from his mother)
  Let me ask you a question. (pointing to Amy) Does she beat
  you up?

This was an attempt to introduce humor and reduce anxiety. Amy
was so much smaller than Larry that obviously she could not beat
him up. Larry, however, was so tense that he didn't even smile. I
was also attempting to counteract the mother's negative comments
about the son by humorously defining the daughter as the initiator
of negative interactions.

Larry: No.
Madanes: Okay. What does she pick on you about?
Larry: Well, you know like sometimes she says, "Do you want to
  play?" or something like that. Then we'll go upstairs and we'll
  start playing and it will turn out to be a fight, we'll fight over
  something.
Madanes: Do you hit her?
Larry: Only if she hits me.
Madanes: Who hits harder?
Larry Me.
Madanes: Can you control it?
Larry: Sometimes.
Madanes: (turning to Amy, who is sitting next to her mother)
  Does he beat you up?

Amy: Not all the time, but sometimes he acts like he's going to hit me.
Madanes: But does he?
Amy: Sometimes.
Madanes: Does it hurt?
Amy: Sometimes.
Madanes: Do you cry? (Cindy makes a gesture as if she wants to talk.) What did you want to ask?
Cindy: Do you guys know, do you realize that — we've had a lot of trips to different places and we've been over to Children's Hospital — do you realize that no matter what you tell Cloé, it is not going to separate our family? We are here to get our family closer together so the more you can tell her about your feelings the more it will help us. Okay?

The mother's reference to the possibility that I could separate the children from their mother is an indication that they have been involved with Protective Services.

Madanes: (to Amy) What do you do that worries your Mommy most?

This question defines the daughter as the initiator of negative interactions with the mother, counteracting the mother's expectation that I would blame her.

Amy: Umm . . . I don't know.
Madanes: Do you say bad things? What do you say, for example, that makes her very upset?
Amy: I call her names.
Madanes: Bad names? And what else? Do you say bad things about yourself? What do you say about yourself?
Amy: I just tell her, when I get mad I tell her that I'm stupid.

Amy was so identified with the mother that to insult her she insulted herself. This was an indication that the suicide threats were probably metaphorical for the mother's despair. If the mother were happier, Amy would not be talking about killing herself.

Madanes: That you are stupid? When you get mad at her or when
     you get mad at yourself?
Amy: When I get mad at myself.
Madanes: When do you get mad at yourself?
Amy: I don't know.
Madanes: When you make mistakes? Like what kind of mistakes?
     When you are doing your homework, or when you do some-
     thing in the house?
Amy: When I get nervous.

I was trying to establish that Amy became angry at herself when
she did something wrong and not because of some internal psychological reason. She did not accept this yet and talked about being
nervous. So I tried another approach and suggested that, if sometimes she said that she was stupid, then sometimes she should also
say that she is smart.

Madanes: And it upsets your mother for you to say that you are
     stupid, right? And sometimes do you say, "I'm so smart"?
Amy: (smiling) Once in a while.
Madanes: Once in a while. Who tells you that you are smart?
Amy: Mommy.
Madanes: Ah, that's nice. That's really nice.

My goal was to raise the mother's self-esteem so that she could
come out of her depression and feel like a good mother. Then Amy
would feel good about herself and would not need to express the
mother's sadness. My immediate goal was to establish that the
mother was good and that the children loved her before I took the
children out of the room.

Madanes: What else do you do that upsets her?
Amy: When I don't listen to her.
Madanes: What else? Tell me all the worst things that you do so
     that we can get it over with. Do you break things? What do
     you break?

I continued to define the daughter, and not the mother, as the
initiator of negative interactions with the mother.

Amy: One time I accidentally — me and Larry were staying home, I was going to throw a pillow at him and then I accidentally broke one of her big jars.

Madanes: But that was an accident. Did you get into trouble for that?

Amy: My Mom just said, "I'm sad that it broke."

Madanes: She's a pretty good mother, right? She tells you you're smart, she doesn't punish you when you break something. What else nice does she do? She works hard, right? She buys you pretty clothes. (Amy nods in agreement.) She protects you from Larry.

I continued to emphasize the mother's kindness.

Amy: Sometimes, most of the time.

Madanes: (to Larry) Who's side does she take usually when you quarrel with your sister? Who's side does your mother take?

Larry: No one, she just tries to keep us apart.

Madanes: Aha, so she's fair also. That's great.

Amy: And also, if we get in a really big fight she'll tell us to go upstairs until we can calm down. We can come downstairs when dinner is ready.

Cindy: And that really makes you crazy lately, doesn't it? When I tell you to go to your room?

Madanes: You don't like to go to your room? There aren't any fun things to do there?

Amy: I have some games but mostly for two people.

Madanes: Aha.

Amy: I'll play some with me and Larry's and Mom's cat. I talk to her.

Madanes: You play with the cat? What's the name of the cat?

Amy: Spider.

Madanes: How nice, what kind of a cat is it?

Amy: It has brown and tan marks on it and white under it's chin.

Madanes: It's a boy or a girl?

Amy: Girl.

Madanes: How old?

Amy: It's four in person and 28 in cat life.

Larry: It's five and a half.

Madanes: I had a cat that I loved and her name was Lucy because she was a redhead. Have you ever seen the show on TV "I Love Lucy"? So we called her Lucy and she lived until she was like about a hundred for our life. So I like cats a lot. Your mother's nice to the cat also, I bet. Who feeds the cat?

I established a bond with Amy through our mutual love of cats.

Amy: Mostly me and Larry do.
Madanes: (to Larry) Do you like the cat too?
Larry: Yes.
Madanes: You're in junior high, right?
Larry: No, I stayed back a year.
Madanes: So you're in your last year.
Larry: Sixth.
Madanes: Sixth, very good. (to Amy) What grade are you in?
Amy: Third.
Madanes: Do you give trouble to your Mom with homework also?
Amy: When I don't understand things . . .
Madanes: You ask her to teach you?
Amy: Yeah, and then she says, "I'm doing something now," and I say, "I'm going to get an E on this if I don't finish," and then I just get mad at her.
Madanes: Aha, so when you want her to help you, you want her to help you now, immediately. And eventually does she help you?
Amy: Yeah, sometimes, after I go outside and play with one of my friends.
Madanes: Aha, so she helps you with your homework too, your Mom, right?
Amy: Yes.
Madanes: That's very good.
Amy: And also my brother does.
Madanes: Does she cook good things?
Amy: She makes me peanut butter and jelly sandwiches, that's my favorite food.
Madanes: That's great. That's very nice. (to Larry) What good things does your Mom do for you?

Larry: Oh, she takes us to get movies and, I don't know, we do a lot of stuff. And I have a Big Brother and he takes me places.
Madanes: That's nice. So she did that for you too, she set that up?
Larry: Uh huh.
Madanes: That's great. Why have you been going to all these different places? You said in the last three weeks you've been going to different places with the children?
Cindy: Well, initially it was to get help for Amy and then I just physically and mentally became so exhausted that I realized that I needed help as much and perhaps I've needed help a lot longer. I think I've been—a friend pointed out that I'm really burned out and I haven't taken vacations for the last three years to pay for their camp and to get the house painted and things, so I haven't taken any vacation time. I've really burned myself out emotionally and now physically, so I want to take care of myself and because I'm so burned out I'm really freaking out about Amy. Amy has expressed verbally, she hasn't done anything physically to herself, she's been beating on me a lot, but she's expressed that she would like possibly to harm herself like to burn up in a fire.
Madanes: What did you say, tell me, the scary, the most scary thing that you said?
Amy: What? (looks puzzled)

Amy's puzzled look when trying to remember her own words was another indication that she had been expressing metaphorically the mother's anxieties.

Madanes: What were the most scary things that you said that you wanted to do to yourself? Did you really say you wanted to burn up in a fire? That's what your Mama said.
Amy: I did not.
Cindy: Yes, you did. It was the night we came back from Children's Hospital and I said that it was time to go to bed and Larry went upstairs, and you said no, you were going to sleep in the living room, remember?
Amy: Uh uh. (negatively)
Cindy: You don't remember? But—

Madanes: Okay. What else? What else scary? Tell me before your Mom tells me.

Amy: I don't know.

Madanes: You don't remember anything? Okay, (to Cindy) what has she said that frightened you so?

Cindy: Well, she raised a fork, I don't know if it was a fork or a scissors, I'm not sure, but Larry was at the table, I think, at me and said she'd like to kill me. And then she said, "I'm just kidding." She tells me all the time that she doesn't like herself and then when I try to explore, I say, "You're a lovely little girl. You know you're very likable." And then she gets angry with me and doesn't want to discuss it or explore it any further.

Madanes: Let me ask Larry, did you hear that? Did you hear Amy say those things?

Larry: Not the first one because I went upstairs to take a bath, I think. I took a bath, didn't I? But I heard her say that she wanted to kill my Mom.

Madanes: With a fork?

Larry: Yeah, with a fork.

Madanes: And why do you think she said that?

Larry: I can't remember.

Amy: I just got mad at her.

Madanes: Why? You wanted something and you didn't get it?

Amy: Ummm.

Once more, I emphasized that Amy was the initiator of unfortunate sequences, not the mother, and that the issue was not a suicide threat but a childish tantrum. Larry confirmed this view.

Larry: I think she asked for a glass of milk, something like that.

Madanes: What did you want?

Amy: I don't know. Oh yeah, because it was my bedtime and I didn't want to go to bed.

Madanes: Aha, and then you were really angry, eh? You have a bad temper, do you think?

Amy: I don't know.

Madanes: Does she have a bad temper? She looks like a sweet little thing. She has a real temper?

Larry: A huh. (agreeing)

Cindy: She's very guarded. It really worries me when she smashes things, not only because I'm wondering what's going on and then she won't even talk about it, but of course I worry about the house. We rent the house and I try real hard to take care of it and we could lose our house. No one wants to rent to people who destroy the walls and the doors.

Madanes: What does she smash?

Larry: Well, when she gets sent upstairs she'll start jumping up and down on the floor and slamming her door.

Madanes: Do you remember doing that? You do that a lot?

Amy: When I get sent upstairs.

Madanes: Aha. (to Larry) What's the worst thing that you do?

Larry: Well, when I was little I used to, you know, I wasn't as bad as Amy but I'd do stuff like her, but now it's probably like when she gets me mad sometimes I'll say, "I hate you."

Madanes: To your Mom? And then you are sorry that you said that because you really love her, right? Does she say, "I hate you," too? (pointing to Amy)

Larry: Uh huh. (agreeing)

Madanes: And you're sorry about that, right? Because you love her, right? Tell her now. Give her a kiss. Say, "I love you, Mom."

Amy: I love you Mom. (She kisses her mother.)

Cindy: I love you too, Amy.

Madanes: Say that sometimes you say things that you don't mean.

Amy: I say things sometimes I don't mean.

I had established that the mother was a good person and her children loved her. By directing Amy to say that she sometimes said things that she did not mean, I was detracting from the significance of her negative statements.

Cindy: So do I. We all do that. We wouldn't be human beings if we didn't say things we didn't mean, would we?

Madanes: (to Larry) Do you want to say "I love you" too, or if it embarrasses . . .

Larry: I love you.

Cindy: I love you, too.

Madanes: That's better. Okay, why don't you two go to the waiting room for a little bit and I'll talk with your Mommy and then I'll bring you back. There's some nice books and magazines to read. (I take the children to the waiting room.)

I could now let the children leave the room after it had been established that the mother was good, the children loved her, and I was not a dangerous person.

Cindy: (After the children leave she is talking about her ex-husband.) He wanted to take Larry out and my fear is—he still denies that there was anything wrong with his assault on my sister, even though he was prosecuted for it, and he wasn't prosecuted for the worst part because the worst, when she was older, happened in Montgomery County, so he would have had to have been tried in two counties. So unfortunately, he got off with assault and battery. But he always says things like maybe one day your sister will tell you the truth about what really happened.

Madanes: She was living with you?

Cindy: No, she would come over for weekends and I would spend time with her. We were very close. My mother was a newly single parent so I would take her for weekends and do things with her and a lot of times my mother would be there. He would wait until both of us were gone, you know, he might let Mary stay with him and Larry, and he would send Larry out in the yard or something and expose himself or get some dirty movies on reel or whatever he was doing the first couple of years. So, no, she wasn't living there, it was just during visits. But I—

Madanes: And then he raped her?

Cindy: Well, by the time there was intercourse, it was several years later and it was somewhat consenting but she was still a child. He primed her or prepped her for it. It was very close to an incestuous situation, because he did more than befriend her, he became almost a father figure. So the first two years were bizarre behavior like exposing himself and then apologetic— you know, "you don't want to tell anybody" and how much he cared for her and playing card games with her—

Madanes: And that's been only with her or with other girls?

Cindy: Well, Rich was married before, and I was visiting his ex-wife after I left him—the kids have three half-brothers from that marriage—and she was surprised that I didn't know that he had attacked his own sister as a teenager. And I said, "Of course, I didn't know it. You know, why didn't you ever tell me?" And she said, "Well, I'm the last person you'd ever believe, right?" I said, "I guess so." I mean, why would I? Perhaps he—that frightened me even more because I realized, well, if he partook in incest as a young man, and then attacked my sister as an adult, then he could easily attack his children.

Madanes: But has he ever done that with children? I mean, by the time he attacked your sister, by the time he actually had sex with your sister, she was 17.

Cindy: 17, yes.

Madanes: And it's been always, it's been girls, not boys.

Cindy: Well, I don't know. At the same time, and of course this would be hearsay in a court of law, at the same time his ex-wife said she always felt, from something that was said in front of them by his mother, that he had attacked his younger brother as a small child. I feel that an adult who at age 33 or 34 might attack or even expose himself leading up to an attack of a small child. . . . I wouldn't trust him with little boys either.

Madanes: That's right. What does he do for a living?

Cindy: He's in construction. He's self-employed but he's covered up his business and taken everything sort of underground so he can get out of paying child support. So he's escaped paying regular child support.

Madanes: Do you know where he lives?

Cindy: No.

Madanes: How come he knows where you live?

Cindy: Because he's been out there to see the children.

Madanes: Oh, so you have allowed that from time to time?

Cindy: Yeah he's been out there about six or seven times over four years.

Madanes: When was the last time?

Cindy: Right before Christmas. He reappeared.

Madanes: Is he married or living with somebody?

Cindy: I really don't know. He's not married as far as I know. And living with someone? I don't know. I got a threatening call from someone, I guess it was a girl friend, today, who told me to stop—I'm not sure what word she used—stop aggravating him. I was killing him. I was putting him in the hospital. Stop aggravating him or the fight would be between me and her. So I just hung up on her and called the Crisis Center to talk with someone because I became really frightened when he called. But I'm not sure, I guess the fear isn't so much for myself. Of course I'm always afraid that . . . yes, I am afraid of him hurting me as well.

Madanes: Who do you have in your family?

Cindy: My family members?

Madanes: Yes.

At this point I had decided that my first strategy had to be to find a protector for Cindy and her children. I asked about relatives.

Cindy: There's my mother, and my father. They're divorced. My father's remarried. My mother is alone. My sister is 22 now. I have a brother who's married with four children who lives about 35 miles away.

Madanes: Okay.

Cindy: And then I have a younger brother who's 30. He is incarcerated.

Madanes: For what?

Cindy: For armed robbery.

I was shocked but it was important to respond immediately with sympathy.

Madanes: (shaking her head) A lot of problems. That must be quite a heartbreak for you.

Cindy: It is. We're very close. He's been through a difficult . . . we've been under a lot of stress. I mean, I'm sure the children felt the impact of that. I've helped Mark recently with a lawsuit against the Department of Corrections for his treatment, which was a successful lawsuit but it took a lot of energy on my behalf to find lawyers who would take it. My mother sold her home to finance it. And I was under stress for the entire two years just, you know, hoping that it would be won for several reasons.

Madanes: And when you win, what do you win?

I questioned the wisdom of being involved in such stressful lawsuits.

Cindy: You know, I thought I would feel so wonderful when he won his lawsuit because it would expose what the Department of Corrections was doing to persons. They were using shackles and chains, and chaining men on the floor to lie in their own body waste for several days and depriving them of food or water. Of course, they denied all of that but they made a mistake of filming one of the incidents and the ACLU got that film for us. So we had a videotape of it. What was your question?

Madanes: When you won, what happened? What did you win?

Cindy: Oh, he won some money but most of it went to the attorneys. He ended up with about $30,000, but most of it he spent on other inmates. Buying them necessities that they needed.

Madanes: So your mother never got her money?

Cindy: Oh no, this is after—he got about $30,000 after it paid for her expenses.

Madanes: Okay.

Cindy: It changed some legislation about the amount and the use of chemicals.

Madanes: You're wonderful! You're a very idealistic person to get into that alone with two children, struggling.

My goal was to raise Cindy's self-esteem, so I had been waiting for an opportunity to express admiration for her. Now the opportunity had come and I could be sincerely admiring of her efforts, knowing that perhaps I wouldn't have had the courage to do what she had done. Cindy was obviously pleased. She hadn't expected admiration from me.

Cindy: Yeah, I probably get too involved in things. I hope one day, when the children are grown, as long as they are healthy, that I can be of some help to society. I want to do some volunteer work in prisons.

Madanes: It seems like you have already been a great deal of help to society. Few people will take on the prison system, you know.

Cindy: I've learned that the hard way. I pay daily for that and they've made it difficult for me to see Mark. And Mark has been in total isolation since last September, in solitary confinement, so they are continuing to make it rough on us.

Madanes: When is he due to come out?

Cindy: I don't know. He has picked up a lot more time while he was in prison, and he has one of the cases on appeal now so that's hard to say. It could be another five years or it could be another 20. And certainly the children have paid dearly too, and I know this, but I couldn't have done otherwise.

Madanes: Why do you think they paid dearly? They seem fine to me!

Cindy: Do they?

Madanes: Sure! They seem wonderful. You should see children who have problems when they come in here. You can immediately tell. Amy and Larry hold a very nice conversation. They express themselves very well. They're very intelligent. They are very thoughtful. They're very caring about you. They are very nice to me, a total stranger with an accent. They're nice.

By praising the children I was reassuring Cindy and raising her self-esteem.

Cindy: Maybe they're guarded.
Madanes: I'm going to talk with them alone and then I'll tell you.
Cindy: Okay.

It was difficult for Cindy to accept praise so I backed off, but I had made my point.

Madanes: But I don't think that they are guarded. What does your father do?

Cindy: My father's retired from the telephone company. He's real ill. He just found out he had emphysema. He's an asthmatic as well. So he doesn't do too much of anything. He didn't take much of an interest in me as a child and he doesn't take much of an interest in my children, but he's really trying. He's trying to turn his life around now that he is ill.

Madanes: What does your brother, the older one, do?

Cindy: Billy was just also incarcerated for a while for substance abuse, possession of narcotics and substance abuse. And by the way, to be very upfront with you, I have had problems with substance abuse but that was back during my marriage.

Madanes: What were you using?

Cindy: Cocaine.

Madanes: And you've overcome that?

Cindy: Oh yeah.

Madanes: That's quite a thing to overcome, let me tell you.

Cindy: Well, yeah.

Even though I was shocked, I used the opportunity to emphasize the positive and praise Cindy.

Madanes: It takes a lot of courage and determination.

Cindy: I had a really bad habit. I think a lot of it was because I realized I was in a very troubled marriage and didn't want to cope with the feelings I was having. My husband introduced me to it. I'm a nurse so I should have known better.

Madanes: I didn't know you were a nurse.

Cindy: Yeah, I'm a nurse. But we were self-employed in our own business so I had stopped practicing. And after a bad car accident where I was having some temporal seizures and I was quite ill, my husband introduced it to me and I was real foolish. I mean, I knew better. From a medical standpoint as well as for many reasons. But I don't think I felt very good about myself and I'm not sure I really cared about anything but the children, but that was right before I left Rich, the year prior to leaving.

Madanes: How many years ago?

Cindy: Five.

Madanes: And how many since you've quit?

Cindy: Well, socially, if I had the opportunity—financially I couldn't afford it—but if socially I ever ran into any friends who had some I would still abuse cocaine.

Madanes: But you would use it occasionally.

Cindy: Occasionally. But a year and a half ago I went to NA with a friend and I was so impressed with the work they were doing there, Narcotics Anonymous, that I picked up a chip and I haven't drank or used any type of substance for a year and a half.

Madanes: That's wonderful.

Cindy: And I didn't realize how much alcohol was probably a problem as well, because I have a real intolerance to it. And even though I wouldn't use a lot, I would become sick when I would use it. So you know it's not really something that I miss in my life now.

Madanes: Is there any man in your life currently?

I was still looking for a protector for Cindy and I was also concerned about her loneliness.

Cindy: No, not for about a year and a half, two years. I was pretty serious about one. We dated for about a year and a half and we were making plans about getting married and then we just had some real differences that I thought were pretty significant. And when I stopped seeing him I made a real effort to date a couple of people, but I think it was at a time in my life when I needed some time alone and needed to really discover what's going on with me. So I have sort of been a recluse for the last year, but I've been very happy with that. I'm ready now to go out and meet people.

Madanes: I think so. You don't seem very happy to me.

It was important to challenge the idea that Cindy was happy as a recluse. She obviously was not.

Cindy: I know. I know. I want to do some volunteer work with an organization called O.A.R., that works with ex-offenders, or offenders, and I'm terribly interested to meet the kind of people that would also volunteer to do that kind of work. You know, what kind of background they come from, because a lot of my isolation over the past few years has been created because of what I went through battling the Department of Corrections! No one really understood.

Madanes: Yeah.

Cindy: Even my dearest friends didn't really understand. I think the only one who did was Mickey, my boyfriend, but he would have understood most anything I decided to do.

For the first time in the session, Cindy smiled broadly, so I decided to go for Mickey.

Madanes: You haven't seen him since?

Cindy: No. He's tried to get in touch and get together but—

Madanes: And? What do you think?

Cindy: Well, I really don't have any interest in doing that because, during a time I was having some real big changes in my life, Mickey became angry and I said some things that I shouldn't have. But within 24 hours he was with another woman, and it wasn't just an affair, it was, he developed a real hot romance with her. They were seeing each other or calling each other every day. And of course, he tried to cover it up so he could have both. You know, have the new romance and maintain our relationship.

Madanes: You know, sometimes men are like that when they get too involved with a woman. They protect themselves from getting hurt by finding another one.

Cindy: Yeah, I told him—

Madanes: It just means that he loved you so much that it scared him.

This reframing of Mickey's behavior preserved Cindy's self-esteem and helped her to consider him, as well as other men, in a more favorable light.

Cindy: Well, I told him that. But yeah, you're right, and that's exactly what I said. I felt that he had a problem with commitments, but I didn't want to get into a marriage then. He had two precious little girls and he had custody of them, and I had my two, so it would have been like the family affair—you know, it would have been four children. I feel very strong about commitments and especially because of the fact that we were engaged to be married and we were even looking for a home. We were looking for this huge home that could comfortably fit six people, where the kids could have their own space, and perhaps I was a little harsh but I just couldn't deal with it. Sent him on his way.

Madanes: Is he still with the other woman do you think?

Cindy: I'm not sure what he's doing. I think he's been through several since.

Madanes: Aha. Well, he sounds like fun.

This was another positive reframing of Mickey's behavior.

Cindy: He's tasting the wine.

Madanes: He sounds like fun.

Cindy: We had a lot of fun times together, but I don't know, I have so many fears still. After what I've been through with my husband, my ex-husband, God forbid. And then Amy, I don't even know if I shared this during my intake call but Amy was sexually assaulted . . .

Madanes: No.

Cindy: At age four. There was no penetration. Her clothes were not removed. It was, I felt, something that I could handle as a parent. The child is now 15. I felt he tried to assault her again. I called the sexual assault unit to see what I should do.

Madanes: What is this? A child in the neighborhood?

Cindy: Yeah. This was one of Larry's friends or ex-friends. He came over to spend the night and the only reason I allowed it was because I knew she was at a friend's house spending the night. But she came home because her friend became ill. So I put her in the bedroom when she fell asleep. They were in the living room, and I went upstairs on the third floor to make a call. I came down to check on things because it was getting real late. I was really on this call for a long time, and I found her in a very awkward position with her panties, you know, pulled down and so I confronted him and of course he denied it. So I asked him to go down to one of the rooms and stay

there and in the morning he ran home and told his mother.
He got real scared.

Madanes: When did this first happen?

Cindy: Oh this happened a year ago. And we went through counseling. Amy didn't know what happened because she slept
through this second ordeal. A lot of anger came out of her
during this counseling. Now the therapist said that she didn't
feel that Amy was suffering from any ramifications.

Madanes: And when she was four years old what happened? Was
she harmed at all?

Cindy: No. She, she was, I was in the kitchen and we were talking
about bad breath and she said, "Yes, Oscar's breath is bad
when he humps me." And I said, "When he what!?" And she
repeated it again and I said, "I'm not sure I know what that
means. Can you show me?" And she got down on the floor
and she went through the humping motions and I thought, oh
dear. I handled it well for a while, until I started talking about
it and, the emotional person I am, at one point I cried and I
think that closed off all communications.

Madanes: But you know she wasn't hurt.

Cindy: She wasn't hurt.

Madanes: An episode like that is not necessarily traumatic, because a child doesn't give sexual behavior the same meaning
that an adult does.

Cindy: Yeah. Well, what I worried about was what perhaps happened between age four and age eight. And I think that when
I called the sexual assault center the intake person took my
name and all and listened to my story, and then she said,
"Why did you let this young man back in your house?" And I
said, "Because he was a friend of my son's." And I did handle
it as a parent. You know, I told him that it wasn't socially
acceptable when it happened, when he was nine, and that
people are even punished by law for touching other people
and it's all right to touch yourself but don't touch other children. And I told him that he had to stay away from Amy and
that I never wanted it to happen again. So she said, "Well, I
just need to let you know that I'm going to call Protective
Services," and I was just shattered. I felt like I had just walked
into a big, fat rat trap! And I said, "What did I do?" And she

said, "Well, are you going to come in so we can show you how to protect your child?" So I was shattered. So I just felt that wherever I go people get assaulted. So I have some fears also about . . .

Madanes: How is it with Protective Services now?

Cindy: Oh, Protective Services never got involved.

Madanes: So you have a fear of—what were you saying?

Cindy: I have a fear that, a mother who, I couldn't detect this in my husband, that he had this problem, it was a total shock when I found out! And I realize how cunning pedophiles are. I have a fear that if I get involved with someone else I may not detect that again. So . . . (tearful)

I realized that this was Cindy's greatest fear and what made her a recluse who avoided men and could not have a normal life. To come out of her depression she had to recover not only her confidence in herself but also her trust in other human beings. First, it was important to reassure her that she was not to blame for her ex-husband and that it was not a matter of bad judgment on her part.

Madanes: You are very demanding of yourself. You're really hard on yourself. It can happen to anybody. For the best therapist in the world that is almost impossible to detect. I mean, I could be speaking with a man here and interviewing him and questioning him and not have the slightest idea. But there's not that many of them around. The chances of running into another one are very slight. Really almost impossible.

Cindy: I know that. I realize.—

Madanes: Now if you keep involved in trying to help prisoners and the volunteers involved in that, you may get to know only criminals. You know, that's a problem, so I'm concerned about that.

Cindy: Well—

Madanes: You want to know, you want to get acquainted with a better kind of man and maybe you should get out of that circle a little bit.

Cindy: Well, I'm not so sure. There are people from the church. A lot of people who are very church oriented do prison ministry work.

Madanes: Oh, okay. All right.

Cindy: But I'm going to probably meet men and women from different ministries. There are sometimes legal students or people who are studying law. They do this as kind of a—

Madanes: Oh, okay, so you will meet some nice people. Let me ask you another question, then we'll go back to your fears. Who is the strongest, most competent man in your extended family or your ex-husband's extended family, whom you're still in touch with?

I was still looking for a protector.

Cindy: Strongest and most confident?

Madanes: Competent. Confident and kindly.

Cindy: My family is a mess. You know, my husband was calling names today. He doesn't have the right to call names but my family is a mess. I was raised in a violent situation. My father was violent. My brother who's married is now violent. My other brother is incarcerated. There's no one in my ex-husband's family whom I would consider competent because they're all substance abusers. They're all a mess. There aren't many male figures in my family or extended family who are very together.

Madanes: Apart from Mickey, do you have any other male friend who's nice?

I gave up on the men in her family and began to look for male friends who could protect her.

Cindy: Uh huh. I met him at my new job, Stan is his name. He worked with me for about a year and a half and then finally transferred, but he keeps in touch. But then I have a friend Bart. I don't know why I didn't think of Bart. I mean, I should. This is ridiculous. Bart is very good to me. Bart is a friend of mine. He's a gay male and we met in counseling five years ago when I came out of the marriage so he knows most everything about me. And I do trust men as friends. I think that it's the intimate relationship that scares me and I hope I'll feel better about that as my kids get a little bit older. I hope I'm only guarded now.

Madanes: There's no reason for you to feel that you are going to find another man who is going to have a sexual problem like that. There's no reason to think that. I know there are theories that a woman repeats, keeps making the same bad choice of partners. That's nonsense. There's no such thing. I don't think it's reasonable to have that concern.

That theory is so popular in the media that I was sure it had influenced Cindy. Even though there might be some truth to this idea, a therapist must believe that she can make a difference in a person's life and prevent a new bad choice of partner. I had that confidence in myself.

Cindy: Well, you know, I have this mother whom I love dearly, but I know it's been very traumatic for her. Since I left home I've come back home to her. I had no place else to go. So there she was with a daughter who had been assaulted and was trying to get through sexual assault therapy and another daughter with two kids, but we argued sometimes and when we did she would attack me. She told me once that I walk around—she covered her eyes and her mouth and said, "You close your eyes." She put a lot of bad thoughts in my head. She woke me up one morning and said, "Come in the room, come in the room. I want you to see this. Larry had Amy in bed." Now Amy was two and a half and Larry was six. So I stumble out of bed and there they sit watching TV in the same bed.

Madanes: Yes. Listen, when I was growing up kids used to touch each other and play and it was considered sexual games. You know, playing doctor and things like that. Nobody called it sexual assault!

It was important to help restore Cindy's common sense.

Cindy: Well, I said to her that day, I said, "You know what, mother? Look at them, she's sitting there, yes, she's just in a diaper, but it was a hot summer night. They are sitting there watching cartoons and you wake me up and all of a sudden—"

I couldn't miss the opportunity to emphasize that Cindy was not only a good mother but better than her own mother.

Madanes: You know what it is? You're a better mother than she was!
Cindy: Mom's a mess. And I know this. She feels her best when I'm at my lowest. And then, when I was living with her, God forbid, I bought the book, *My Mother, My Self*. And in an argument once she even held that up and she asked what I was telling the counselor. "What are you saying about me?" We both went through mental hell. So I understand the relationship, but . . .
Madanes: So you shouldn't take her seriously when she says that.

Again I was reinforcing Cindy's self-confidence.

Cindy: I know, but when you're the sensitive person I am, sometimes—
Madanes: What do you do for fun?
Cindy: I haven't done anything for fun in a long time.
Madanes: It shows.
Cindy: I know. I want to change that.
Madanes: How do you expect your daughter to be happy and to feel good about herself if she has a mother who doesn't feel good about herself and doesn't have any fun?

Fun is important, not just as an antidote to depression but to provide balance in life. I knew that Cindy was so depressed that she would not be motivated in that direction for her own sake. But for the sake of her daughter she would do what she would not do for herself.

Cindy: I know. You mean if I got out and did more for myself I could see a change?
Madanes: Sure! And if she saw that you were happy, if she thought you had good self-esteem, liked yourself, were happy, were pleased with yourself, she would be pleased with herself. She looks like you. She's just like you! So you come all depressed and she sits there all depressed.

Cindy: That makes a lot of sense.

Madanes: I'm not saying you should do it for her sake. You should do it for your sake, but it would also help her.

I was capitalizing on the mother's love and identification with her daughter.

Cindy: Well, a lot of it has been because I have isolated myself, but a lot of it has been my fatigue, too. I've been invited to things sometimes and really wanted to go. I was so exhausted that I couldn't have come home, taken Amy to somebody—because when I go out for an evening I don't like to leave the children alone yet. And if some of the violence between them could slow down—I've even thought about paying both of them, not just one, and saying okay, this money would go to a sitter or I would inconvenience a friend for an evening, and you guys could earn money. But I have a lot of people saying, "You'd leave your daughter alone with your 13-year-old son?"

Madanes: Oh, he seems very responsible.

Cindy: I think I should trust him and I think it would be a good idea. I think it would make them feel really good. When I did go to a P.T.A. meeting once, I came home, they had the house vacuumed and they had all the clothes folded.

Madanes: It shows how much they love you.

Again, I did not miss the opportunity to make the mother feel good about herself.

Cindy: I know they love me. Sometimes I wonder if they don't love me too much! You know, that they have to—

Cindy had difficulty accepting praise. I accepted that difficulty and backed off, but my point had been made.

Madanes: Listen, as a mother let me tell you there is no way that your children can love you too much. It's never too much! It's like you can never be too thin or too rich. Right? It's great to have children love you. Write this down. I want you to do some things.

Cindy: All right.

Madanes: "Fun" at the top of the page. That's your first priority. Okay?

Cindy: Right.

Madanes: You are going to make yourself look nice and you are to go out and do fun things. You are to be cheerful and show the children that you are happy. So, in order to have fun you're going to call these three men, Mickey, Stan, and Bart. A gay guy is wonderful to have fun with, you know.

The directive "to do fun things" is given in the context of showing the children that she is happy. When a woman is afraid of men, it is easier for her to date two or three men rather than one. In this way each man protects her from the others. If one of them does not treat her well, she knows that the next day she can see another one. She is also protected from becoming too involved with any one man, which is what she fears.

Cindy: I love him. We go dancing sometimes. He has a friend who's more fun right now so I've done that to myself. I think the last few times I went out with him I wasn't too much fun.

Madanes: Okay, so you've got to renew that friendship. Call Mickey and say that you are available. That you need some cheering up.

Cindy: Before I do that—no, I will do that because I've had fantasies of riding on the motorcycle again.* I love to go scooting on motorcycles. But the one thing that scares me, and again I'll share with you why, Amy said to me one day out of the blue, "I hate Mickey!" I thought good, we'll explore this right now. I said, "Why? Did Mickey ever do something to you?" She said he was so mean to his girls. He is a strong disciplinarian. I—

Madanes: You know, children get jealous. I'm not saying marry Mickey. Go out and have some fun!

Cindy: Okay. And keep it totally separate from the children because—

*This chapter is titled "Easy Rider" because when Cindy begins to come out of her depression she remembers her joy in riding on the motorcycle.

Madanes: Don't be rigid about it. If he wants to visit he can visit. I wouldn't go by what a little girl says. You know, she might have been jealous.

Cindy: But you don't think we should explore that at all?

Madanes: I don't think that you should explore anything. Talk with her about childish things.

Cindy: Okay.

Madanes: Not about adult relationships. It's none of her business. She couldn't understand. Have a good time with Mickey, and with the other guy, Stan.

Cindy: Okay.

Madanes: And if it gets really good with Mickey, then don't see the others. Stay with Mickey. But it's better to have three because if it goes badly with Mickey then you can always have Stan.

Cindy: Stan and I have been entirely platonic. But I've often wondered if he wanted more. And I think he feels the same about me.

Madanes: Do the same as Mickey. He likes to have two at a time. You can have two at a time also.

Cindy: Yeah. Well—

Madanes: It gives it more balance. You will be nicer to each one because you know that you will be going out with the other one. That gives you time to make up your mind about what you really want. It's less pressure. You are very young. You are very attractive and here you are all focused on the children. Whether you are a good mother. You know your life goes by while you worry about this.

Cindy: I sure would like to go out to dinner to a nice restaurant again. I would like to go dancing and have some laughs with an adult. I mean, I laugh with my girlfriends, you know, we get pretty crazy when we get together, but it's too family oriented. They come over and they bring their children and we go places with our children. You know?

Madanes: It's important for you to have a network of friends to replace your family network because in your family there are so many problems. So you have to create an artificial family of friends who will compensate for all the trouble, all the aggravation that you get from your real family.

Cindy: It does, but you see that happens when Lisa—Lisa is a friend of mine whom I met when we were 10 years old, so we've been friends for 24 years. It's a wonderful friendship, and she has a son John who is a month older than Larry so it's wonderful. But she came out and spent Easter weekend with us and it was real bizarre. You know Amy doesn't just use a bad word. She likes the word *fuck*! And, so she'll call someone a fucker and she'll say it over and over and over.

Madanes: Obviously she's very possessive. Every episode like this that you tell me shows she's possessive of you. She's jealous if you're having a good time with somebody else.

Cindy: Yes! Yes! And Lisa was totally caught off-guard. I said, "I know this is bizarre. You know, I'm sorry." She said, "Don't apologize. I'm worried about you." You know, both of them — Larry, he acts out like a little child.

Madanes: You know what would be good when Amy gets like that is to say to her, "I know that you mean that you love me. I know you love me dear, you don't have to say it like that."

Cindy: Oh, she'd get so angry that she'd say, "I don't love you! I hate you!"

Madanes: And then you'd say, "Oh, all that passion! You don't have to tell me so much."

Cindy: Then they'd accuse me of teasing. Believe me, I've tried it.

Madanes: Then good! Just have a good time with it.

Cindy: I dance for them. I dance for them.

Madanes: That's great.

Cindy: You know, one thing I did the other night, and I don't know, these are the things I need to explore. Coping mechanisms. She started kicking me. She likes to beat on me these days. So when she kicked me I grabbed her by the ankles and I looked at her and I took her knees and I started going back and forth and I said, she was still kicking very angry, I said, "You know I used to do this when you were a little baby when I changed your diaper." And she didn't want to laugh but she couldn't help it.

Madanes: Uh huh.

Cindy: And I said, am I doing the right thing or am I really setting up something? Is that okay?

Madanes: Sure. That's wonderful. That's great. That's great. Also, when she sees you happy all that anger will stop.

Cindy: Okay.

Madanes: She's angry at the world because the world is doing something bad to her mother. And for a while she's going to escalate a little bit—

Cindy: Yes.

Madanes: —because she's also jealous and possessive.

Cindy: Yes.

Cindy came to therapy with the idea that Amy was angry because she had done something bad to her. Now it has been established that Amy is angry not because the mother is bad, but because the world has done something bad to her mother.

Madanes: You have to give her a little time. But when she sees that you are happy and having a good time, she'll stop worrying about you and be able to think about things that are appropriate for her age.

Cindy: Well, do you know, things have gotten much better. I've been home now for four days. I went to work Monday. Cleaned up my desk and left and things are better already. And I told them, I said, "Mommy needs a little time off. Mommy's been working real hard!"

Cindy is now smiling and visibly more cheerful.

Madanes: Sure.

Cindy: "—and I need to get some help for us." And that's really all I've done. I've still been depressed.

Madanes: Okay, let me tell you more so you will stop being depressed.

Cindy: All right.

Madanes: No more. You stop going places. You don't call the Crisis Center, Children's Hospital, Protective—what else did you call? Sexual assault—

Cindy: Uh huh.

Madanes: All these places. All these counselors. You are over counseled. If you need anything you call here. You get in touch with me. But don't call—no more social workers, nothing.

Cindy: Okay.

Madanes: No more of that.

Cindy: I've called every crisis center in the country!

Madanes: You realize you get all these intruders into your life that just upset you and make you feel insecure. They have to make a living and so they have to find something wrong with you—

Cindy: Uh huh.

Madanes: —so they can justify their job. Stop it.

Cindy: You make it sound so easy. But I'm going to believe you. I'm going to give it a chance. Okay?

Madanes: Well, you know, has all that helped you? (Cindy shakes her head negatively.) Okay, so then don't do it anymore.

Cindy: I'm very analytical, so I could do a lot of damage. But I haven't been good to myself. I haven't given myself vacations.

Madanes: That's right.

Cindy: I've been put on an antidepressant so when my level goes back up—

Madanes: What are you taking?

Cindy: I haven't started it yet. I pick it up tonight, Elavil. And I asked—

Madanes: Oh, don't take that.

Cindy: I asked for a very low dosage.

Madanes: Don't take that. You've been on drugs before. You don't want to get into that. Don't pick it up. Really, take my advice. Don't start with that! And you're a nurse. You know that if you start with one thing and then the temptation to do more—don't do it. And it's also very bad for you because—

Cindy: Elavil?

Madanes: Oh sure. The downs from it are terrible.

It was important to discourage Cindy from medication that could lead her back to drugs.

Cindy: Well, it shouldn't bring me down. It slowly brings the—

Madanes: Don't! You don't need that. Go to aerobic classes. That will bring your mood up very quickly and help you to—you obviously have a very good figure—it would make it better.

Cindy: Well, I have a bicycle and last night for the first time I had the fantasy of getting on my bike and riding. So I'm going to do that.

Madanes: Sure. You mean not on a standing bike but on a real, outdoor bicycle, right?

Cindy: Oh, a real bike. I'm going to ride all over the village while—

Madanes: That would be the best thing for your mood. If you can get into an aerobics—

Cindy: Well, I can't afford that but I will take my bike out.

Madanes: You know, there are these very inexpensive ones in recreation centers and places like that and you'll make new friends.

Cindy: Yeah, well I'm on no pay for two weeks.

Madanes: Okay. Ride your bike. But find out about that. Write that down. Find out about the aerobic classes.

Cindy: All right.

Madanes: Because they might be for free even!

Cindy: Well, I always get coupons every week that I throw out because I don't have the time. And it's free. Two classes are free.

Madanes: Right. Also I have seen people—you go up to theeacher and say, "You know, I can't pay today but I really need to life my mood. Would you let me take the class and I'll pay for it eventually? In a couple of weeks I'll start paying you." They always say, "of course." What do they care? There's a bunch of women there, one more or less doesn't make any difference. And it's fun. You meet other women. You're jumping up and down.

Cindy: You know what? I'm so vain too. I always get my children everything that they need. Not everything. I mean—

Madanes: They need their mother to be happy. They need that much more than food, clothes, anything!

Cindy: But I would not go into aerobics class unless I had something suitable to wear. Either jogging shorts with little tights and leg warmers—

Madanes: Wait until you see these fat women jumping up and down in horrible clothes! (Cindy laughs.) I can see that you haven't been there!

Cindy: No I haven't.

Madanes: Just wait until you see them!

Cindy: Okay.
Madanes: Write: Don't pick up medication!
Cindy: All right.
Madanes: Don't do that, really. It's dangerous for you.
Cindy: Okay.
Madanes: And it's going to alter your mood in a way that you are
    going to appear weird to your children.
Cindy: Even the antidepressant?
Madanes: Oh especially! You're going to be weird to your children.
    You're not yourself. You're not the same person and then
    that's going to give them problems.
Cindy: He wanted to give me Valium and I said no way!
Madanes: Oh no.

Elavil, and especially Valium, would just have increased the
chances that Cindy would go back to drugs.

Cindy: I said, I am a zombie sitting here today. I am not going to—
    please—
Madanes: But you don't need the Elavil. Look, you have two men
    to go out with—
Cindy: Uh huh.
Madanes: and a gay one to have fun with! That's what you need!
    Not Elavil! If you're depressed, call Bart.
Cindy: Uh huh.
Madanes: That's the gay one, right?
Cindy: Uh huh.
Madanes: Sure. And I would just say straightforwardly to Mickey,
    "Listen, you know, for old times sake, I really want to see you
    again. I need to have some fun. I need to be happy."
Cindy: Uh huh. "Let's go for a ride on the motorcycle."
Madanes: Right. Right.
Cindy: That's a great idea. He'd even take the day off so we'd have
    the whole day while the kids were in school. And then I
    wouldn't have to worry about them freaking out. What are
    they going to do? How are they going to feel? I'll tell them,
    when they ask what I did, I spent all day out, you know,
    cruising around.
Madanes: Sure! That's right. Having fun. Okay. Your ex-husband.

Cindy: Uh huh.

Madanes: Your fear is that he might come to the house and do what?

Cindy: Well, when I was about to leave Rich he went into great detail about a murder he had committed and was never, ummm, no one ever knew who did it.

Madanes: Hmmm hmmm.

Cindy: You know. At the time I thought, is this for real or is he saying this to terrify me so I won't leave? But I believed it was real. One thing one of the crisis centers suggested today was, with Rich's history, they said go talk to Legal Aid and get an attorney and see about getting a restraint order to keep him away from me and the children.

Madanes: Right.

Cindy: How do you feel about that?

Madanes: Sure. I would do that.

Cindy: I mean, as long as the children know I'm doing it to protect them. They can see how upset I was and I didn't mean to— you know, I always try to act real strong towards their father.

Madanes: Sure, it's an injunction against him. I would do that right away!

Cindy: Okay. And especially because he's being really irrational by putting women on the phone whom I don't even know and having them call me and threaten me. So he doesn't need to see those children.

Madanes: No.

Cindy: They don't need that instability in their life. So that's okay?

Madanes: Yes. I would do that right away, on Monday.

Cindy: Okay.

Madanes: Let me see what I have forgotten. Oh, write down, no more discussions with the children about their feelings, their thoughts, their opinions about relationships. Talk with them about TV shows or about their schoolwork or their friends.

Cindy: Okay.

Madanes: You're so uncertain about whether you're a good mother that you keep asking them all these things, and then they get worried about things that they shouldn't be worried about.

Cindy: I know. I'm an analytic personality with not enough adult companionship.

Madanes: That's right! So you should analyze those things with people your age. Talk with girlfriends about that. Not with men because men will escape, you know? They don't want to talk about that. So you are going to have a network of friends. The three guys?

Cindy: Uh huh.

Madanes: And you have three girlfriends. Right?

Cindy: Uh huh.

Madanes: And so if you get upset, if any problem happens you call one of those friends. No professional helpers anymore.

Cindy: Okay.

Madanes: Okay?

Cindy: Okay.

Madanes: What else? Is there anything else that is troubling you? I think that the dreams, the premonitions, and all those feelings just have to do with your being so bored. For the same reason that you talk with the children about all these things— it's just out of boredom. It happens when people are very bored. They begin to imagine things.

I went back to her first statement, at the beginning of the session, and included it as part of the rationale for having more fun. I wanted to address all the complaints that she had presented and to find some solution for each one.

Cindy: Yeah, but—well, I used to feel that my dreams were just bizarre, but I've dreamed too many things that have happened. You know, things that—and I haven't really explored it in reading about it—

Madanes: But that's not a problem. That's an asset.

Cindy: Yeah.

Madanes: A quality so—

Cindy: And I know I shouldn't let myself—

Madanes: It doesn't mean, it also doesn't mean that *every* dream is a premonition.

Cindy: Yeah.

Madanes: So you shouldn't think of it like that because otherwise you go crazy.

Cindy: Absolutely not! Oh absolutely not. Especially when they're bad.

Madanes: Right.

Cindy: Immediately I just discard it as—no. But, you know the kids and I have been through a lot. We really have. I know right now I'm looking like a basket case that can't get through something simple—

Madanes: Look you've been through a lot and you've done wonderfully!

I did not miss the opportunity to emphasize success.

Cindy: But I've been too hard on myself in the past. My boss keeps saying, "Don't be so hard on yourself!" He knows how strong I am. He always says, "My God, you commute 60 miles a day. Why don't you move closer?" I said, "Because I love the village; it's been so wonderful to us." Maybe one day, if I find something else that—

Cindy is responding better to praise and emphasizing her strengths.

Madanes: Or maybe it would be nice at some point to move within the village but to an address that your ex-husband won't know.

Cindy: That's true. That is true.

Madanes: And a phone number that he won't have. See, I was going to suggest that you change your phone number, but if he knows your address that will make it worse. It would be better to move.

Cindy: Well, they told me that. And I said that to them. They said change your phone number and make it unlisted. I said, "Look if I do that—"

Madanes: Then he'll come over.

Cindy: He would have a legitimate excuse to show up unannounced.

Madanes: That's right.

Cindy: And I would find that very frightening.

Madanes: No, you can't do that. But when possible, move, even if
it's just next door or a block away, but to an address that he
won't know. Then you can be at a phone number that he
won't know.
Cindy: Yeah, well I made the mistake by allowing him to come over
out of curiosity. That's the only reason why he comes by. He
didn't care for his first children from his first marriage. Why
should I expect him to feel any differently towards ours? You
know? I don't even feel that they are his. But I think I could
cope with that. He hit me when I was very vulnerable. I was
just feeling so low. But I feel like this is the first time in a long
time that I really want to take care of myself. I'm saying I'm in
trouble and usually I don't. Usually it's very easy for me to
just blame it on something else. I could see myself doing that
when I was up at Children's. I was saying, "My daughter
needs help." I heard two doctors say, "It sounds like you do."
And it wasn't just that alone that hit me. It was a lot of things
that hit me. You know, I do need help but I need some rest
and I need to take care of myself.
Madanes: And you need to have some fun! At the top of the page
right? Fun. That's what you need, not rest. Are you eating
well?
Cindy: No.
Madanes: Okay. If you are not eating well, you could gain a few
pounds.
Cindy: Yeah, I just lost about eight this week. Just in a couple of
days. And I don't know how one can lose weight so fast—
Madanes: Okay, you're a nurse, so you don't need me to explain.
You get on a good diet and eat healthy and feel good. And get
some exercise and go outside and play. Children like to see
their parents play.
Cindy: Uh huh.
Madanes: You know, they think that life should be a little bit of
work and a lot of play.
Cindy: They do. They do like that.
Madanes: You don't play.
Cindy: Larry caught me dancing once. I mean, he didn't catch me
because I do it openly. I do my own aerobics you know.
Madanes: Uh huh. Oh, that's nice.

There has been quite a change in Cindy during the course of the session. She is now cheerful, smiling, and presents a very different view of herself.

Cindy: But I had the *Flashdance* song on and he came down and he was so impressed he said, "You look just like the woman in *Flashdance*."
Madanes: That's great.
Cindy: So I was performing for him, you know, and he laughs. Now sometimes he doesn't think I'm very funny but—
Madanes: He looks a lot like you also.
Cindy: Oh yeah. He does.

I had been waiting all through the session to point out that Larry was like his mother, in the hope that Cindy would accept the resemblance. Had she thought that he was like his father, I would have had a difficult task encouraging her to identify with him, since she could not have been a good mother to a son who was like her hated husband.

Madanes: He is like you. He looks exactly like you.
Cindy: I hear that all the time. But they laugh at me and I think sometimes they laugh because they are very happy that, you know, I'm doing something that's totally off the wall and funny and they realize—
Madanes: But it would be better even if they saw you doing that with friends your age.
Cindy: Uh huh.
Madanes: Particularly boyfriends.
Cindy: Rather than alone.
Madanes: Right. Rather than alone. It's not right. So the problem is that they feel that they have to entertain you. And then Amy might get into her head that if she really scares you, it's entertaining. So she says, "I'm going to burn myself," and things like that.
Cindy: You really don't think she means it?
Madanes: I am sure she doesn't.
Cindy: Well, you're going to talk to her.
Madanes: I am going to talk to her, but I'm sure she doesn't.

Cindy: Boy that scared me.

Madanes: She couldn't even remember that she had said that.

Cindy: I think she remembered. I think that she—

Madanes: She remembered the fork. She remembered, "I hate you." She didn't remember the burning.

Cindy: I think she remembers it. She's—Amy is very honest, but she is very guarded here.

Madanes: Okay. In any case, whether she meant it or not, what you have to do is show her that you feel good about yourself. That you love yourself. That you are happy. That you are happy with yourself. Then she can be happy with herself. You know, she looks up to her mother. She looks like you. She's so much like you. Whatever you are, she's going to be.

Cindy: Okay. I'll try very hard. It's going to be a long haul. I'm going to—

Madanes: I don't think so. Look at all the resources you have. Whenever you've set your mind to doing something you just did it. And you've succeeded. I don't think it's going to be a long haul at all!

Cindy: Yeah.

Madanes: You are going to come in transformed next time!

Cindy: Oh come on! (laughs) I mean you're asking for miracles!

Madanes: You're going to call Mickey tonight!

Cindy: Tonight? Okay.

Madanes: Okay. And Stan and Bart also tomorrow.

Cindy: Stan's had, Stan just had surgery, I'm going to—

Madanes: It's a good excuse. You can go visit him.

Cindy: Yeah, well he wanted me to come over.

Madanes: You should. You have to keep those friendships. And you might make some other friend.

Cindy: Uh huh.

Madanes: Okay, let me talk to the children and you can think about this. Maybe you'll remember something else.

Cindy left the room and I brought in Amy. I wanted to evaluate her emotional condition, having not yet discarded the possibility that she might hurt herself. I also wanted to arrange for Amy to have a happier situation at home and for her to help me to help her mother to be happier.

Madanes: (sitting on the couch next to Amy) What could help you
to have a better situation at home?

Amy: If I would try to get along with everybody in my family and
if Larry wouldn't tease me.

Madanes: If you were trying to get along? Or if you did get along?

Amy: I did.

Madanes: Do you think it's possible for Larry to stop teasing you?
I've never known a big brother who doesn't tease his little
sister. Do you know any? It's the way he shows you that he
really loves you. You know he can't say it. He's a boy. He can't
say, "Hey Amy, I like you." He has to tease you.

Amy: Uh huh.

Madanes: He takes care of you also? He's a good boy. How does
he tease you? What does he say?

Amy: He, when he used to stay home, he had the chicken pox, he
used to boss me around and then we would start to get in a
real big fight.

Madanes: He makes you do things for him? Like, "Bring me this,
do that, go here, go there," kind of thing?

Amy: He tells me to turn the channel and then I say, "No, you have
two legs, why can't you do it?" One day he started, he came
down and he said, "Amy, can you change the channel to that
channel?" And I said, "No. Why can't you?" And then I just
went upstairs. I just left him alone.

Madanes: Would you like him to play with you more?

Amy: Well if I do, it starts out for the big fight. So I'm going to try
to leave him alone from now on.

Madanes: But you have friends that come over and play with you,
and you go outside and play?

Amy: I go outside and play.

Madanes: Who is your best friend?

Amy: April.

Madanes: April? Is she nice? (Amy nods.) And your second best?

Amy: Hmmm, Jenny.

Madanes: Do you have a boyfriend?

Amy: Yes, but he doesn't love me.

Madanes: He doesn't love you? How can he be a boyfriend if he
doesn't love you?

Amy: I just like him.

Madanes: You like him? But he doesn't like you, do you think?

Amy: Yes.

Madanes: How do you know? Your girlfriend asked him?

Amy: Because he told me.

Madanes: He told you? Or he told April?

Amy: He told me.

Madanes: What did he say?

Amy: He said he didn't like me.

Madanes: Oh, boys are like that. And you still like him?

Amy: Hmmm hmmm.

Madanes: So what are you going to do about it? How are you going to get him to like you?

Amy: I don't know.

Madanes: Maybe you could like another one.

Amy: No. I like him.

Madanes: Do you like him? For how long have you liked him?

Amy: Since like March. Beginning, like, let me see—(counts with her fingers)

Madanes: Almost four months?

Amy: Let me see. Probably, let me see, probably, I started to like him in March first.

Madanes: Ha! And today is April 10, that's a long time to like somebody. Do you send him little notes? No? Little hearts? What do you do? Do you talk to him?

Amy: No. I just say "Hi" to him.

Madanes: Do you talk to April and Jenny about him?

Amy: Yes.

Madanes: Do they like him also?

Amy: As friends.

Madanes: Ah. Do they like some other boys?

Amy: Yes.

Madanes: What's his name?

Amy: Neil.

Madanes: Neil. Okay. Listen, I know that you don't like to be sent up to your room, right?

Amy: Yes.

Madanes: Would your life be easier if you weren't sent up to your room—

Amy: Yes.

Madanes: —all the time? Do you feel that would make you a nicer person around the house?

Amy: Yes.

Madanes: You'd be nicer to your mother?

Amy: Yes.

Cindy had said that Amy didn't like to be sent to her room. I mentioned this here because I was looking for a way to negotiate with Amy so that she would stop threatening to hurt herself in exchange for the privileges she wanted.

Madanes: What else does she do or say that really gets on your nerves?

I talked about "nerves" because that is the language that Amy had used.

Amy: Sometimes she just repeats things over when I'm talking to Larry and I just tell her to shut up because I get so nervous. I said, "Mom, I can't talk with two people at the same time."

Madanes: She interrupts you?

Amy: No, she doesn't interrupt me. She just starts talking.

Madanes: She just talks over you.

Amy: Yes.

Madanes: She talks to you or to Larry?

Amy: She talks to me and I say, "Wait a minute," and then she says, and then I say, "Help, I can't talk to two people at the same time."

Madanes: You don't like to be sent to your room because you like to be with your mother? I can understand that. She's very nice.

Amy: Because she likes to play with me, my games with me.

Madanes: Is there any other punishment that she could use that wouldn't be as bad, that you wouldn't mind?

Amy: Like if we had a treat that I couldn't have it.

Madanes: Okay, I'm going to write this down because I'm going to get all these things for you. You'd better think. This is your chance. "No sending to room. Take away treat instead."

Amy: You write fast.

Madanes: Yes. It comes from going to school for so many years. All right. "Don't interrupt." No, "Don't talk over her. Don't talk over Amy." What else? Do you want her to play a game with you every day or to read you a story, to tuck you in at night, give you a kiss?

Amy: Oh, I know one, she does that all the time—when I need her, to help me on my homework, if she's not doing anything that she really needs to do that's important.

Madanes: Okay. "Help with homework if not doing something very important." Okay. Any special place that you like to go to or a special thing that you like to do with your Mom?

Amy: No. My mother's taking me out to dinner somewhere tonight.

Madanes: That's good. That's good.

Amy: I want to go to McDonalds.

Madanes: Okay, listen. If these things work out—she doesn't send you to your room if she needs to punish you, she takes away a treat. She doesn't talk over you. And she helps you with your homework as soon as you ask her rather than say wait and all that. And if Larry tries to tease you less—that's the difficult one, we're going to try for that too. Do you think that will help you to say nice things about yourself? So that you don't say "I'm stupid" or "I'm going to hurt myself" or "I hate you" or "fuck you" or things like that? It will help you? Hmmm? You'll manage? Instead you're going to say. "I'm happy, I'm smart, I'm pretty, you're very pretty."

Amy: Okay.

I've made a bargain. This strategy can be called "the offer that can't be refused." It is based on the principle of simplicity. Instead of complicated hypotheses about the presenting problem, the therapist assumes that changes can be negotiated and finds out exactly what the child wants. She then proceeds to arrange for that. It is best to inquire with the child alone so she can be sincere. Then the mother has to be convinced, also in private, to accept the changes.

Madanes: You'll do that? Do you think? It'll make it easier for you. Because I can see when you have to go up to your room all the time it's a bore. You get disgusted with yourself. Then you say

· 179 ·

"I'm stupid" and "I hate you." Do you like your Mom's friends?

I switched to the subject of the mother's friends because I wanted to find out if Amy disapproved of any of these friends, I wanted Amy to collaborate with me in arranging for the mother to have some fun with people her age. This collaboration was very important because Cindy was so involved with her children that, if they disapproved, she would refuse to go out.

Amy: Yes. She used to have a friend. She met her when she was in sixth grade. She's like my aunt to me because she works at this shop and on one Saturday she's going to take me home with her and then we are going to go out shopping.

Madanes: Oh, that's great. That's wonderful.

Amy: And she has a little niece and she's going to come too. And her name is Sheryl.

Madanes: Ah, that's great. That's wonderful. It's great to have an aunt who's not a real aunt, but you call her an aunt. Do you know what I mean?

Amy: Yes.

Madanes: They are better than real aunts. That's great. Okay, you are going to have a good time. I'm going to help your mother have a good time too.

Amy: Oh, good.

Madanes: In the next few days she's going to have some fun, and you are going to see her much happier. She's okay. I just think she needs to play a little bit more, don't you think? She doesn't go out enough, right?

Amy: Yes. Because when she gets home she hardly gets any fresh air because she works like, eight a.m. to five o'clock p.m. So she hardly gets to go outside unless she goes out to lunch like to a store. And she usually works on the bills when she gets home.

Madanes: Oh, so she has to go out and play more. She told me she has a bike. She's going to ride her bike.

Amy: She only used her bike like two times.

Madanes: She's going to do that and she told me she's going to call some old boyfriends and go out and have some fun. Wouldn't that be good? So you be sure when she goes out with someone that you say to her, "Oh Mommy, you look so pretty!" Say, "You look just like me." Because you are very pretty. And help her dress and put on her makeup.

Amy: All right. (Amy smiles with pleasure.)

I wanted Amy not only to give permission for her mother to go out, but also to collaborate actively in this plan.

Madanes: Okay? She's a good dancer too. She was telling me. Are you a good dancer also?

Any: She thinks so. I took dance lessons once. She was going to look for dance classes for me but it was too expensive.

Madanes: Oh, she'll be able to find some I'm sure. But anyhow, she has a lot of very nice friends. Do you remember Mickey?

Amy: Yes.

Madanes: And then there's Stan?

Amy: Yes.

Madanes: Ah huh, and Bart?

Amy: Yeah.

Madanes: So she has all these other boys to go out with. Not that she's going to get serious with anybody, but she needs to have some fun.

Amy: Well, she goes out with Bart sometimes.

Madanes: She should go out more, with several. Make sure to tell her that it's all right and you want her to have fun and that she looks pretty. Will you do that?

Amy: Yeah.

Madanes: Which of her boyfriends do you like best?

Amy: Ummmmm, Stan. He's real funny.

Madanes: Oh, that's great.

Amy: He invited us to a crab feast before.

Madanes: Okay. Is there something nice that you would like to do for your mother, that you would like to plan to make her feel nice?

Amy: I usually surprise her and I wash the dishes and clean up the house.

Madanes: She told me that. That's wonderful. You're so little to do all that. That's great.

Amy: Larry helps. And he mows the lawn because he has a job and for the big yards he gets six dollars and for the small yards he gets three dollars.

Madanes: Oh, that's great. Listen, although all that work is wonderful for you to do, doing the dishes and all of that, try just a little thing—even just like saying to her "You know, Mom, you're pretty like I am." And, "I'm happy with myself. I like me." She'll like that. Say it to me. Say, "I like me."

Amy: I like me. (Amy smiles through the whole conversation.)

Madanes: Point to yourself.

Amy: I like me.

Madanes: Good. That's good. You're going to say that to your mother every day? Okay? At least once a day, maybe twice? Okay. There's just a lot to like about you. You're really great. You're very smart and you're very sweet. And you're very caring of your mother. And very pretty. Even if this—what's the name of this boy who you say doesn't like you?

Amy: Neil.

Madanes: Neil. How could I forget? I have a friend called Neil also. He probably is just pretending not to like you. You know? Boys are shy. Do you think that's it? I'm sure that's it. Okay. Anything else?

Amy: Ummm. When I go into my brother's room and if he tries to push me out, instead of fighting with him, I just walk outside immediately.

Madanes: Yes. You know what you can say? You can say to him, "Larry, be nice to me. Remember what Cloé said." I'm Cloé. Okay, and then you walk out. Okay? Does he really scare you or is it more that he just teases?

Amy: Well, sometimes he wears these masks and he comes and usually hides from me and he comes into my room and he sneaks under, he usually sneaks behind the walls and when I come upstairs he'll go "Ahhh!" And he scares me.

Madanes: You know that there is somebody here at the office who does that to me all the time? I'm afraid to walk down the hall because I think that he's going to be behind the door and scare me. Some boys are like that, right? Okay. It was great talking to you. I am going to see Larry for a few minutes.

Amy: Okay.
Madanes: And then I'm going to see your Mom and then I'll see
      you again in about a week. Okay?
Amy: Okay.

I brought Larry into the room and sat across from him.

Madanes: Is there something particularly that worries you, that's
      on your mind about your Mom or your sister or yourself?
Larry: Well, kind of with my sister because she's been having a lot
      of troubles lately. You know, because, you know, when she
      starts yelling at my Mom I just, you know, feel like I don't
      want to live in the house because, you know, when she starts
      up it's, you know, kind of weird.
Madanes: Hmm hmmm.
Larry: I just don't like being in the house when she starts yelling.
Madanes: She yells so loudly?
Larry: Yes.
Madanes: So bad, eh? She's such a little thing to make so much
      noise. It's hard to imagine how she would. You mean when
      she says "I hate you" or swears or something.
Larry: Yes.
Madanes: Well, I've had a talk with her about what are the kinds
      of things that would make her feel better about herself so that
      she doesn't need to do that so much. And so she told me that
      one thing she doesn't like is to be sent to her room. That she
      would prefer another punishment.

I need Larry's approval of my plan with Amy as well as with his
mother. The three of them are so close that everyone's collaboration is essential.

Larry: Uh huh.
Madanes: So she suggested to take away some treat, for example.
      And so I'm going to suggest that to your Mom because I think
      that Amy is very fond of your mother, and so she doesn't like
      to be sent away—
Larry: Uh huh.

Madanes: —you know, away from her. And another thing that she said was that she doesn't like her mother to talk over her.

Larry: You mean like—

Madanes: She's talking to you and your mother talks to you at the same time.

Larry: Oh.

Madanes: And she wants your mother to help her with her homework. When she asks. Right away. But the most important thing that she said was that she wants you to be nicer to her. She doesn't want you to tease her. So a lot of it—

Larry: On that one we are both going to have to work together.

Madanes: Yeah. Do you think you can do that? I mean, she has some good times with you. She was telling me how you scare her and that you come into her room with a mask or something.

Larry: That, I used to do that a long time ago.

Madanes: But I think that she probably, because you are so big and so much taller than she is, probably when you tease her sometimes she's not sure whether you're teasing or you're really going to hurt her.

Larry: Uh huh.

Madanes: So you have to find some way of saying to her "This is just play, don't be scared."

Larry: Yeah.

Madanes: Or just not to tease her. How old are you, 13?

Larry: Yes.

Madanes: And she is nine, right? There's a big age difference and you are very big and strong, and you have to get some practice anyhow with girls. So maybe you can practice with her. Talking differently and playing games. Does she bother you a lot that you tease her? Does she come and tell you things? What does she do?

Larry: You know, she'll, like, like when we're downstairs, like Amy—I'm not saying my mom favors her more—but usually she's downstairs before me and she's watching TV and let's say I come down. And I say, "Oh darn, I wanted to watch something." And then she'll say, "Well I'm watching this, you can't watch it." Then Mom says, "She asked me first Larry." And so then a fight will start and then the teasing will start.

Madanes: Do you think you could make some money to buy yourself a new TV set?

Larry: I have a TV set but it's black and white. I want to get color.

Madanes: Well, maybe you can work towards that and then you'll have your own. It must be hard to be the man in the family with two women.

Larry: Every time I fix something Mom always says like, "You're a real handy man, or something like that.

Madanes: Well, I told Amy that if you tease her and if she's bothered she's going to say to you, "Be nice to me, remember what Cloé said!"

Larry: Uh huh.

Madanes: That's me. She's going to try and remind you.

Larry: Okay.

Madanes: You do that and you try to tease her less and to work things out.

Larry: Okay.

Madanes: You know, sometimes as you grow up—and you're almost a man now—you have to give in to girls a little bit.

Larry: Uh huh.

Madanes: It's life.

Larry: Uh huh.

Madanes: And you can do it?

Larry: Uh huh.

Madanes: Do you have a girlfriend?

Larry: Uh huh.

Madanes: Ah. What's her name?

Larry: Jackie.

Madanes: Oh. And she has her own way also?

Larry: Uh huh.

Madanes: So you have three women who always get their own way.

Larry: Yeah.

Madanes: How old is she?

Larry: Twelve.

Madanes: She's in your same class?

Larry: Well, she's in my math class.

Madanes: Uh huh.

Larry: And then, you know, I see her some other times.

Madanes: Is she pretty like your sister and your mother?

Larry: Uh huh.

Madanes: Blonde also?

Larry: No, she has brown hair.

Madanes: Okay, let me tell you. I talked to your Mom, and I told her that she needs to have more fun. She needs to go out and play more. She needs to be with adults.

Larry: Uh huh.

Madanes: So she's going to do some of that.

Larry: One of her friends, well, one of her friends said yesterday when she was talking to her, she said—because she's always helping my Mom out—and she says, "You ought to get out. I can watch your kids for you." And she said "That's all you need—four terrors running around the house."

Madanes: Well, your mother is so concerned about you. She's so worried about doing the right thing.

Larry: Uh huh.

Madanes: That it would be nice if once in a while you would just say to her, "You know, Mom, you're a good Mom, go have some fun. I'm all right."

Larry: Uh huh.

Madanes: "And I'm going to take care of Amy and she'll be happy too!"

Larry: Uh huh.

Madanes: Your mother has a couple of good girlfriends.

Larry: Yeah.

Madanes: And she knows a few guys also to go out with. And so she's going to be calling them and going out with them.

Larry: Yeah.

Madanes: She's going to be seeing Mickey, Stan and Bart.

Larry: Uh huh.

Madanes: Do you know them?

Larry: Uh huh.

Madanes: So it's good, don't you think?

Larry: Yup.

Madanes: Okay, so you are going to tell her it's good, to go out with them. "They are nice. Have a good time."

Larry: Uh huh.

Madanes: Okay? She's also going to take her bike and go riding to get some exercise and fresh air.

Larry: Yeah, because she's only used that bike like once or twice.

Madanes: Yeah. Do you approve of her doing that?

Larry: Yeah.

Madanes: Okay. Is there anything that you would like her to do differently that you disapprove of or that she shouldn't be doing?

Larry: I don't think so, no.

Madanes: Okay. Because your opinion is very important to her. So even if she doesn't ask you she's thinking it. So say to her, "You know that's nice, you look nice, have a good time." That kind of thing.

Larry: Uh huh.

Madanes: And she'll be all right and Amy will be all right. She just has a little bit of a temper.

Larry: Uh huh.

Madanes: And you know, as you said, you went through that. And she'll outgrow it.

Larry: Uh huh.

Madanes: You look like a very calm guy. You are? Do you fight a lot?

Larry: No.

Madanes: Yeah, I could tell that.

Larry: No, I don't like picking fights.

Madanes: That's right. You look very controlled, very calm.

Larry: Yeah.

Madanes: How long have you had this girlfriend?

Larry: About six or seven months.

Madanes: Oh, that's almost like marriage. That's great. Very good. Okay, well, things will be better.

Larry: Uh huh.

Madanes: Is there any way that you can, that I can ask anything of your mother or of Amy so that you have fewer conflicts with Amy?

Larry: Well, what she told you, you know, that's pretty good for right now.

Madanes: Okay.

Larry: I just want to see what she acts like and I'll tell you the next time we come here.

Madanes: Okay. Very good.

I took Larry to the waiting room and brought Cindy in. I talked to her about the change in punishments that Amy wanted.

Madanes: So can you do that?

Cindy: Okay.

Madanes: She explained to me that she really likes to be with you. Near you. Around you. And to be sent to her room is like the worst horrible thing.

Cindy: That scares her. That frightens her.

Madanes: Well, I think that she misses you. You know, usually you're working and she doesn't see that much of you.

Cindy: Uh huh.

Madanes: And so when you are there, she wants to be near you.

Cindy: Okay.

Madanes: So don't punish her by withdrawing yourself from her.

Cindy: Okay.

Madanes: Okay? It seems reasonable to me.

Cindy: Okay.

Madanes: She also doesn't want you, when she's talking to you or to Larry, she doesn't want you to talk over her. And you know, she's so sensitive about that. She's very sensitive.

Cindy: Okay, I don't quite understand that.

Madanes: Well, she says that, for example, she says something and as she's talking you're talking also.

Cindy: Okay, I'll try to be aware of it.

Madanes: Yeah, some people don't mind that at all and other people are very sensitive. I myself talk over everybody. But, you know, it's a personality trait.

Cindy: Okay. So she picked that up?

Madanes: Yes.

Cindy: I'll be darned.

Madanes: She's very bright.

Cindy: Perhaps I do that. You know, I lunge into it to keep things from happening and I'm causing more frustration with her. Okay.

Madanes: And she has a very little voice. So she's very easy to talk over.

Cindy: You should hear it when it's not so little. (laughs)

Madanes: Okay. She says that when she asks you for help with her homework—

Cindy: Uh huh.

Madanes: —if you're not doing something very important she really would like you to help her. Because I think that she gets very frustrated if she doesn't understand something and she doesn't want to wait for the explanation. It makes sense.

Cindy: Uh huh.

Madanes: She also wants Larry not to tease her. So I told her to say to him, "Larry, be nice to me, remember what Cloé said." And so she said that she would do that. And then I talked with him about that also, so he's going to try and work that out.

Cindy: Uh huh.

Madanes: You should write these things down.

Cindy: Uh huh.

Madanes: So, "No sending to room. Take away treat instead."

Cindy: Okay. (writes)

Madanes: "Don't talk over Amy. And help her with her homework right away."

Cindy: I really wasn't aware I was doing that because usually—I mean I might be making a pot of coffee because that usually is the first thing I do when I come in is put on some coffee. But that only takes five minutes.

Madanes: Oh, you mean as soon as you come in she asks you for help with her homework?

Cindy: Well, it's nice now. She wants to hit the playground. They just built a playground—

Madanes: It's also good that she's responsible and wants to do the homework first.

Cindy: Hey, we—this is one thing now that's better, we used to have screaming fights. She'd say she's not doing her homework. So she'd have to stay in the house and she still wouldn't do her homework.

Madanes: So you've accomplished that. That's a big major thing.

Cindy: And then she wouldn't let me sit with her. You know, I'd sit down and she'd go, "Get away from me!" I mean, any excuse, you know.

Madanes: Okay. They were both very interested in the idea that you are going to go out and play more.

Cindy: Good.

Madanes: They approve of Mickey, Stan, and Bart.

Cindy: Really? Mickey?

Madanes: Yes. They both said that they liked him and it was great for you to go out with him. And they are going to be supportive.

Cindy: Amy too?

Madanes: Yeah.

Cindy: Well maybe she was—I don't know what happened that day.

Madanes: You should have seen her. She brightened up at the idea you were going to go out and have some fun.

Cindy: Did she? I'll be darned. I was thinking about something while I was out there, making up excuses. I'm going to cover this quickly because I know that Larry is dying to get to this birthday party, but Mickey was very introverted and I was good for him. He was very good to me. But sometimes he's terribly, terribly shy, I mean painfully shy, not with me but in public. He also mumbles and grumbles a lot about his problems and, you know, never could seem to find a solution for anything. I really don't want to get into a heavy relationship. But that's not what you're suggesting.

Madanes: No, no, no, no. That's why I'm telling you, have at least two.

Cindy: Okay. I didn't want you to be disappointed in me. My first thought when I sat out there was "I can't call him." Because I know he's going to want to get into a heavy relationship. But I can—

Madanes: No, just say to him, "This is going to be light."

Cindy: Uh huh.

Madanes: "I just need to have some fun, that's all."

Cindy: Okay.

Madanes: And so you can say to him "Now don't go and break up with your girlfriend or anything like that."

Cindy: Okay. That's true, it takes two!

Madanes: Sure.

Cindy: I was responsible for having him become very serious.

Madanes: That's right.

Cindy: I'll tell you, after being with one person for so long—I've been on my own for years now, but this relationship, the dating game and all, is a real trip!

Madanes: Well, it's fun. It's nice to be liked. Okay. Let me take you out there and we'll make another appointment. Remember to do all these things.

Cindy: Okay.

A week later, Amy reported that her mother was beginning to change. She had forgotten to say, "I like me," but she had not said "bad" things about herself. Threats of suicide and of burning herself were no longer a problem for Amy. The mother had gone out once and had changed her hairdo, which is often an indication of other changes. Cindy had contacted all three men and was planning to see them.

As it happened, Mickey was very interested in her. They began to see each other and soon Cindy reported that she realized she was no longer attracted to him. However, he painted her house and did many repairs before she concluded she didn't really want him.

In a few weeks, Cindy and the children were much better. Yet she still seemed disturbed and preoccupied, so I began to think that perhaps there was still another problem that I did not know about. I asked Cindy what was the worst thing, the most bad thing, she had ever done.

She told me, with great anxiety, that when she visited prisoners she sometimes brought contraband into the prison and one time, in a fight over the goods, the inmates had burned a man alive. I said that her intentions had been good, she had wanted to bring some solace to their lives and she had never imagined that her good intentions would lead to such horror. But, I emphasized, that is why it is important to obey the law. When something is banned, particularly in prison, it is because over many centuries of careful thought, it has been foreseen that these tragedies might happen. The lesson to be gained was to obey the law. Now I understood why Amy had talked about burning herself. Angry at her mother, she offered the most deeply painful metaphor to her.

Cindy began to date the hairdresser who had cut her hair after the first session. Soon after she met another man to whom she was very attracted, a body builder, and began to date him also. He was a very good influence because of his interest in exercise and health. The body builder and the hairdresser, who was from the Middle East, became the protectors that I had been looking for, and the ex-husband did not bother Cindy again.

As Cindy changed, other family relationships also changed. Cindy began to ask her mother to babysit so she could go out. The mother complained about Cindy's late hours and was concerned about her lifestyle. Cindy was about to give her up as a babysitter but I suggested that she should simply accept that a mother has the right to nag and complain and a daughter has the obligation to keep her mother young with stories of love and adventure. In fact, I suggested that Cindy should talk about men with her sister in her mother's presence, so they would help each other by helping the mother to enjoy a more exciting life vicariously. When Cindy followed my suggestions, this brought her closer not only to her mother but also to her sister (whom her ex-husband had molested).

There was no intervention with respect to Cindy's father but he spontaneously became more involved with her and the children. By the end of the therapy, about four months later, he was contributing money to buy clothes for the children and he had given them a trip to Disneyland.

Amy began to do very well at school and Larry continued to develop normally. Cindy was cheerful. She disengaged from her brothers and from her involvement with the prison system. She was never promiscuous and did not go back to drugs or alcohol. By the end of the therapy she was exclusively involved with the hairdresser, who was very conservative.

On follow-up at one and two years later, Cindy was involved in her work. She had become a union representative and was planning to go back to school. Her relationship with the hairdresser was stable and good. She also worked out regularly and was looking very attractive and healthy. The children were fine and no new problems had developed.

Conclusion

This transcript demonstrates how a large number of problems can be addressed therapeutically in one interview — suicide threats, temper tantrums, dreams and premonitions, fears, depression, loneliness, sexual abuse, sibling rivalry, low self-esteem, drug addiction, and violence. A general strategy can be chosen that specifically benefits each individual family member while improving the relationship of each one to the others. Every statement by the therapist can be a therapeutic message targeted to a specific goal.

III

Special Issues

9

SEX THERAPY
IN SPECIAL CIRCUMSTANCES

There is no end. There is no beginning. There is only the infinite passion of life.

—*Federico Fellini*

SEX THERAPY AND directives about sex have been and still are sensitive and controversial. Almost a century ago Freud was attacked for suggesting that mental illness was related to a lack of sexual fulfillment. He believed, for example, that hysterical symptoms were the consequence of sexual repression. But, in a Victorian society, he was unable to direct single young women to experiment with sex. Instead, he offered insight into their problem, hoping that they would some day fall in love with someone who would reciprocate (Freud, 1908, pp. 195–198).

It should be expected that by the 1990s sexual fulfillment would be considered natural and human. As therapists we should be able to encourage our clients toward a satisfying sex life, just as we encourage them to work, to enjoy their leisure time, and to love their families.

Alfred Kinsey, Masters and Johnson, and other American pioneers have informed us about the many mysteries and technicalities of sex. But do we encourage our clients to fulfill their needs? Have we accepted Freud's idea that lack of sexual fulfillment is related to anxiety, depression, psychosomatic symptoms, and disturbed behavior? If Freud were a family therapist today, giving directives rather than interpretations, would he, for example, be encouraging bulimics to have sex instead of vomiting? If he suggested that a sexual affair is a cure for depression, would he be expelled from the American Association of Sex Educators, Counselors and Therapists? If, instead of medication, he prescribed sex to a depressed single mother, would he be able to renew his malpractice insurance?

I am Freudian in the sense that I believe that sexual problems are at the root of a variety of emotional difficulties and that a good sex life is often the cure for a variety of problems. As a strategic therapist I find myself encouraging people to enjoy sex for pleasure, for fun, and because it is important in a person's life.

Many therapists think of giving directives about sex only when sex is presented as a problem. However, often sexual directives are useful even when sex is not the presenting problem. Sexual interactions can replace pathological interchanges and bring people together quickly and dramatically. Directives about sex can be used to counter violence and to help a depressed person recover a sense of humor.

During my many years as a teacher of marital and family therapy I have noticed that couples who have a good sex life more easily solve all kinds of marital and family problems. In contrast, if sex is not good, the bond that helps a couple to stick together through all kinds of difficulties is missing. So, I always ask spouses about their sex life and do my best to help them improve it if it is not good. I don't think I could be as successful with many problems if I eliminated playful teasing and seduction from my repertoire of therapy strategies.

Sexual issues are just as important to homosexual couples as to heterosexual ones. This chapter is about solving the sexual problems of people who do not have a regular sexual partner, of homosexuals, and of those with homosexual fantasies.

Two women had been doing co-therapy for a long time with a middle-aged lesbian couple. They brought the couple for consultation. I was observing the therapy session from behind a one-way mirror. The therapists were stuck with a difficult problem. For years the younger woman had complained of lack of sexual desire and had rarely had sex with her older partner, who was very much interested in sex. Recently, the older woman had discovered that the younger one was frequently unfaithful to her with a variety of women, with whom she did not have lack of desire. When confronted, the younger woman declared that she was not going to give up her lifestyle. In the session the older woman cried, begged, and reproached the other for her cruelty.

My suggestion was to tell the older woman that it would be impossible to enforce faithfulness when the other was so clear in her refusal; however, a favorable contract could be arranged. Every time the younger woman had sex with somebody else, she had to have sex five times with her partner. A sexual act was defined as one where each woman had at least one orgasm. The younger woman accepted the contract and the older woman was delighted.

The intervention solved both the problem of infidelity and the problem of low sexual desire. What the older woman had resented was that others were getting what she was being deprived of. With this arrangement, the more others got, the more she would get. Once her freedom was respected, the younger woman responded to the older one with interest and affection, salvaging her self-esteem by talking about how she truly loved her and did not want to separate from her. The couple stayed together and settled into a relationship that was satisfactory to both.

Three years later, however, the roles were reversed. The older woman fell passionately in love with someone else and the younger one decided to kill herself. She said goodbye to her therapist and to all her friends. I was called to an emergency consultation and helped to arrange a postponement of the suicide for three months. During this time the therapist organized the network of friends to make life so interesting (including romantic involvement) that suicide was postponed indefinitely.

We all have the potential for many different kinds of sexual activities. Sometimes people have sexual experiences that are incongruous with their view of themselves. Sometimes sexual needs are used in a power struggle that leads to confusion and to a weakening of the sense of self. Some people's potential for sexual enjoyment is so broad that they have to make arbitrary decisions about their sexual preferences.

It used to be that therapists had to discourage homosexuality, but since homosexuals were liberated from psychiatry in 1974, we now have a choice. Sometimes we have to decide what type of sexual behavior to encourage.

A wife requested therapy because she said that her husband was homosexual (see Chapter 11). They had been married for 15 years and had three children. Their sex life in the past had been very good. The husband had experimented with homosexuality in his late adolescence and young adulthood, but he had decided to abandon that life, fell in love and married. Recently, he had been troubled by what he called "homosexual fantasies seething in his breast" and had decided not to have sex with his wife until he resolved the problem of these bothersome fantasies.

From behind the one-way mirror I noticed that the spouses were in a power struggle. The wife accused the husband of being insecure, not working hard enough, not making enough money, and neglecting her. He retaliated with implicit or explicit threats that he was truly homosexual and would eventually leave her. She used criticism and interference to block him from being involved with the children, feeling that she was protecting them from him. He escalated his threats of homosexuality and refused to have sex with her to punish her. When each was asked what he/she wanted most from the other, he said that he wanted to be closer to the children and she said that she wanted him to be a more responsible father.

The therapeutic strategy was obvious. He was put in charge of the children. In exchange he was to have sex with her whenever she wanted and in a way that was pleasing to her. In two months, the relationship had greatly improved, but the husband was still, from time to time, making innuendos about his possible homosexuality. These comments put him in a superior position to his wife because they threatened her; at the same time they put a distance between them that took the joy out of their marriage. To end the strife between them, the therapist explained to the wife, in the presence of the husband, that she had been misled in believing that the husband was a closet homosexual. In fact, the opposite was true. His alleged homosexuality was a coverup for his tendency toward a macho domination of her. He covered up the fact that he always got his way by appearing to be delicate, sensitive, and tormented by homosexual impulses, when in fact all this was a way of manipulating her. In the past she had thought that she wanted to save him from homosexuality, when in reality she needed to transform him from being a brutal John Wayne into being a sensitive and respectful person. In this way the therapist arranged for her need to reform her husband to be respected and preserved but *how* she would reform him to be changed.

Sometimes the best sex therapy has to do with common sense and changing a person's expectations and point of view. A 60-year-old woman consulted me about a problem with depression. Divorced for many years, she had three grown children and several grandchildren, and an interesting job that kept her flying between east and west coasts. She had been in therapy with a colleague of mine for a long time for what she referred to as her anxiety and depression, which she related to problems in a sexual relationship. She was pleasant looking, rather short and plump, well dressed but certainly not glamorous or beautiful. With great difficulty, as if it were a big secret, she told me that for years she had been tormented because of an affair she was having with a man a few years younger than herself, successful in her field, attractive, but plagued by guilt feelings. As a young man, he had gone to seminary and almost become a priest. He had chosen a different profession, but had always felt that perhaps the priesthood had really been his calling. He had never married and always valued a celibate life. When he met her, he had become desperately passionate about her. For years they had had wonderful sex together, but he always talked about how it was sinful and wrong and made him feel guilty. He sometimes said that he saw her as a temptress and a whore but couldn't resist her. She wanted to be respected and be friends with him, but every time he saw her he was tormented with desire and guilt. Lately, he had been seeing her less. She was so upset with the situation that sex was no longer good for her.

I asked her how this was related to her depression. She asked, didn't I realize that she was being humiliated, not treated with respect, just wanted for sex, and that was obviously depressing? I told her that if, when I'm 60, I have an attractive, compassionate, intelligent man, who just wants me for sex, and who is tormented by passion and guilt, I'll be ecstatic. In fact, I would like her to teach me how she does it. She had been crying most of the session, but now she smiled through her tears. I told her to play along with her lover's fantasies and talk to him about how sex is sinful. She said, "But isn't it wrong to have a relationship that is totally based on sex?" I answered that, in fact, that idea was only a fantasy. She and her lover were both in the same profession and probably spent a great deal of time talking about their work. Also, she wasn't exactly a spring chicken or a sex symbol, so surely he liked her for other reasons. However, probably their passion was kept alive by not seeing each other very frequently, so she should compensate by having other close friends. Some men cannot be everything in a woman's life. What she had was wonderful; she shouldn't ruin it. She said she would follow my advice.

This brings me to the issue of solving the sexual problems of single people, particularly when loneliness and sexual deprivation are related to depression. In the last chapter, we met Cindy who came to therapy extremely depressed and worried about her nine-year-old daughter, who was threatening suicide. For two years, since she broke up with Mickey, she had not had sex with anyone.

In the first session I gave Cindy a piece of paper and asked her to write down her prescription: at the top of the page, the word "fun." I told her that it wasn't healthy for a woman her age to lead a celibate life. To make sure that she had enough fun she needed to go out with two or three men. The idea was not necessarily to become sexually involved but to resume adult relationships without ruling out the possibility of sex. She soon began to go out with two men. On follow-up two years later Cindy told me that she had dated two men for only a couple of months and had settled into a very good monogamous relationship with one of them. Their social life revolved around the health spa and there was no involvement in drugs. I agree with Freud that sex is often a very good cure for poor health, depression, and anxiety.

It is interesting how often sex is linked to spiritual issues. It has been so for thousands of years in all religions, even though today we sometimes think of sex lightly. Sex can bring out the best and the worst in people. Without kindness, compassion, and joy, the experience can be more degrading than any other form of aggression. I think this is true for both men and women. It is important that sex therapists recognize this link between spirituality and sex and that we do our best to encourage sex in a kind and compassionate context. Since sex involves people in unusual ways, common sense and a sense of humor are invaluable in untangling constraint and misery.

A friend called to refer the daughter of a wealthy family who was involved with some kind of guru. The parents were desperate to save her. A few days later the young woman called me and said she wanted a spiritual therapist. I said she had come to the right person, because I consider myself a Buddhist. She was pleased and told me that she was 21 years old and had very strong reasons to suspect that she had been sexually molested as a child by her father or by someone else. She wanted to be able to remember whether or not she had been molested and by whom. I said that I would try to help her and that I needed her family to be present in the first session.

The mother and father and her two sisters came to the session. Debbie explained that she had been in school in California, where she had become involved with a teacher who had become her lover and her spiritual guide. He was 43 years old and she was 20. After a few months, she had become doubtful about whether she wanted to be in this relationship. At that point she decided to go home for a while and visit her parents, leaving the teacher with her apartment and her car. Once home she began to feel more and more that she didn't want to talk to this man and she didn't want to go back.

One day he called her and said that in meditation he had had a vision that she was being raped as a child by a big man who could have been her father. Further, he had told his own guru, an old man who had also moved into the girl's apartment, about this vision and the guru had confirmed that he also felt she had been raped and it had been her father.

Debbie was very upset on hearing all this and said that she had always had the feeling that something like that had happened to her. When she confronted her parents with this information, they were bewildered. Her father flew to California to confront the teacher and convince him that he had not molested his daughter. But after spending a day with him, in the girl's apartment which the guru now occupied, he ended up feeling so sorry for the man, because of his poor physical condition and unkempt appearance, that he gave him a considerable amount of money.

I asked Debbie's mother and sisters whether they thought that the father and Debbie were very kindly and easily taken advantage of and they agreed that they were. I asked Debbie whether she had considered the possibility that the teacher was desperate to get her back and was using the story of the vision as a way to separate her from her family and bring her back to California. She said there might be some truth to that, but she had the feeling that something terrible had happened to her in her childhood and she wanted to talk to me privately about it. I agreed. But before dismissing the family I said that it was important for Debbie to have a spiritual leader and also a boyfriend, but that they should be two separate people. Everybody agreed with this.

I stayed alone with Debbie, and she told me that ever since she was a small child she had thought that she was a witch possessed by demons. There were creatures living in her bedroom that scared her and moved things around and she had done many bad things. I asked her if she had hurt anyone—people, children, animals. Very tense and agitated, she said no. I said I could understand if she didn't want to tell me, but that it would be better if she told me what the worst things she had done were, so she could get it over with.

All of a sudden she shouted, "They're here, they're here," and she began to jump up and down with tremendous strength, looking at the ceiling as if she were seeing something flying around the room. She jumped and screamed with such strength that a couple of paintings in other rooms in the building fell. I looked at the ceiling and said, "What is here? You're scaring me shitless." With this she stopped and began to cry and said that all her childhood there had been these demons that made her do bad things and that she had suffered terribly, particularly because her parents thought it was her imagination and didn't believe her or offer her any reassurance or comfort.

I commiserated and asked her once more to tell me something very bad that she had done. Crying, she said that she used to stick vegetables into her vagina and hurt herself, and she would keep on doing it even after she was hurt because it was the demons that made her do it. Another time she poured a can of soup on her crotch and let the dog lick it and once a baby boy was sleeping in the house and she had touched his penis.

I said all that didn't sound very terrible to me. Had she hurt the vegetables? No. Had she hurt the dog? No, he had probably liked it very much. Was the little boy hurt? No, he didn't even wake up. I reassured her that many girls stick vegetables in their vagina without being possessed by demons. In fact, I said some sex therapists are now recommending vegetables instead of vibrators because they are more natural. About touching the boy's penis, certainly she had to know that many girls did that. And about the dog, that was really not such an uncommon practice. Did she know that people make fun of french poodles because they say that French courtesans used to do that with them?

She said she had never heard any of this, and I said that, if she liked, I would give her the literature. I said that she was a very kindly, spiritual person who, even in her terror, had never hurt anyone but herself.

I realized that I needed to integrate her experiences with the vegetables with her ideas about having been molested and I had to do it in such a way that she could overcome both. I also realized that the guru still had a great deal of power over Debbie and if I contradicted him I might lose her. The dilemma for me was how to reframe the situation without contradicting the teacher and yet reassure Debbie about her sexuality and her relationship with her father.

I made a quick decision and said that what was most important was that now I understood the whole situation with her teacher. His vision had been true. He had probably seen in a vision that as a little girl she was being hurt by something that looked like a big penis in her vagina. Naturally, since he was a man and was in love with her, he had assumed that it was a penis that belonged to a big man, because no man likes to think that a cucumber is bigger than a penis. In fact, when as a child she masturbated with a cucumber she probably thought about her father, or maybe he was in the next room or maybe he had even interrupted her, and that was why he was in the guru's vision. But it wasn't her father; it was a cucumber. In this way I arranged for the guru to be right and her father to be right.

She said that she still had the feeling that somebody else might have molested her. I said to her, "You know, Debbie, such a high percentage of little girls in the world are sexually molested in some way. What does it matter for you to know whether it happened to you or not? Their memory is your memory and their pain is your pain. You carry with you the painful memory of all those women who were molested as children, as if it were your own memory, because you are such a sensitive spiritual person."

She thought for a moment and then said, "All right, it's all over, you're right. I'm never going to see demons or think about being molested or feel that I'm possessed or a witch again. Call my family in and please tell them that I'm all right and it's over."

I said I would, but first I wanted to ask her to remember that if she ever had bad thoughts again she should think about the way I reminded her of her kindness and spirituality. I also wanted her to stay home for a while and not return to school for a semester. She was to find herself a nice simple boyfriend, one her own age, preferably not very bright or very handsome, with whom she could have ordinary sex as a way of practicing for when she found the right man. Also, for the next six months I didn't want her to read anything having to do with religion, spirituality, or philosophy.

When the other family members came into the room, I explained to them that Debbie was over her problem, that she knew her father had not molested her, that perhaps some other man had bothered her in some way but that she didn't need to know because it was enough to share in the painful memory of so many other women who had been molested.

I saw the family for three more sessions and dealt with issues that concerned Debbie and that are characteristic of the family situation when a young person presents psychotic behavior. The father had just been forced to retire from his favorite sport, which left him depressed and seeking his wife's company at a time when she had gone back to school. She was involved in an all-male department full of lonely divorced professors, whom she kept bringing to the house, as she tried to make them friends of the family. Debbie thought that her mother might be bored with her father and ready for a sexual affair. She feared that her mother might find such an affair emotionally disturbing and that it might destroy her marriage.

I talked to the mother and suggested that this was a time when she had to be careful about taking very good care of herself and alluded to the importance of being discreet. I asked both parents to reassure Debbie that, no matter what the future might bring in terms of their marriage, they would always love and take care of each other.

I told the family not to leave Debbie alone for a few months and if she was ever frightened again to take turns holding her until the fear went away. I talked alone with Debbie about sexual problems that concerned her. Although she had had several sexual encounters, she had only enjoyed sex with the guru. She was concerned about feelings of dissociation and of putting on a performance during sex. I explained that it is not uncommon for young women to prefer sex with older men because they are more patient, but that she shouldn't feel stuck with him for that reason. I suggested that she practice having sex with a young man her age who was not particularly attractive but with whom she could have a friendly, comfortable relationship rather than a romantic or passionate one. The therapy ended with plans for Debbie to transfer to a college close to home.

As we approach the next century we need to take the risk of opposition and deal more frankly with sex. Here are three simple, reasonable ways to approach sex in therapy:

1. Affirm each individual's right to have a satisfying sexual life.
2. Encourage sex as therapy for depression, anxiety and other problems.
3. Discourage guilt and emphasize sex as kindly and compassionate.

As a family therapist, when I have wanted to give credit to someone for saying something about sex, I have had to go back to Sigmund Freud, who had the courage to take a position on the importance of sex in human life. He wrote: "Sexual love is undoubtedly one of the chief things in life. . . . [A]ll the world knows this and conducts its life accordingly, science alone is too delicate to admit it" (Freud, 1915 [1914], pp. 169–170). As family and sex therapists, let us not be too delicate to admit it.

10
FAMILY THERAPY TRAINING
AS ENTERTAINMENT

People think the Beatles know what's going on. We
don't. We're just doing it.

— *John Lennon*

FAMILY THERAPY TRAINING coordinates the traditional transmission of knowledge and skills with the modern technology and culture of entertainment. The word "Entertainment," defined here as imaginative presentations that make money, is a specialized form of popular art that is not subject to the aesthetic and political scrutiny reserved for "real art." In this sense television, Hollywood movies, wrestling and other popular sports are all entertainment, even though some, such as French author Roland Barthes (1966), have argued that they are art.

In contrast, traditional education communicates information through lectures and readings, as well as through apprenticeships, where a disciple learns a trade from a master. While entertainment relies heavily on metaphorical communication and often plays with confusion and misunderstandings, in education such confusion and misunderstanding have no place. The exception might be the teaching of therapy, when the subject to be taught is how to solve the problems of living. When posed a question, the Zen master may offer a metaphor. When asked about a problem in therapy, Milton Erickson would tell the story of another patient. In this sense the teaching of therapy is metaphorical.

Much has been said about whether therapy is a science or an art. Political implications have been addressed, and the importance of aesthetics has become an issue. But if therapy is an art, who is the audience? If there is an audience, it is a very limited group. There are no exhibits, no auctions, no performances for the general public. Compared to the audience for the mass media, this audience is limited in numbers, even though recently it has expanded to include large numbers of people at conferences and workshops who expect to be instructed in entertaining ways. These people are interested in acquiring a practical education with the least possible effort, so it could be said that if therapy is an art, it is a form of entertainment to be assimilated as effortlessly as possible.

This is not to say that therapy is not also a science. We understand the stages of life, the organization of the family, hierarchy, power, the function of a symptom, institutionalization. We know how to change sequences, reverse hierarchies, use paradox, change metaphors. When we try to teach these skills, however, we can only do so through metaphor. Generalizations and rules are difficult if not impossible to make. The respect for the uniqueness of each individual and each family that characterizes a systems view makes classification, the basis of science, anathema to the approach. As teachers, we vacillate: Should we attempt to be scientific, should we teach as the Zen master does, or should we offer an entertaining performance?

To make the dilemma even more peculiar, there are critics from within and outside the field. Some critics say that all attempts to intervene in a system are futile or detrimental; others see therapists as agents of social control; some evaluate therapy on the basis of whether it is aesthetic; and the whole field is said to have deliberately or unwittingly collaborated in the oppression of women, homosexuals, and social deviants. Even the very idea that there should be a profession that attempts to solve the problems of living has been questioned. Some of the criticisms are similar to the attacks on television, "where owners of thousand-dollar sets think nothing of calling them 'idiot boxes,' and where a well pronounced distaste for TV has become a prerequisite for claims of intellectual and even of ethical legitimacy" (Marc, 1984). There have even been serious proposals for the elimination of television. But television, like psychotherapy, is part of the mind industry. It is beside the point to think that either could be arrested or abolished.

These dilemmas of art, entertainment, science, political oppression—even whether therapy should exist as a field at all—are the context in which we have to teach. And all this while we try to do something about the concrete problems of real people, and while we attempt to teach some skills to real students.

I know of no other field dealing with practical issues that is so consistently self-critical. The effect this criticism has on teachers is that we teach what we know while simultaneously attempting to justify (1) the fact that we are teaching, (2) the content of what we teach, and (3) the idea that there is anything to teach at all. This is where entertainment comes in. When teaching must take place at many levels, a teacher must rely on metaphors, symbols, and narratives that will influence the audience directly and indirectly. Drama becomes essential. But how can we produce this drama without violating the privacy of the therapist's office? How can we create the theater in which the student will be the audience, a sensitive and understanding witness to the human dilemmas that will become his or her area of expertise? Here technology enters: the one-way mirror and the video camera. With this technology a family therapy training institute begins to share more and more the elements of the world of entertainment, with which we are all familiar.

The students sit behind the one-way mirror watching the drama unfold on the other side of the glass. Sometimes they watch the action on a television screen that reproduces with close-ups and at different angles the view from behind the mirror. They take turns being the therapist, the observer, and the observed. The supervisor is the drama's director, organizing the action on both sides of the screen and arranging simultaneously the solution to the client's problems and the education and the entertainment of the students (whose attention span seems to become shorter every year, as new generations raised in front of the television set expect fast-paced action, and who engage in the learning process while simultaneously eating and conversing). Some sit, mesmerized and spaced out. Others rise to the occasion—to consciousness—and are able to preserve their integrity and autonomy by analyzing and comparing what they see on the screen or on the other side of the mirror with other therapies of the past or of the present. Similarly, television's most interesting moments occur, as David Marc points out, when new series are compared to reruns. "Miami Vice" and "Hill Street Blues" make "Starsky and Hutch" obsolete, while "Dragnet" and "The Mod Squad" have lost all credibility as police mysteries and have become comedies of obsolescence.

It is important to distinguish between taking television on one's own terms and taking it the way it presents itself. The television viewer who watches a rerun or a soap opera with an understanding that emerges out of the culture of television itself is protected from the homogenizing, authoritarian influence that is claimed by television's pessimistic critics. Similarly, the student of therapy can save himself or herself from the monolithic, authoritarian teacher through the autonomy of his or her imagination and through a knowledge of the culture of therapy.

Some of today's therapy students, accustomed to the world of the sitcom, where months become weeks and years become months, are bored with long-term therapy. In the television soap opera, each episode ends with uncertainty as to the possible rescue of characters from danger, torture, or even apparently hopeless anxiety, which device is used to entice the viewer to watch the next episode in the series. In the sitcom, on the other hand, the central tensions are almost always alleviated before the end of each episode. Each episode resembles a short, self-contained play.

Modern therapy has incorporated aspects from both of these modern television genres, mostly through the use of the directive as the main therapeutic tool. The use of the directive creates suspense within the session as it addresses the family drama: What directive will the supervisor come up with? Will the student be able to deliver it? How will the family respond? There is drama beyond the confines of the interview, however: Will the directive solve the problem? Will the clients return to the next session transformed? Will they return at all? These are the elements that create tension between sessions and entice the students to return to the next day of training.

The movie screen and the television set have limitless possibilities for thrilling the audience. The viewers can be flooded with hordes of characters, transported out of this world, and made to suffer innumerable illusions. The possibilities of the theater, in contrast, are limited to what can transpire on a stage, where there are obvious physical constraints, and where editing to create distortions is impossible. The ideal play, in terms of the expense of production, is one with three actors and one set. Modern playwrights struggle to produce thrills, action, and drama within these limitations.

The supervisor in modern therapy suffers from similar restrictions. The set of characters is limited. Even though relatives and friends of the family in therapy are invited, they often do not come to sessions. There is usually one therapist. The set is always the same. The possibilities for action and interaction in the therapy room are limited by the code of ethics of the various professions. In most therapies, sex, violence, nudism, and anything but restricted physical contact are discouraged. Furthermore, in general terms, the plot is always the same. Family members come in, distressed by what appears to be an insurmountable problem, estranged from each other, unhappy. The therapist questions, prods, sets up a different scenario. The problem is solved, and the family ties are strengthened. The ending must be happy, or the therapy has failed.

If it is impossible to arrange a happy ending, it is essential to bring out in the therapy all the qualities of a warm human drama. There is almost as much satisfaction for therapists in revealing the unsolvable dilemmas and the tragedies of life as in finding the best possible solutions. Just as in theater, where the audience can be entertained by the tragedy of *Hamlet* even though they know what the outcome will be, so the audience of therapists can be fascinated by how family members came to be as they are, irrespective of the outcome of therapy or of any effort to influence them.

What are the possibilities for the supervisor as playwright, who assumes the task of entertaining by writing, for each family and therapist, a script that will produce a happy ending or reveal a warm human drama within a very limited context? One possibility is intelligent questioning that will reveal unsuspected elements and uncover carefully concealed secrets, thereby unraveling right in front of the eyes of the student glued to the one-way mirror the mystery of why the family has come to be the way it is. Among strategic therapists, the Milan group (Selvini Palazzoli, Boscolo, Cecchin, and Prata, 1978) excels at this skill, although we can all claim a certain proficiency. It is the basis for the drama that will subsequently unfold.

Another possibility is enactment. The family members can be asked to reproduce their conflicts and difficulties in the therapy room. In this way some action is introduced; the clients may stand up and move around the room. The most famous playwright of enactment is probably Minuchin, who has reproduced in the therapy room the struggle of the parents of anorectics to feed their daughters during his now classic lunch sessions (Minuchin, Rosman, and Baker, 1978).

As in a play or a novel, once the characters and the conflict have been introduced, the obstacles to the resolution of the conflict must be presented. These obstacles must be serious enough to create tension, but they cannot be insurmountable, since the ending has to be happy. Reframing is one way to present such obstacles. The therapist explains to the family that the origin of the problem, the motivations of the characters, and the nature of the conflict are not as they appear. That is, family members come to the therapy with one view of the obstacles that they find overwhelming. The therapist transforms these obstacles into new difficulties that can be solved.

The members of the Mental Research Institute are the most famous reframers, having proposed that the obstacle is the attempted solution to the conflict (Watzlawick, Weakland, and Fisch, 1974). Virginia Satir, however, probably made the most memorable contribution in her famous reframing of a murderous husband who, she said, had been running after his wife with an axe because he was trying to reach out to her (Haley, 1984a). With reframing, magic is introduced: Hatred becomes love, avoidance protection, and rebellion submission.

Vargas Llosa (1985) has said that fiction was created to appease people's appetite for a life different from the one they lead. The truth of the novel does not depend on facts. It is written and read to provide people with lives they are unresigned to not having. Similarly, reframing introduces to the family meaning, drama, and the possibility of being someone else, of relating and living in ways that have gone unsuspected. The truth of the reframing depends on its own persuasive powers, on the skill of its magic. Every good therapy tells the truth and every bad therapy lies. Truth in therapy is to make the client experience an illusion; manipulation and lies mean to be unable to accomplish that trickery. Therapy has its own ethic, one in which truth and falsehood are secondary concepts.

Reframing involves taking what is presented by the clients and throwing a new light on it. A different approach is to introduce totally new obstacles. Milton Erickson was probably the best known master of this. In his therapies, the obstacle would often become climbing Squaw Peak, enduring the desert sun, approaching a stranger. This was a therapy of adventure, where the main action occurred outside of the therapy room. There was no video or live supervision in Erickson's day, and he entertained his disciples with stories of his own feats and of those of his patients. The adventures he proposed involved overcoming not only physical obstacles but also intellectual and spiritual ones, and his characters changed as they struggled to solve a puzzle, understand a difficult subject, and improve themselves in a various way.

Once the obstacle has been redefined, or a new obstacle has been created, it must be overcome. Here is where directives and metaphors come into play. Directives may be simple or complex, straightforward or paradoxical, to be carried out in or out of the session. They may be an ordeal to be performed as a punishment if the problem occurs, or they can be pleasurable experiences. Erickson was the originator of directive therapy, and Jay Haley (1973) has probably been the most thoughtful presenter and theorist of the approach. It is in the directive that the greatest possibilities for entertainment exist, and where the future may bring the most spectacular developments. It is also where therapy may become comedy or slapstick, when clients are asked to do what appears absurd or ridiculous. Here is also where it is possible to develop the play within the play. For instance, I have asked families to pretend to have other problems than those they offered and to pretend to solve these imaginary problems in make-believe ways (Madanes, 1981, 1984).

Sometimes, metaphors are used instead of directives. Erickson used to tell stories to his patients in which fictional characters solved problems that were similar to the clients' problems. I have developed this approach into what I call "prescribing the metaphor." The clients are given the ingredients of a fictional situation that resembles their own conflict and asked to resolve it in the form of an essay, story, movie script, or play. This is another type of play within a play, where the clients create their own metaphors and are influenced by the metaphorical solutions that they themselves create. As they solve the problems of their fictional characters, they extend the solution to their own situation, which the fiction represents.

It is currently in the realm of directives that the most creative work, as well as the most interesting theorizing about interpersonal influence, is being done. The directives and theories can become so sophisticated that supervisors are protected from noticing that their efforts are often focused on banality and trivia, such as the problem of a 12-year-old who refuses to take out the garbage, or of spouses who quarrel over who will do the dishes. Therapists and teachers in the past dealt with mental illness and with emotional problems. In the present, perhaps because of our attempts to get away from the medical model, perhaps because of a need to drum up business for ourselves, we find that we are working more and more with banalities. Just as popular sitcoms deal with trivia—little everyday problems that are cheerfully resolved by the characters in shows such as "Three's Company," "Family Ties," and "The Cosby Show"—so also do therapists deal with the normal difficulties of living related to the stages of development of family life.

What is normal is important for television. A program is successful if it portrays what is currently normal in the culture. Similarly, a teacher of therapy is concerned with normality and must be constantly in tune with what is normal in the culture, so that student therapists can adjust to that "normality" and can in turn help their clients to do the same. Cultural norms come to us through the mass media, so that culture determines what television will portray as normal and television tells us what we should tell our families is normal, except for the problem of censorship.

Hollywood used to produce only musical comedies, romances, or police dramas because there was an implicit rule that the mass media should not discuss certain ideas or make certain issues explicit. Apart from constraints on the subject matter, there were also constraints as to what moral could be derived from a story. For example, it used to be that nobody could be portrayed stealing and not go to jail. Gradually, other unhappy endings became possible, and script writers were able to arrange imaginatively for the thief to die in an accident, or become maimed for life, or lose the woman he loved.

Censorship both in entertainment and in therapy is primarily self-imposed. Explicit rules and regulations are not necessary, but a healthy fear of financial ruin is useful. A television show might be taken off the air; a therapist might be sued for malpractice. Our freedom to decide what should be done in a therapy is sometimes determined more by the apprehensiveness of a therapist concerned about malpractice suits than by the particular needs of a client.

Family therapy has its own shows and its own microcosmos of mass media. Just as the sitcom presents its own abbreviated version of life, so we edit our videotapes and present our own abbreviated, censored version of therapy to the large crowds that come to our workshops for training. Those of us who provide training for large groups of students must often create training materials in the form of videotapes that have to be as entertaining as television shows, lest we lose the attention of our students. Errors, hesitations, and instructions from the supervisor are edited out, and students admire the smoothness and intelligence of therapists who are becoming performers as they grow accustomed to carrying out instructions from behind the one-way mirror. Just like the director and the actor, supervisor and therapist are lost without each other. The supervisor's instructions can make a timid therapist appear bold or a boring therapist hilarious, and the final edit of a videotape can make a rambling therapist look intelligent and precise.

The interest of the audience determines the success of the show, and there is no question that family therapy is quite a show. More than 7,000 people attended the "Evolution of Psychotherapy" conference sponsored by the Erickson Foundation in 1985. I know of no other field of scientific endeavor that attracts an audience turnout worthy of a rock concert or a political rally. This is a unique phenomenon of therapy in our times.

In the old days, music and therapy were live and could only be enjoyed on stage or through audio recordings. Today, with clever marketing, the endless technological improvements carried out behind the closed doors of the studio result in pop videos available for rent or for purchase. A whole new market has opened.

With the "Live Aid" benefit concert, rock and roll became a major political force, bridging the lack of communication between nations and making us all one big family. Just as rock music has broadened its audience, so have we. Some therapists are now admitting the general public to their workshops, since they also deserve to be enlightened. Perhaps this is what the future holds. We are truly entering the world of real entertainment.

11
NO MORE JOHN WAYNE: STRATEGIES FOR CHANGING THE PAST

with Ingrid Keim, Genine Lentine, and James P. Keim

If she can take it, I can take it. Play it, Sam.

— *Rick Blair (Humphrey Bogart) in* Casablanca.

OUR LIVES ARE stories and we are both characters and authors of our plots. However, unlike authors, who have the license to discard a first draft, to eliminate characters, or to rewrite dialogue, we have little power to revise our lives once the present has receded into the past. We cannot retrospectively change an event, but we can "change" the past by changing the representation of it through the stories we tell about our lives. When we narrate an event from our personal archives, we have the license to present ourselves in any light we wish, changing details here and there to effect a variety of presentations of self. Narratives about our lives are offered to impress, to elicit sympathy, to make the other feel superior, to build solidarity, to ask for help, or as a metaphor for another message.

By telling stories about ourselves we assume authorship over our lives. The process of authorship consists of choosing what we want others to know about our experiences, constructing a coherent version of the past by selecting information, and organizing and presenting this sequence of experience in a particular style. As people tell stories about themselves, they construct versions of events that provide ways of understanding what has happened to them and communicating this understanding to others. Motivations, causes, explanations, and interpretations are offered as part of the narrative.

Given this power to revise our lives by retelling, we are understandably hesitant to yield this power to another author—hence the typical discomfort of listening to someone else telling an anecdote from our lives. Authorship is claimed with varying degrees of intensity, depending on the context in which the telling takes place. A story from one's life may be offered to a friend or acquaintance when he or she has no information or power to change the story. The telling of the story may take place in a context of sympathy and support or disapproval and criticism. In either case, this kind of interlocutor accepts the story as such and does not attempt to change it.

At the other extreme is the context of therapy, where the teller offers the story to the therapist to be changed by interpretations, attribution of motivations, change of emphasis, causal explanations, etc. In therapy the client relinquishes authorship over his or her life story to the therapist with the hope that it will be changed for the better. Sometimes a client in therapy refuses to relinquish authorship. Instead he or she tells the story with the purpose of eliciting sympathy and support or of justifying questionable actions. A story may also be used to convince the therapist to influence relatives or a spouse to accept the client's version of certain events.

Related to the idea of authorship are the concepts of personal and family myths. Since the time of Freud, psychotherapy has been fascinated by concepts of myths. In 1963, Ferreira's paper "Family Myths and Homeostasis" sparked much interest in this subject. In his paper, Ferreira described the function of family myths in simplifying and distorting reality. Family myths have been much discussed in the literature (Berne, 1978; Ferreira, 1963, 1966; Lederer and Jackson, 1968; Selvini Palazzoli, Boscolo, Cecchin, and Prata, 1978; Paolino and McCrady, 1978; Sager, 1976; Steiner, 1974), and currently, most models of family therapy employ a concept of family myths and/or legends (Bagarozzi and Anderson, 1989; Byng-Hall, 1982).

We have chosen to use the term "legend" to describe certain distorted perceptions of reality that some of the above authors might refer to as myths (the term legend shall later be better defined). The concept of multiple possible realities described by Minuchin and Fishman (1981) has been of particular interest to us. They say:

> A family coming to therapy presents only their narrowed perception of reality. . . . They want the therapist to repair and polish their accustomed functioning, and then hand it back to them, as it were, essentially unchanged. Instead, the therapist, a creator of worlds, will offer the family another reality.

Madanes (1981, 1984, Chapter 2 of this book) describes various strategies for changing the drama of a family through pretending techniques and for changing the genre from tragedy to comedy and the theme from violence to love through the use of humor.

In the pages that follow we examine the significance of personal narratives—telling stories about our lives—in face-to-face interaction. To illustrate the dynamics of personal narratives we present two examples, one from fiction, Woody Allen's film *Manhattan*, and one from the therapy of a couple. Our discussion assumes that the process of authorship takes place on two levels: a stylistic level at which the teller manipulates the presentation and content of a story through a variety of verbal techniques, and an interactive level at which the telling of a story in a particular way and by a particular person affects the status of the relationship between the teller and the listeners.

Basic characteristics of a story may change if it is told many times. Usually, a particular story is selected for frequent retelling because it contains important information about the teller. The story may represent a preferred view of the past and may be the vehicle for a favorite presentation of self, even though the content of the story, the style in which it is told, and the significance of the narrative may undergo a variety of transformations as it is repeated.

There are different kinds of stories with different levels of significance. Some stories are best described as legends to be told over and over again, to be shared by family members, or to be the object of dispute: Who has the correct version of the legend? Certain legends and the disputes surrounding them may become so commonplace in a family that the legend may even be given a title, such as "The Legend of Grandfather's Whorehouse," with grandchildren arguing for years over whether (a) a whorehouse existed and their grandfather owned it; (b) the story was made up by enemies of the family to malign their grandfather; (c) their grandfather rented a property to someone who, unbeknownst to him, opened a whorehouse.

Although all legends are essentially stories, legends are different from other kinds of stories in various ways. A legend is a story that:

1. Has been repeated many times;
2. Is a relatively vague and imprecise account of events that took place in the past;
3. Contains facts that are not easily subject to verification or contestability, and/or contestability of such facts is rendered irrelevant by the significance of the story (see 5 below);
4. Has its meaning in either (a) the way in which the literal content is significant to the life (or lives) of the teller(s), or (b) the communicative purpose and effect of telling the story within a given interaction;
5. Contains literal content that is less important than its "meaning" and what it reveals about the teller as well as the other people depicted in the story.

When a story has become a legend, a struggle over its authorship may become central to a person's life, taking place in many different ways and involving various people. In the movie *Manhattan*, the protagonist struggles unsuccessfully to retain authorship over a significant event in his life. In the example from marital therapy, the spouses disagree over the significance of a legend involving the husband. By manipulating the authorship of the legend on both a stylistic and an interactive level, the therapist is able to successfully change the nature of this legend and thus change the effect that this legend has on the relationship between the husband and wife.

Manhattan

Woody Allen's film *Manhattan* is punctuated by various retellings of one incident. When one traces the development of this incident in the film, it is apparent how it ceases to be an objective event and takes on the status of legend, as the protagonist attempts to represent the event in the way most flattering to himself and becomes considerably anxious when others usurp his authorial power.

The incident in question involves the main character, Ike, his ex-wife, Jill, and her lover, Connie. Ike allegedly "tried to run over Connie with a car." There are a few objective or agreed upon facts surrounding the event: It was dark; it was raining; a car with Ike at the wheel came close to hitting Connie. These basic facts are present in most of the retellings of the event. In the movie, the incident has become a legend, as characters begin to talk of it in a language used to speak about pieces of literature. The transition from event to story to a legend which can be treated as an entity unto itself is symbolically underlined by the fact that Ike's ex-wife is in fact turning the events of their marriage into a book. In the following example Ike and Jill are talking about her book.

Ike: You're gonna put all the details in the book, right?
Jill: (interrupting) No, I'm not gonna dwell on the part where you tried to run her over with a car.

In this exchange, Ike is reluctant to accept his ex-wife's terms, which reduce him to a character in a story of which she is the author. However, for Jill, his life has clearly become a story, as she refers to the event under discussion as a "part." In the following exchange between two of Ike's friends, Mary's question to Yale also reveals a tendency to treat the incident as a literature-like legend:

Mary: Did you hear the one where he tried to run her lover over?
Yale: Oh, yeah.

Mary does not say, "Did you hear about the time when he tried to run her over?" in the way one might refer to an event which has not become a legend. Rather, "the one" characterizes the incident not as a thing that happened but as something that is told. This reorientation of a story away from its content, an actual event, and towards its role as a thing to be told is characteristic of stories that have become legends.

In the film, Ike, acting as author, constructs a story out of his life in order to make it coherent and to mitigate his own responsibility. The process of authorship involves the speaker's manipulation of the details of a narrative. As author the speaker is accountable for the meaning of the utterance. By the way he chooses to offer an account of an incident, a speaker is able to impart structure, coherence, and a sense of motivation upon a world of events which are, in themselves, rarely clear-cut and accessible. In the following exchange, Ike and Mary have just met and are discussing Ike's reason for his divorce and his reaction to it.

Mary: Well, okay, tell me, why'd you get a divorce?
Ike: Why?
Mary: Yeah.
Ike: I got a divorce because my ex-wife left me for another woman. Okay?
Mary: Really?
Ike: M-hm.
Mary: God, that must've been really demoralizing.
Ike: (shrugging) Tsch. Well I don't know, I thought I took it rather well under the circumstances.
Mary: (still reacting, shaking her head) Phew-wee.
Ike: I tried to run 'em both over with a car.

In this exchange Ike tells Mary about the incident as a way of explaining how he felt when his wife left him for a woman. He categorically tells Mary that he tried to run his ex-wife and her lover over with a car. The agent in this sentence is clearly Ike. In the following exchange, Ike uses his authorial power of manipulation to change the story. In this exchange, Ike, Mary, and Yale are discussing Jill's book, and Mary brings up the story that Ike had told her earlier.

Mary: Did you hear the one where he tried to run her—her lover over?

Yale: (looking at Mary) Oh, yeah,
Ike: (to Mary) Whose side are you on?
Mary: (looking at Ike) What do you mean?
Ike: (ignoring Mary's question) No, I didn't try and run her over. It
    was raining out. The car lurched. Jesus, now everybody in
    town is gonna know all—

Here Ike mitigates his agency for the action and responds to Mary's comment as if she had betrayed him by uttering it. In a sense, she does betray him by giving voice to this story, which undermines his reputation. She also betrays his confidence by retelling a story that he had told her in another context. She is usurping authorship by choosing to repeat it. She repeats it in exactly the same way, but Ike responds to her as if she changed it somehow. By telling Ike's story (to fulfill her own communicative goals), and thus assuming authorship of his life, Mary does not significantly change the overt form of the story; rather, what she changes is the context and Ike's license to present his own story to a new audience in a way he designs. Ike revises her version of it by saying that he in fact did not try to run Connie over. He attributes the alleged attempt to other agents: the rain, the car ("the car lurched").

    Throughout the film, Ike manipulates the telling of the story in order to achieve various desired presentations of himself and of the events in the story. With such delicate processes of manipulation possible, it is no wonder that Ike becomes uneasy at the prospect of having his ex-wife retell his story. In the following passage, Ike has stopped Jill on the street to question her about her intentions to write a book about their marriage. He goes on to plead with her not to write the book.

Ike: Hey, don't write this book. It's a humiliating experience.
Jill: It's an honest account of our breakup.
Ike: Jesus, everybody that knows us is gonna know everything.
Jill: Look at you, you're so threatened.

Jill's book, which is to be published, sold and read, represents her ultimate play for authorship. To Ike, it represents an ultimate loss of authorial power over his own life. Hearing one's story told to others by someone else is perhaps one of life's most vulnerable positions. When someone else assumes authorship, the power of the subject, who is reduced to a character, is usurped, and the subject no longer has the power to manipulate details. The character is completely at the mercy of the author. When the author is malevolent, or even ambivalent, this prospect is particularly frightening, because just as an author has the power to manipulate details to his own advantage, to put himself in the best possible light, so a malevolent author treating the subject as figure has the power to manipulate the details to put the figure in an unflattering light. Even an ambivalent author attempting to portray the subject objectively, without shadings, usurps a subject's power. There are few situations where we willingly hand over authorship of our lives to others.

In *Manhattan*, Ike is on his way to regaining control of his life when he decides to go back to writing one of his own short stories. Authoring a story based on his life, Ike is again in the powerful position of being at once a figure, author and principal. Throughout the film the process of writing and publishing is symbolic of power and control. The film in fact begins with the voice of Ike as he explores ways of representing himself by testing out different openings for his novel. He is demonstrating the process whereby we consider different versions of stating the same story in order to present a suitable picture of ourselves.

Ike: "Chapter One. He adored New York City. He idolized it all out of proportion." Uh, no, make that: "He—he romanticized it all out of proportion. Now . . . to him . . . no matter what the season was, this was still a town that existed in black and white and pulsated to the great tunes of George Gershwin." Ahh, now let me start this over. "Chapter One. He was too romantic about *Manhattan* as he was about everything else. He thrived on the hustle . . . bustle of the crowds and the traffic."

In this passage, Ike takes the same characteristics and molds them into different descriptions. At first the character is agreeably romantic; then he is romantic to the detriment of all else. The difference between these two versions is merely the slant of the perspective. Ike continues to try out perspectives with alternate openings:

Ike: "Chapter One. He adored New York City, although to him, it was a metaphor for the decay of contemporary culture. How hard it was to exist in a society desensitized to drugs, loud music, television, crime, garbage." Too angry. I don't want to be angry. . . . "Chapter One. He was as tough and romantic as the city he loved. Behind his black-rimmed glasses was the coiled sexual power of a jungle cat." I love this. "New York was his town. And it always would be."

Considering different versions of his story, Ike takes part in a deliberate effort to slant his presentation of self. Writing a story requires more of a conscious design than telling a narrative spontaneously in personal conversation, but nevertheless, the processes are the same and serve the same purpose.

In *Annie Hall*, Woody Allen's main character also refers to authorial power in the lines, "What do you want? It was my first play. You know, you know how you're always trying to get things to come out perfect in art because it's real difficult in life." This type of authorial power is not confined only to art as it is defined in this quotation, but is also operative in the art produced by speakers in the form of discourse narratives. Authorial power is exercised whenever there is an opportunity to provide a representation of an event in place of the event itself.

No More John Wayne: The Therapy of a Couple

Much of the communication in therapy has to do with past events that the clients present as determining the present and the future. Often a therapist needs to change the clients' version of the past so that the present and the future may change. As in *Manhattan*, the central issue in many therapies is the struggle to arrive at an acceptable version of one's life. In the following transcript of a marital therapy, two spouses offer stories about their lives and the therapist changes these stories.

A wife called the institute asking for marital therapy. She said that the problem was that her husband was more physical and she was more spiritual and that he was homosexual. She had recently been disturbed by finding a pile of male pornography magazines in the basement. The couple had been married 15 years and had three children, two boys and a girl.

The therapist was Richard Belson, a middle-aged man with a strong New York accent. As the supervisor, Cloé Madanes sat behind a one-way mirror and called the therapist with instructions over a direct telephone line.

In the first session, husband and wife, John and Jane, appeared very attractive, intellectual and charming. They avoided the issue of the husband's alleged homosexuality and talked about communication difficulties, intellectual interests, and how the husband was more physical and the wife more spiritual. At one point the therapist abruptly asked the husband: "What is it that your wife does not pay enough attention to that binds the two of you together in a fierce kind of way?"

This question aims at eliciting a particular kind of story from the clients. It takes for granted that there is a strong, passionate (fierce) bind. It capitalizes on the information that the husband is more physical and the wife more spiritual (it is the wife who does not pay enough attention to the fierce bind) and gambles on the possibility that what the spouses are trying to say is that the husband wants sex more frequently than the wife. Instead of asking, "Do you have a sexual problem?" which would put emphasis on the difficulties of the marriage, he emphasizes togetherness and harmony, setting the tone for a therapy focused on bringing out the positive.

Belson: What is it that your wife does not pay enough attention to that binds the two of you together in a fierce kind of way?

John: Sex is something that binds married people together. And Jane and I have very different sexual needs. My sexual needs seem to overwhelm her at times.

Belson: How is that?

John: Well, I kind of view myself as being a typical male, and as a result — well, two things. I think it's legitimate to say my sexual needs are far more material, that is to say physical, than they're spiritual, and Jane's tend to be far more spiritual than they are physical.

Belson: (smiling in a teasing way) What's a spiritual sexual need? You mean like a lot of intercourse?

John: No, quite the contrary. I think, put in oversimplistic terms, my sexual needs are more purely physical, that is to say animal, not sex-crazed animal but just —

Belson: Are you a sex-crazed animal? (laughing)

John: I hope not. I don't think so. (laughs) Without the kind of, you know — it's an old conflict between men and women — without the kind of gentleness and lovemaking that isn't as physical. Jane would prefer a more gentle, spiritual person who isn't just interested in getting his rocks off!

Belson: Do the two of you have sexual relations?

John: Oh yeah!

Belson: How many times a day do you usually make love?

John: A day? You didn't mean a day. (laughter) Is that a joke?

Belson: A joke? I'm dead serous.

Jane: Five. When we were first married.

Belson: So that you were reaching five, you never went beyond five?

Jane: A day?

Belson: A day.

Jane: No, not when we were first married. That was enough. I —

Belson: Five was your peak?

Jane: It was more than my peak!

Belson: What do you mean — "more than your peak"? I thought that you were a Swedish Irish?

Jane: I'm more interested in reading. (laughs)

Belson: You can read while you make love too.

Jane: No you can't.

Belson: You never wrote poetry? You recited poetry.

Jane: I might have recited poetry.

John: You certainly wrote poetry about lovemaking.

Belson: That's right. Have you saved those poems?

Jane: I don't know. I have to go back and look.

Belson: So you reached five times a day.

Jane: That was on our honeymoon. And I was pissed.

Belson: You mean, even when you were angry you went up to five. If you were in love you could imagine what would have happened.

Jane: I thought I was pretty nice. We were in Europe and we were at the Salzburg Festival and Mozart was playing and I was looking at the pension's ceiling and I kept thinking, "We're in Europe! We can do this in America."

Belson: Let's go on just to make sure I'm on the right track. You were saying, how many times a day did you reach? Do you remember five, too?

John: That seems excessive. I would say an average—

Jane: This is a Woody Allen movie!

Belson: What do you mean?

Jane: It's *Annie Hall*. Don't you remember—did you see *Annie Hall*? The split screen. "How many times do you make love?" And she says, "Three times a week—so often I can't stand it." And he says, "Never enough—two or three times a week."

Belson: Do you like Woody Allen, incidentally? Do you?

Jane: Very much.

Belson: So both of you like Woody Allen. So that happens to be an important sign in terms of a relationship.

Jane: I bet it does. (points to husband) I like him. I mean, you know—

Belson: Well, that's very clear. Any two people who like Woody Allen always like each other; it's a mathematical, rational equation. In fact, logic has indicated that psychologically.

John: I don't remember numbers as high as that, but we're talking about, you know, the first six to twelve months of a marriage and it's normal for people to taper off—

Belson: It took you a whole, almost a whole year to taper off from five!

Jane: Five years.

John: Five years?

Jane: He told me that if you didn't have an orgasm every day it wasn't good for your health. So I believed him! For five years I believed him.

Belson: So you were making love five times a day?

John: Once a day.

Jane: No, no, it was after we had been married five years we got down to once a day. It was in the morning before you went to work and when you came home after school.

John: Really? Scandalous.

Jane: And then in the evening. John, after you finished studying.

John: But it was always enjoyable, I think.

Belson: Was it enjoyable for him?

Jane: For him I think so, yes.

Belson: Was she orgasmic?

John: Yes.

The therapist had been correct in assuming that there was something that bound the couple together in a fierce kind of way. The therapist's question elicited a story that perhaps had never been expressed in this way, about the husband's "typically male" heterosexual interests and about his heterosexual prowess. Before the husband's alleged homosexuality is even mentioned in the session, he has defined himself as heterosexual and very interested in his wife. After this positive framework has been established, the therapist continues.

Belson: What is the secret of your problem? Why don't you give me a hint of what the real problem is? (to husband) What would you say is the secret that she hasn't said?

John: One of the overwhelming problems, and Jane knew this when she married me is that I'm homosexual. Or at least I was a practicing homosexual in Boston.

Belson: When you got married?

John: When I lived in Boston I was in the life, and then I decided that was just a foolish whim. So I came back to Philadelphia, finished up my degree, met Jane, fell in love with her and married her, convinced that it was the right thing to do and that that part of my past which was adolescent and not productive would be left behind me.

Belson: Why was it adolescent and not productive?

John: Well, certainly the way I was living and the way most of my friends were living. It was a kind of hedonistic and adolescent way and the sexuality of our lives was all that was talked about. It's as if I knew people and all they ever talked about

was baseball, and even though they were bright and interesting they couldn't talk about any other subject. You know, this
relates to this rational thing. I have, during my life, made
some very difficult but very rational decisions about what I
want to do and this was one of them. The business about
being gay didn't really bother me, except off and on, until
very recently. (to wife) Within the past year?

Jane: Before that. You started talking about the fact that it was
torturing you.

John: And it creates problems because it's still there, seething in
my breast.

The husband's story about his homosexuality is best understood
as a legend primarily because, for reasons that will be discussed
later, the significance of the story does not reside in its validity.
This story is perhaps the most crucial legend in the life of the
couple, and the husband tells it using the strongest possible language. He describes the problem as "overwhelming," he says that
he is a "homosexual," that he was a "practicing homosexual in
Boston," he depicts himself as having been "in the life," and says
that his homosexuality is "still there seething in my breast." At a
later point in the interview the therapist learns that the husband
had never in fact had an orgasm in a homosexual relation. As John
and Jane discuss his homosexual "life" in Boston, it becomes in-
creasingly unclear to what extent he was ever a homosexual at all.
It is also evident that he provokes and threatens his wife with his
alleged homosexuality, making statements such as, "It's still there
seething in my breast." He has also decided to refuse her sexually
until he resolves this issue of his homosexual impulses.

The hypothesis of the supervisor is that there must be a power
imbalance in the marriage, that the husband must be in an inferior
position to the wife in some way, that she must be putting him
down in a way that has become intolerable, and that he retaliates
by punishing her with threats of homosexuality. These threats are a
source of power for the husband, since they humiliate the wife and
threaten the marriage, but they are also a source of weakness, since
in our society it is not considered a strong position for a husband
and father to be homosexual. From the point of view of the wife,
the husband's alleged homosexuality puts her in a position of pow-

er as the one in the couple who is not conflicted sexually, but the tacit threat that he might become involved with a man is humiliating and weakening. An incongruous hierarchy is defined in the couple's relationship, where the husband's homosexuality is simultaneously a source of power and weakness for both spouses.

The husband presents little factual evidence for his homosexuality and no accounts of particular events during his allegedly homosexual period. Rather, the part of the story pertaining to his homosexuality is told in a vague, general manner with no specific details, despite his use of decisive language. It appears that this story is not told with the intention of communicating an event or set of events which occurred at a given time; rather, the husband seems to tell this story for the sole purpose of presenting himself as a homosexual. The validity of the facts in the story, or that there be any facts at all, is irrelevant to the intention of the story. In contrast, in what follows, the wife's story about finding a box of pornography is told for the purpose of informing the therapist of the event which eventually led the couple to seek therapy at this particular institute.

Jane: When it finally came to a head was when I went down to the cellar quite innocently one time to look for a paint brush and found a huge box of homosexual pornography and confronted him about it. He got very upset and wept and said it wasn't something that he wanted to do. I had been in group therapy with Mary O'Donnell for a year and a half. I don't know if you know her or not, she works out of Our Church of the Savior. So I called her up and I said, "What am I supposed to do?"

Belson: Does she save homosexuals?

Jane: I don't know; that's just the office she works out of. I called her up and I said, "You know, it's kind of upsetting and it offends me. I mean, any kind of pornography offends me. I don't know why, it just does."

Belson: Well, YOU don't have to like it.

Jane: Yeah, I don't like it. But I don't mind if he—he can go to dirty movies if he wants, it doesn't bother me, that's his business. She [her therapist] just laughed and said, "Oh, he's been waiting for you to find that box for a long time. You just haven't found it in time!" That felt a lot better, but she said, "You really have got to—you know, this is an opportunity for growth for both of you and you really should go see if you can find some help." And she recommended this institute.

The wife's story about finding the box of homosexual pornography is a good example of a story that has not yet become a legend. This story is different from a legend in the following ways:

1. It is a relatively precise account of an event that took place.
2. It is open to factual verification and contestable in part because it is relatively detailed—it could be described as anecdotal.
3. The meaning of the story resides in its literal content.

The conversation with the therapist continues:

Jane: And she recommended this institute.
Belson: This institute? You mean as a cure for pornography?
Jane: No, no, as a cure for working on the relationship, because there are a lot of other areas we haven't talked about. Like willpower. I feel his will is not very strong. He sets out to do things and he doesn't finish them, endlessly. He doesn't have much strength of will in pursuing his career so we live on very little.
Belson: So that money is an issue between the two of you?
Jane: It's a terrible problem.
Belson: You know, I wanted to ask you what is it that you're worried about? Are you worried that, for example, there is another man in his life now?
Jane: No, that doesn't really worry me. I kind of freed myself of that kind of anxiety. I had to. I had to do a lot of inner work on that one. And let him live his own life.
Belson: Are you worried that he might have an affair?
Jane: No, I think it's because I worry about the stance for my children.
Belson: Are you worried that he'll leave you for another man?
Jane: I have to be honest and say it's crossed my mind. I think about it. I have thought of ways to be financially independent if that should occur, because I feel that that would be the last

straw for my children. I do feel that would not have to be necessarily the end of the marriage but it has been something I've been very aware of.

Belson: Have you asked him about what his intentions are?

Jane: Yes, I have, and he said he had no intentions of doing that and I think he doesn't.

Belson: Was that reassuring to you?

Jane: Yes. But I also am a realist in the sense that I know that people sometimes follow their peckers places they never intended. I've seen it happen to other friends and in other marriages, especially at this age.

The supervisor's hypothesis had been that the husband was using his alleged homosexuality as a source of power over the wife in order to balance his lack of power in other important areas. As the interview progresses, the wife provides information as to what these areas may be. She criticizes him for lacking willpower and for not making enough money; also, she appears concerned that he might be both a bad influence on the children and a threat to their well-being because of his homosexuality. She has probably blocked him from relating to his children. It can be hypothesized that the husband responds to the wife's fears and criticism with further threats of homosexuality, which in turn increases her fears, and so they escalate. Later in the interview a strategy was formulated to end this escalation and to restore the husband's position in the hierarchy as a father to his children.

Belson: Are you aware of the clinical definition of homosexual?

John: Probably not.

Belson: Would you mind if I tell you?

John: Sure.

Belson: A homosexual is someone who practices sexual relations with a man.

John: Mhm.

Belson: Are you?

John: No.

Belson: I don't want to argue with him any further. (to wife) Anyway, are you aware of the fact that that's the definition of a homosexual?

Jane: That's how I always felt about it. And even for all his hang-
ing around the gay people when I first met him, he had never
had an orgasm in a homosexual relationship. And at that
time I had gone through a lot of adolescent readjustment
crises, real crises, from when I was 19 to 22. I was then seeing
a psychiatrist and he encouraged me to develop this relationship with John because he didn't believe that John was a
homosexual. I was very hesitant at first because we had — how
we met was very interesting. We had an English teacher at the
university who had him in one class and me in the other. And
she felt we should meet each other and had us for dinner. So
that there were all these connections in our lives intellectually
and a lot of other connections. I mean, we both love the
ocean and we both like to do things with our hands. And we
had a lot of things that connected us when we first met and
were married. And I never felt that that was really as big an
issue for him as he felt it was. And then after we had been
married a while it seemed that it was more of an issue for him
than I had thought and I think part of the reason I married
him was because, you know, I was raised a very religious
Catholic and you know you're always supposed to save someone and this was a kind of form of ultimate salvation that
probably appealed to me a lot.

Belson: You mean to save a man.

Jane: To save a man from this kind of horrible life — which he
described as a horrible life!

Belson: What did you want to marry her to save her from?

John: Going crazy.

Belson: Going crazy over you?

John: Going crazy.

Belson: That's a metaphor, going crazy. Going crazy is people go
crazy for love.

John: Literally. Jane was, when I first met her, a very emotionally
distraught young woman with great — wonderful — qualities
and I saw the wonderful qualities being damaged by her emotional instability. And I discovered that her feelings toward me
were sufficient that I could make her see the good side of
herself and not give in to the bad side. And while I married
her for a lot of reasons, one of the things that was in my mind

· 235 ·

was that here's—I guess I've never articulated this before. I didn't think, "Here's someone I could save," the way Jane felt about me, but I certainly felt that, "Here is someone who has got some wonderful qualities and if she doesn't marry me or someone like me the bad side of her is going to destroy her life."

Belson: It's really very touching what he just said to you. He's very spiritual.

Jane: I think he is. I've always thought so.

So far in this first interview the spouses have related the following legends in chronological order:

1. *The homosexuality legend*: The husband's account of his homosexuality and his homosexual "life" in Boston.

2. *The psychiatrist's encouragement legend*: The wife tells of her psychiatrist's encouragement of the relationship to show that she had never believed he was really a homosexual and that her psychiatrist had not thought so either.

3. *The legend of how they first met*: They were introduced by an English teacher and they had many interests in common.

4. *The saving of the husband legend*: The wife describes how, being raised a very religious Catholic, part of the reason she married her husband was to save him from being a homosexual.

5. *The wife's craziness legend*: The husband's extended version of how the wife was about to go crazy when they first met had he not saved her. This includes an allusion to the wife's version of the psychiatrist's encouragement legend.

The therapist has responded by opposing many of the basic features of the legends as they are presented. His responses can be viewed as a series of counter-interpretations or counter-tellings of the legends. The following are examples of the ways in which the therapist counters the couple's legends.

1. Challenging the clinicality of the problem

a. Jane: (referring to her previous therapist) So I called her up and said, "What am I supposed to do?"
   Belson: Does she save homosexuals?

b. Jane: And she recommended this institute.
  Belson: This institute? You mean as a cure for pornography?
2. Challenging factual validity
Belson: A homosexual is someone who practices sexual relations with a man. Are you?
3. Random playful challenging
(The husband has just said he married the wife to save her from going crazy.)
Belson: That's a metaphor, going crazy. Going crazy is people go crazy for love. (The therapist is not willing to accept the pathological characterization of the wife.)

As the conversation continues, the therapist incorporates the couple's legends into a new legend about success and accomplishment.

Belson: You know, clearly he's very spiritual and you're very sexual, but I want to. . . . I think by the way that you have succeeded, and I think that you have too. I think that one of the great erotic fantasies of a woman is to save a man from, supposedly, his homosexuality, which he wasn't, though he had these thoughts and feelings. It's a very exciting thing for a woman —
Jane: It is.
Belson: — to do this. And I think that you (to husband) have succeeded because you have been living together — how long?
Jane: Fifteen years.
Belson: Fifteen years you've managed to save him!
Jane: Well, we've been living together longer than that —
Belson: And I think that you have saved her because clearly your wife is a mature and kind and well-put-together woman and I think that you have succeeded in doing that.

Belson succeeds in changing the spouses' legend about their lives. In contrast, in the film *Manhattan*, Ike not only cannot get his ex-wife, his girlfriend, or his friend to agree on his version of his life, but also cannot change the legend that they have constructed. Belson works on changing the husband's and wife's stories about their own lives. Ike works on changing other people's stories about *his* life. Ike attempts to take charge of his life. Belson attempts to take charge of his clients' lives. Ike works on his own behalf; Belson works on the couple's behalf.

Because the couple has, after all, sought therapy, there is a sense that any account of the past presented as directly or indirectly leading to this moment is an account of failure. In the above section the therapist manages to retell some of the legends elicited from the couple in such a way as to ensure that these will be perceived as stories about success.

The therapist goes on to ask what it is that they want to solve in the present.

Belson: What is your current problem? What is it that's wrong now? What is it that you want to do now that you're not doing? I'd like to ask each one of you that. What is it that you want next week?

Jane: I want more rhythm in the day for the children.

Belson: More rhythm in the day for the children? That sounds very sexual. You want more rhythm; you mean you want more sex from him?

Jane: No, I want him to be consistent with them and I want to be supported when I discipline them. Even if I'm too angry—at 5 o'clock mothers are very tired. I want him, when he agrees to do something, to do it. And if the children are supposed to be in bed at 9 o'clock—see, I work three nights a week, I'd like to see them be washed when I come home and asleep in their beds with their teeth brushed, having had a story read to them in a way that I know is best. Also, all last year I would say, "Let's go out and do something," and he didn't want to go anywhere. He never wants to do anything except go to this Irish bar and drink.

In the middle of the conversation about the husband's homosexuality, the wife changes the subject in an abrupt and unexpected way to issues of child-rearing (more rhythm for the children, having their teeth brushed, etc). She also shifts to the characteristic complaints of lack of intimacy (he never wants to go anywhere). The association between the husband's homosexuality, the children, and their lack of intimacy indicated to the supervisor that the original hypothesis had been correct. The husband's position as a father to his children had to be restored if he was to be once more a husband to his wife. The wife's associations served to suggest what the intervention should be. The husband confirmed this hypothesis even further with his next statement.

Belson: What do you want from her?

John: I think Jane spreads herself too thin. Too many activities—work related, social. I don't want to use the word compulsive, because I don't think it's a compulsion, but she's always doing something. She's not as relaxed maybe as I am. We just had two weeks of vacation. It was wonderful. It was one of those ideal vacations. We really had a good time. And Jane did something very interesting. Well, I'm getting away from the answer to your question, but Jane did something interesting. She let me assume a lot of responsibility for things that she normally would have done, especially with the kids, in scheduling events and stuff like that and, you know, it worked out very nicely.

The husband's statement that it was an ideal vacation because his wife let him assume responsibility for the children further confirms that this is what he wants and needs. It is necessary to arrange for the wife to stop protecting the children from him so that he can be closer to them and feel fulfilled as a father. The therapist proceeds to instruct the couple along these lines, instructing the wife to allow her husband to be in charge of the children in exchange for having the husband be more attentive to her sexual needs.

Jane: What does HE have to agree to?

Belson: Aha. Okay. It did sound one-sided. I would like him to follow your own sexual needs. And he should be tuned in to that. Let him follow your own sexual desires in the next five weeks as a reward for that. So that, as you move out of his space he'll move correctly in and out of yours. (to husband) Would that be agreeable to you?

John: Sure.

Jane: I try to tell him what I like?

Belson: Directly or indirectly, but he will follow your own needs. In other words, you'll contract your space physically and materially. He'll expand his space spiritually so that he can be the father he doesn't need your help to be. He will then follow your space sexually according to your wishes. You can tell him directly or indirectly, and he agrees he said to do that. How does that sound? Would you agree to do that?

John: Yes.

Belson: Is that an agreement?

Jane: Mhm.

Belson: Okay, could the two of you shake on that?

John: Certainly, we can shake on that. (They shake hands.)

Jane: We haven't set up the fall schedule yet for the children. Does this mean I just don't say anything and let him set up the schedule?

Belson: I would say that it would probably be a good idea, just to give you a rest for a while. Put him in charge of the children for the next five weeks till we meet. That doesn't mean that you couldn't have some input, but let him make any final decisions necessary and that will give you a rest for five weeks.

Husband and wife left the session cheerfully. Obviously the husband had wanted to be closer to the children and the wife had wanted to resume their sexual relationship.

Five weeks later they came to a second session and reported remarkable changes. The husband had been successfully in charge of the children. The wife had been angry about this at first but then she was happy as they resumed their sex life. The husband had also taken over the family finances for the first time in the marriage. He took over a difficult task at work and had spoken in public at a large national meeting, which was something that had previously frightened him. The wife reported that he was much nicer to be with and much less critical of her.

At a third session four weeks later the therapist asked the husband:

Belson: This delusion that you had in the past of being a homosexual—

John: Now that I'm convinced—

Belson: You know, such thoughts will still linger a little bit as you come to the realization that it was a delusion and that you could be interesting to her apart from that. But did you have any thoughts about it during the month that you reported to her?

John: I don't think I reported it to her. But I disagree with you about your characterization of me as having a delusion of being homosexual. I may think about it a little, not as much as maybe two, three, four months ago.

Jane: You were obsessed with it in the spring time!

John: Well, obsessed with the conflict.

Jane: You talked about worrying about it all the time.

Belson: As you begin to give it up, is your wife going to find you an interesting person apart from this interesting thing about you?

John: Oh, yes.

Belson: Yeah, you're so sure?

John: Oh, absolutely.

Belson: Why are you so sure?

John: Because I'm an intriguing person.

Belson: You don't mind if I'm a little bit more cautious than you people? (to the wife) What part of his homosexuality do you think that you still want to keep?

Jane: Just his sensitivity I guess.

John: That has nothing to do with homosexuality.

Jane: It does, I think it does. I was thinking about it the other day, of what kind of men notice things like the way the woodwork is in a building and door knobs, and he notices things like that.

Belson: He notices even the kind of door knobs? That's very remarkable.

Jane: I know it is.

Once the husband's homosexuality had been accepted as a legend from the past it was time to transform it into a piece of fiction. Fictionalizing the past is an effective way of controlling and changing it. Among the various ways of changing a current characterization of a person, one is to make the characterization a thing of the past, another is to make it not only a thing of the past but a literary, or make-believe, characterization of the past. This is a second-order step into the realm of unreality. Looking back on our lives, it is difficult for us to decide what was true and what was real.

In Greece, a place famous for both its history and fiction, a tour guide once pointed at some fallen stones and said, "Those are the ruins of the house of Hercules." A timid tourist asked, "But wasn't Hercules a mythical character?" The guide answered, "In Greece fact and fiction are always intertwined." The same is true of our lives, and as important stories recede into the past and become legends, so they can change from legend to pure fiction depending on the emphasis and skill of the storyteller.

In the case of this couple, the supervisor called the therapist and suggested that this was an opportunity to change the whole situation into a piece of fiction by arguing that the husband's alleged homosexuality was nothing but a coverup for his macho brutality and exploitation of his innocent wife. That is, under the guise of his alleged homosexuality, the husband took advantage of the wife, materialistically, like a typical male, as John Wayne might do in one of his movies. The wife was deceived by his apparent sensitivity, which really covered his John Wayne brutality.

At the beginning of the first session, the husband had talked about how he was more physical while his wife was more spiritual and about how he was a typical male with a typically male approach to sexuality. The therapist is now able to use the husband's own words to reverse the meaning of the presenting problem. The issue no longer has to do with the husband's covert or true homosexuality. Now the issue is that all through the marriage the husband had used the threat of his alleged homosexuality to take advantage of his wife. The wife, who in the past had devoted herself to saving him from his homosexuality, could now devote herself to saving him from his macho, John Wayne brutality. An important pattern of the relationship of the couple is preserved. He needs to be reformed and saved, and she devotes herself to saving him. However, the homosexuality, which had become too painful and dysfunctional, no longer serves as the focus of the saving. Instead, the husband must now be saved from his macho brutality. With these instructions from the supervisor, the following dialogue ensued.

Belson: You know, once a problem starts to recede, sometimes you become aware that things are just the opposite of what you thought. And now that I see that you are getting ready with this ritual to say goodbye to his homosexuality, it becomes clearer what he's really about. The notion is that he can play behind the homosexual mask, he can play with the idea of being weak and effeminate and gushing over door knobs and other artifacts, when really his tendency is to be the opposite, a kind of John Wayne character, rough, aggressive and tyrannical.

Jane: He's been all those things.

Belson: That's right! So the problem is the opposite of what you brought in. He's being finally unmasked and the tyrant, the rough guy who doesn't know how to cherish, is coming out. Your problem is not to get rid of his effeminate homosexual nature. Your problem is the opposite. Your problem is to help him be more gentle.

Jane: I think so. With the children, too. You have this idea that you're very gentle but you're not, especially with the boys.

Belson: He's really a brute. That's what his problem is. It's finally emerged. Now you're faced with a more serious problem about how to bring some sensitivity and mellowness into him, how to make him more sensitive.

Jane: Well, it's not as though he's not sensitive —

Belson: For door knobs he's sensitive.

Jane: That's right.

Belson: That's right, for artifacts he's sensitive, but for human beings he's insensitive. He's like a macho man, that's what this guy is.

John: I can't sit here and go undefended.

Belson: What can you do to help bring some warmth and kindness into his heart? (to husband) Do you want to ask her for some help with this problem?

John: You're right for a large part what the two of you are saying, that I'm afraid to be loving and gentle.

Belson: (to wife) The thing is, he took advantage of you. He pretended to be, you know, a, quote, homosexual. He pretended to be a sensitive guy. You know, he could gush over door knobs and other artifacts. In effect he was hiding this very aggressive, brutish kind of nature. So he took you unawares and put you in a difficult position, because he's even stated the wrong problem to you. You've been worrying about how to get rid of the, quote, homosexuality, when the real problem is how to get rid of this macho masculinity.

Jane: He's got an artificial need for it.

Belson: No, it's not artificial. That's what he is. See, the game was that he was doing this as a defense for his homosexuality. I think it's just the other way around, that he fooled you and played games with you to convince you about this to hide his really brutish way of dealing with you and with other people.

Jane: He always said he deceived me, and I never believed him.

Belson: Well, now you know! I want to ask you, when you caress him, does that warm him? Sometimes these Wayne types warm up to a woman's touch.

The therapist goes on to suggest that they try an experiment in which the wife caresses the husband in order to observe how he reacts. The gesture leads to a discussion of how the husband has trouble responding to affection in any way that is not sexual.

Belson: You know, you can try different things. One way that I find sometimes helps—it's only one of a hundred different ways. Do they have a place in Philadelphia where you can make up T-shirts with slogans?

John: I'm sure they do.

Belson: It could say "no more John Wayne." Wear that. "No more John Wayne." (to wife) I think that, again, he could learn to control his passion and let it just be, you know, warmth. To get rid of this kind of—I mean it's terrible, it's a terrible quality in a man. That's what he's been fighting against himself. I don't think he wants to be like that forever, but it's a terrible quality, a certain ruthlessness towards women and children. (to husband) Why don't you decide right now what would be three things you could do that would be the expression of a more sensitive, delicate kind of feeling towards the other person and that you'd be willing to do on an ongoing basis in the coming month, and that would be an expression

not of a John Wayne kind of thing but of a more contemporary attitude?

John: One thing we used to do that I enjoyed is reading. I used to read to her, poetry, short stories.

Belson: So that would be one thing. What are two others?

The couple agreed on several activities that would bring out the husband's sensitive side. The therapy continued with a focus on improving the couple's relationship and on helping the husband to become more sensitive and considerate. They wrote a humorous one-act play that they read out loud in a session. The play was about the night they first met at their English professor's house. Interestingly, the film *Manhattan* opens with Ike fictionalizing his life by presenting himself as a legendary character in the story that he is writing, while the therapy "no more John Wayne" ends with the spouses fictionalizing their relationship by writing a play about their first meeting. This play is a new, humorous version of the homosexuality legend. In both the movie and the therapy, there is an objectification from oral narratives to concrete written pieces of fiction.

The No More John Wayne Strategy

Clients seeking therapy can be viewed as searching for a more comfortable version of their own lives, just as a movie producer unhappy over a scene in a script might look for a screen writer to revamp the scene and make it consistent with the rest of the movie or with the movie's desired outcome. The therapeutic process often involves giving up authorship over one's own personal story to a therapist. This rewriting of the client's personal scripts, this tem-porary taking over of the clients' authorship, we have dubbed the "no more John Wayne" strategy. It consists of the following stages:

1. The client(s) tell one or several stories from their past and the therapist listens carefully, discovering patterns, identifying themes, incorporating the language used by the clients and memorizing words and phrases that are discrepant with the

main theme being presented and that may be used in the future to rewrite the stories while still using the clients' own words.

2. The therapist expresses sympathy, understanding, respect, and appreciation of the clients. At the same time, the therapist makes several brief, friendly, sometimes humorous attempts at challenging or reframing the clients' stories. Questions are aimed at eliciting a particular kind of story and the therapist challenges the clinicality of a problem and/or its factual validity. These small reframings prepare the clients to accept major rewriting and other directives later in the therapy and give the therapist an idea of how best to influence the client(s).

3. The therapist makes an effort to understand the basic needs, desires, and deprivations in a person's life. The idea is that, if these deprivations can be resolved, problem behaviors will be abandoned. (In the case of Jane and John, the husband was being deprived of his position as a father to his children.)

4. The therapist offers a major rewriting of the clients' scripts.

5. The therapist gives directives aimed at aligning the clients' actions, thoughts, and feelings with the new story of their lives. These directives mainly invoke kindly actions, an essential aspect of the "no more John Wayne" strategy.

Skillful use of authorship requires that the new version of a story be more satisfying and clarifying than the version the therapist is trying to replace. When offered two different versions of a legend from respectable sources, a person will choose the one that explains events more comprehensively and in a more satisfying manner. The accepted version will be more consistent with the client's expectations of human behavior.

In addition, a new version presented by a therapist might offer a less painful way of perceiving a story. For example, a client might be encouraged to remember pleasant events from an otherwise painful childhood; the therapist might then inform this client that, if he can remember these few nice moments, there are many others that occurred that he is unable to remember. Not only would this new version of the client's childhood be a truer (all of us have experienced more happy moments than we can recall at any point in time) and more comprehensive version of the past, but it would also be a less painful way for the client to view his childhood.

Outside the context of therapy, a person might be just as likely to choose a less pleasant version of two legends. In *Manhattan*, the friends of Ike are offered both Ike's version of the car "accident" and his wife Jill's less pleasant version. Among the reasons that these friends choose Jill's is that it is more consistent with their expectations of human behavior (Ike's wife had left him for another woman) and with the theory that the breakup was so devastating that it drove Ike to date a 17-year-old girl. In the "no more John Wayne" case, an equally acceptable explanation of the husband's behavior was provided; in addition, the new story was more satisfactory because it empowered the wife and allowed the husband to think of himself in a more masculine manner.

If a therapist must have a theory of personality, then the most helpful one is that of an identity as a mental, abridged anthology of stories, any one of which can be replaced by a story from the total collection. Therapy thus involves editing the abridged edition of perceptions of the present and past. A change in these perceptions is a change in the personality, and a change of shared perceptions is a change in the relationship.

BIBLIOGRAPHY

Allen, W. (1982). *Four films of Woody Allen*. New York: Random House.

Barthes, R. (1966). *Critique et verite*. Paris: Seuil.

Bagarozzi, D. A. & Anderson, S. A. (1989). *Personal, marital, and family myths*. New York: Norton.

Berne, E. (1978). *Games people play*. New York: Ballantine.

Bradbury, R. (1951). The Veldt. *The illustrated man*, pp. 15–30. New York: Doubleday.

Byng-Hall, J. (1982). Family legends, their significance to the family therapist. In A. Bentovim (ed.) *Family therapy: Complementary frameworks of theory and practice, Vol. 1*. New York: Grune & Stratton.

Ferreira, A. (1963). Family myths and homeostasis. *Archives of general psychiatry, 9*, 457–463.

Ferreira, A. (1966). Family myths. *Psychiatric Research Reports of the American Psychiatric Association, 20*, 85–90.

Frankl, V. (1960). Paradoxical intention: A logotherapeutic technique. *American Journal of Psychotherapy, 14*, 520–535.

Freud, S. (1908). "Civilized" sexual morality and modern nervous illness. In J. Strachey (trans. and ed.) *The standard edition of the complete psychological works of Sigmund Freud, 9*, 177–204. New York: Norton.

Freud, S. (1915 [1914]). Observations on transference-love. In J. Strachey (trans. and ed.) *The standard edition of the complete psychological works of Sigmund Freud, 12*, 159–171. New York: Norton.

Goffman, I. (1959). *Presentation of self in everyday life*. Garden City, New York: Doubleday Anchor Books.

Gyatso, Tenzin, Dalai Lama XIV. (1984). *Kindness, clarity, and insight*. J. Hopkins (trans. and ed.) & E. Napper (co-ed.) Ithaca, New York: Snow Lion Publications.

Haley, J. (1967). *Advanced techniques of hypnosis and therapy: Selected papers of Milton H. Erickson, M.D.* New York: Grune and Stratton.

Haley, J. (1973). *Uncommon therapy*. New York: Norton.

Haley, J. (1976). *Problem-solving therapy: New strategies for effective family therapy*. San Francisco: Jossey-Bass.

Haley, J. (1980). *Leaving home: The therapy of disturbed young people*. New York: McGraw-Hill.

Haley, J. (1984). *Ordeal therapy*. San Francisco: Jossey-Bass.

Haley, J. (1984a). Personal communication.

Haley, J. (1985). *Conversations with Milton H. Erickson, M.D., Vol. I, Changing individuals*. Rockville, Maryland: Triangle Press.

Haley, J. (1987). *Problem-solving therapy*. 2nd ed. San Francisco: Jossey-Bass.

Keim, I., Lentine, G., Keim, J., & Madanes, C. (1988). Strategies for changing the past. *Journal of Strategic and Systemic Therapies*, 6 (3), 2–17.

Laing, R. D. (1969). *Self and others*. London: Tavistock Publications; New York: Pantheon Books.

Laing, R. D. (1967). *The politics of experience*. Harmondsworth: Penguin; New York: Pantheon Books.

Laing, R. D. (1969). *The politics of the family and other essays*. New York: Random House.

Lederer, W., & Jackson, D. D. (1968). *The mirages of marriage*. New York: Norton.

Madanes, C. (1981). *Strategic family therapy*. San Francisco: Jossey-Bass.

Madanes, C. (1984). *Behind the one-way mirror: Advances in the practice of strategic therapy*. San Francisco: Jossey Bass.

Madanes, C. (1984). Family therapy training—It's entertainment. In H. A. Liddle, D. C. Breunlin, & R. C. Schwartz (eds.), *Handbook of family therapy training & supervision*. New York: Guilford.

Madanes, C. (1987). Advances in strategic family therapy. In J. Zeig (ed.) *The evolution of psychotherapy*. New York: Brunner/Mazel.

Madanes, C. (1989). The goals of therapy. British *Journal of Family Therapy*, (2).

Marc, D. (1984). Understanding television. *The Atlantic*, August 254 (2).

Minuchin, S. (1974). *Families and family therapy*. Cambridge, Massachusetts: Harvard University Press.

Minuchin, S., Rosman, B., & Baker, L. (1978). *Psychosomatic families*. Cambridge, Massachusetts: Harvard University Press.

Minuchin, S., & Fishman, H. C. (1981). *Family therapy techniques*. Cambridge, Massachusetts: Harvard University Press.

Paolino, T. J., & McCrady, B. (1978). *Marriage and marital therapy: Psychoanalytic, behavioral and systems theory perspectives*. New York: Brunner/Mazel.

Sager, C. J. (1976). *Marriage contracts and couple therapy*. New York: Brunner/Mazel.

Selvini Palazzoli, M., Boscolo, L., Cecchin, G., & Prata, G. (1978). *Paradox and counterparadox*. New York: Aronson.

Steiner, C. (1974). *Scripts people live*. New York: Grove.

Vargas Llosa, M. (1985, June). Is fiction the art of lying? *The Writer*.

Watzlawick, P., Weakland, J., & Fisch, R. (1974). *Change: Principles of problem formation and problem resolution*. New York: Norton.

INDEX